Peace-building in Post-Conflict Societies

Rehabilitation of Former Child Soldiers in Northern Uganda

Adonis & Abbey Publishers Ltd

St James House
13 Kensington Square,
London, W8 5HD
United Kingdom

Website: http://www.adonis-abbey.com
E-mail Address: editor@adonis-abbey.com

Nigeria:
Suites C4 – C6 J-Plus Plaza
Asokoro, Abuja, Nigeria
Tel: +234 (0) 7058078841/08052035034

British Library Cataloguing-in-Publication Data
A catalogue record for this book is available from the British Library

ISBN: 9781906704278

Peace-building in Post-Conflict Societies
Rehabilitation of Former Child Soldiers in Northern Uganda

By

Arthur Bainomugisha

ADONIS & ABBEY
PUBLISHERS LTD

Acknowledgements

The work that goes into a book of this nature is largely a collective responsibility. To this end, I am pleased to acknowledge the tremendous intellectual, moral and material assistance that I received from different people in the course of doing my doctoral programme. Suffice to say is that since many people contributed to the work in many different ways; it would be impossible to mention everybody in this acknowledgement.

My first debt of gratitude goes to my mentor, Professor David Francis, whose intellectual guidance, oversight and comments were of paramount importance to this project. Professor Francis's critical comments and encouragements were critical for my persistence to complete this book. I am also grateful to Professor Donna Pankhurst for her intellectual guidance.

A number of other academic mentors, colleagues and friends deserve mention for their insights and moral support. They include Dr Joao Gomes Porto, Professor Shaun Gregory, Ms Michele Mozley, Professor Michael Pugh, Dr Job Akuni; Tereza Wamuyu; Dr Sarah Njeri; Dr. Fred Rwecungura and Dr Elias Omondi Opongo. Particular recognition goes to Professor Kenneth Omeje who read and made useful comments on most of the chapters in this book.

I am particularly indebted to Onesmus Mugyenyi and Associate Professor Winstons Wilson Muhwezi, my colleagues at the Advocates Coalition for Development and Environment (ACODE), for their sacrifice and multi-faceted support which was critical for me to undertake research for this book.

I am sincerely grateful to my dear wife, Hope Asiimwe Bainomugisha for all her love, sacrifice, and support, as well as for the challenges she endured to make sure that I complete research for this book. I will not forget to appreciate my children - Amanzi Ananura Bainomugisha, Mandela Arinanye Bainomugisha and Kwame Asiimwe Bainomugisha and King David Bainomugisha for their love, encouragement and endurance.

Finally, I am particularly thankful to my mother Mrs Mangyeri Katsigaire and my father Apolo Wilson Katsigaire for their vision and sacrifice to have me educated at a time when most parents in my locality did not consider education important for their children. I will forever be grateful to my parents. I entirely accept liability for any shortcomings and limitations of this work. I am also thank full to my elder brother Abel Muhwezi who smuggled me from grazing cattle arguing that I was old enough to start school when my parents still considered me too young. I have never looked back. I am also grateful to my research assistant Arthur Owor who helped me in conducting field work and to interpret for me the local language in the geographical area for material in this book. Finally, I am indebted to former child soldiers who freely shared their lived experiences captured in research for this book. It is my hope, that this book will make a contribution in the eradication the vice of child soldiering across the world.

Table of Contents

Map of Uganda Showing Areas of Affected by LRA Conflict

Source: Allen and Schomerus (2006), originally obtained from UN OCH

List of Abbreviations

AC	Amnesty Commission
ACODE	Advocates Coalition for Development and Environment
AGOA	African Growth and Opportunities Act
ANC	African National Congress
ARP	Amnesty Reintegration Programme
AU	Africa Union
BBC	British Broadcasting Corporation
CAP	Community Action Plan
CAR	Central Africa Republic
CBOs	Community Based Organizations
CEDAW	Convention on the Elimination of All Forms of Discrimination Against Women
CPA	Concerned Parents Association
CPU	Child Protection Unit
CRC	Convention on the Rights of the Child
CSOs	Civil Society Organizations
DDRR	Disarmament, Demobilization, Reintegration and Rehabilitation
DRC	Democratic Republic of Congo
DRT	Demobilization, Resettlement Team
FDC	Forum for Democratic Change
FRELIMO	The Liberation Front of Mozambique
GoSS	Government of Southern Sudan
GUSCO	Gulu Support the Children Organisation
HRW	Human Rights Watch
HSM	Holy Spirit Movement
IDA	International Development Assistance
IDPs	Internally Displaced Persons
INGOs	International Non-Governmental Organizations
IPI	International Peace Institute
KAR	Kings Africa Rifles
KIDDP	Karamoja, Integrated Disarmament and Development Programme
KIWA	Kitgum Concerned Women's Association
LRA	Lord's Resistance Army
LTTE	Liberation Tigers of Tamil Eelam
MPs	Members of Parliament
NGOs	Non-Governmental Organizations
NRA	National Resistance Army
NUREP	Northern Uganda Rehabilitation Programme
NURPI &11	Northern Uganda Reconstruction Programme
NUSAF	Northern Uganda Social Action Fund
OAU	Organization of African Unity
OHCHR	Office of the High Commissioner for Human Rights
OPM	Office of the Prime Minister
PRA	Peoples Redemption Army
PRDP	Peace, Recovery and Development Plan for Northern Uganda

RENAMO	The Mozambique National Resistance
RLP	Refugee Law Project
RLPI	Religious Leaders Peace Initiative
RR	Reintegration and Rehabilitation
RUF	Revolutionary United Front
SAF	Sudan Armed Forces
SPLA/M	Sudan People's Liberation Army/ Movement
TRC	Truth and Reconciliation Commission
UDN	Uganda Debt Network
UHRC	Uganda Human Rights Commission
UN	United Nations
UNDP	United Nations Development Programme
UNFPA	United Nations Populations Fund
UNHCR	United Nations High Commissioner for Refugees
UNICEF	United Nations Children's Fund
UNIFEM	United Nations Development Fund for Women
UNITA	The National Union for the Total Independence of Angola
UNLA	Uganda National Liberation Army
UPA	Uganda People's Army
UPDA/M	Uganda Peoples Defence Army/ Movement
UPDF	Uganda Peoples Defence Forces
UPE	Universal Primary Education
UPF	Uganda Police Force
USE	Universal Secondary Education
VTIS	Vocational Training Institutes
WACA	War Affected Children Association
WWI	World War I
WW II	World War II
YOP	Youth Opportunities Programme

CHAPTER ONE

Introduction

Contextualising the Book Focus

The level of brutality and violence against children abducted and forcefully conscripted by the Lord's Resistance Army (LRA) in Northern Uganda pricked the conscience of humanity. The suffering of the people in Northern Uganda was described by Jan Egeland, the former United Nations Under-Secretary for Humanitarian Affairs, as 'the biggest forgotten humanitarian crisis in the world'. This book is primarily concerned with the plight of ex-child soldiers in Northern Uganda and how their effective reintegration and rehabilitation using indigenous psychosocial support systems could become an effective tool for peacebuilding.

Psychosocial support based on traditional and indigenous resources is an aspect of peacebuilding neglected by the dominant liberal peacebuilding intervention framework in most war-torn societies. For example, while traditional and indigenous resources in Northern Uganda have been instrumental in the effective rehabilitation of many former child soldiers, most scholars and policy makers have largely paid attention to the dominant official government and United Nations structured top-down interventions that emphasize Western approaches to peacebuilding. More dismally, the official western-centric approaches have tended to marginalize the former child soldiers in the reconstruction and peacebuilding processes of Northern Uganda. It is this philosophical and empirical gap which fundamentally hurts the post-conflict reconstruction and peacebuilding processes in Northern Uganda that this study seeks to help fill. Far from completely dismissing the orthodox Western approaches, this book critically explores their contextual utility in peacebuilding in Northern Uganda and argues that

11

they can be integratively used to complement the indigenous psychosocial resources and remedy their practical shortcomings.

The coming into power in Uganda by President Museveni in 1986 sparked off a violent protracted conflict in Northern Uganda popularly known as the Holy Spirit Movement led by a self-styled prophetess Alice Lakwena which was violently crushed by the victorious National Resistance Army (NRA) in 1987. An offshoot of this conflict was the Lord's Resistance Army/Movement (LRA/M) rebellion led by Joseph Kony, which caused untold suffering to the people in Northern Uganda. Critical to gross human rights violations and human suffering caused by the LRA rebellion are the children who are abducted and forcefully recruited into the LRA ranks. Most of the abducted girls was turned into sex slaves of rebel commanders. By the end of 1987, the LRA had successfully brought under one command the remnants of the forces of the Holy Spirit Movement; the defeated Uganda National Liberation Army (UNLA): the former the government army (1979-1985) that was overthrown by the National Resistance Army/Movement (NRA/M) led by President Museveni. By 1994, the LRA rebellion that initially had enjoyed the local appeal and support of the population in Northern Uganda, particularly in Acholi sub-region, lost the support largely due to its brutality. This forced the LRA to resort to abduction and forceful recruitment of children (Lucima (ed.), 2002:68). It is estimated that 80% of the LRA fighters are abducted children. Humanitarian organisations such as the World Vision International estimate the number of children abducted by the LRA to be 30,000, although the actual figure may be much higher (World Vision Report, 2005: 17). Available information also implicates the Government army in the recruitment and deployment of rescued child soldiers in offensives against the LRA rebels (Human Rights Watch Report, 2003).

As a strategy for the LRA to prevent children from escaping from the bush, they were harshly brutalized and indoctrinated so as to instil in them fear of ever thinking of going back to their homes. Most of the children returnees told stories of how they were forced to kill fellow children who attempted to escape. The guilt of having murdered their own relatives or friends using crude methods left permanent scars on the minds of the child soldiers (Anderson et al, 2005:130).

After the resumption of peace negotiations in 2006 between the Government of Uganda and the LRA, mediated by the Government of

South Sudan (GoSS), the rebels relocated to South Sudan, the Democratic Republic of Congo (DRC) and Central Africa Republic (CAR). This scenario resulted into the return of relative peace in Northern Uganda. With the return of relative peace in the region, the challenge became how to effectively reintegrate and rehabilitate former child soldiers as part of the overall peacebuilding process in the region. As scholars (Wessells, 2006; Singer, 2006) have observed, unless former child soldiers are effectively reintegrated and rehabilitated in most war-torn societies, they can become a threat to peace and security and constrain post-conflict reconstruction processes. This is because former child soldiers have the potential to join criminal gangs and fuel the crime rate; they can be re-recruited into fresh rebellions or they can be hired by warlords to fight in other on-going regional conflicts, thereby threatening regional peace and security. With an estimated 30,000 children having been abducted and forcefully conscripted into the rebel ranks, it becomes apparent that if not effectively reintegrated and rehabilitated, former child soldiers could pose a serious security threat to the peace dividends already registered in Northern Uganda.

In this book, I argue that the effective reintegration and rehabilitation of former child soldiers into civilian and productive life would contribute to conditions of peace and security in Northern Uganda. Secondly, I argue that the neglect of former child soldiers in most of the reintegration and rehabilitation processes in war-torn societies causes more wars, increases criminality and hampers any efforts towards building durable peace (Singer, 2006; Honwana, 2006). The third argument is that the provision of psychosocial support based on traditional and indigenous resources which is the neglected element of peacebuilding, is very crucial in the reintegration and rehabilitation of former child soldiers as the case in Northern Uganda demonstrates.

The arguments made in this book in favour of providing psychosocial support for ex-child soldiers based on cultural and indigenous resources does not mean that other interventions in the reintegration and rehabilitation of former child soldiers are not important for peacebuilding. Rather, it is intended to underpin the argument that the provision of psychosocial support is ostensibly the most contextually relevant instrument in the reintegration and rehabilitation of former child soldiers. Most crucially, psychosocial support is effective if it largely relies on traditional and indigenous resources rather than the Western approaches that have contextual and cultural limitations. This book

13

offers a critique of the liberal peace approach to peacebuilding, which is usually top-down, time-bound, lacking long-term financial commitment by the international community and governments, and overlooks local knowledge and resources (Pugh et al, 2007). The liberal peace approach to peacebuilding is discussed extensively in Chapter Three. For example, this research shows the resilience of former child soldiers in Northern Uganda who have empowered each other by establishing their own associations relying on local resources.

Most of the academic and policy studies on the conflict in Northern Uganda have mainly focused on its political and ethnic dimensions as well as the abduction and use of children in the conflict by the LRA, without paying sufficient attention to their reintegration and rehabilitation using indigenous psychosocial support mechanisms as an essential bulwark of peacebuilding. This research is informed by the realization that in spite of the suffering child soldiers endure during civil wars, in most war-torn societies, they are often marginalized in the reintegration and rehabilitation processes (Singer, 2006:183). Yet, failure to plan for effective reintegration and rehabilitation of former child soldiers makes them pose a threat to peace and security in the post-conflict period (Singer, 2006; Honwana, 2006). Consequently, the effective reintegration and rehabilitation of former child soldiers in Northern Uganda is crucial in order to contribute to conditions of durable peace.

The provision of psychosocial support based on traditional and indigenous resources in the RR (Reintegration and Rehabilitation) of child soldiers is generally a neglected element of peacebuilding in most academic and policy circles. This research shows that in spite of the limitations of traditional and indigenous resources, which include the fact that they have been weakened and undermined during the long period of the civil war, colonialism, domination and gender biases towards women, they can play a crucial role in the reintegration and rehabilitation of former child soldiers. As the subsequent chapters of this research show, traditional and indigenous resources have been crucial in the reintegration and rehabilitation of former child soldiers in Northern Uganda. However, while the research acknowledges the relevance of traditional and indigenous resources, it also recognizes their limitations and the importance of Western approaches of psychosocial support in the RR of child soldiers. To this end, the book proposes an integrated approach of psychosocial support that blends the two processes.

Furthermore, available information on child soldiering in Uganda shows that there is an apparent limited expertise in handling reintegration and rehabilitation of child soldiers. For example, when the then rebel National Resistance Army (NRA) led by President Museveni captured power after five years of guerrilla warfare in 1986, government attempted to demobilize, reintegrate and rehabilitate thousands of child soldiers from the army with limited success. Child soldiers were simply sent back to schools and were subsequently re-absorbed into the army upon completion or dropping out of schools[1].

Moreover, there are reports that in Northern Uganda, some of the former child soldiers who are now fully blown young adults remain psychologically traumatized and socioeconomically dislocated not only because of their horrendous experiences in the war but also aggravated by the failures of post-war efforts at reintegration and rehabilitation. Cases where former child soldiers ended up on the streets of Gulu town in Northern Uganda and abandoned to their own devices are common. Ethnographic evidence from the study location indicates that this scenario is especially more prevalent among child mothers who were rejected by their parents because of the "fatherless" children they returned with from the bush. There are also documented cases where rescued children who failed to put up with their families and communities had to run back to the LRA rebels or were absorbed into the Government army (Coalition Global Report, 2004). With complete breakdown of the local economy and the weakening of the traditional institutions in Northern Uganda, the reintegration and rehabilitation of former child soldiers remains challenging.

This book recognizes the important role played by agencies such as UNICEF, World Vision and Gulu Support the Children Organization (GUSCO) in the RR of child soldiers in Northern Uganda. However, most organizations used Western approaches of psychosocial support in the RR of child soldiers such as one-on-one counseling which have cultural limitations and are not sustainable in the long-run (Kostelny, 2006). The study further explores the role of official and unofficial peacebuilding interventions, their limitations and challenges in the RR of

---

[1]Interview with Lt. Col Felix Kuluyagye, the spokesman for Uganda Peoples Defence Forces and Ministry of Defence which took place in Kampala in March, 2010.

former child soldiers. It is hoped that this study will contribute to the deeper understanding of the child soldier problematic and how traditional and indigenous resources are important in the RR of former child soldiers particularly in Northern Uganda.

Methodologically, this study is based on a mix of secondary data (academic literature, policy reports, media resources, etc) and qualitative fieldwork data. The fieldwork data for the analysis of the work were mainly derived from assorted interviews with a range of ex-combatants and former child soldiers in Northern Uganda, as well as officials of civil society organizations, international organizations, faith-based organizations, community based organizations and relevant government agencies with field operations in the study location. Focus group discussions were also conducted with some former child soldiers in urban and rural Northern Uganda. Data interpretation and analysis have proceeded using simple qualitative techniques such as thematic analysis of excerpts, deconstructive interrogation, and application of relevant theories.

Anecdotal Note

My interest in this book is rooted in my practical experience in conflict intervention, policy advocacy and stretches over 10 years of my involvement in the various peace processes aimed at contributing to the end of the 24 year old violent conflict in Northern Uganda. While working with the Church of Uganda in 1998, I was involved in implementing a peace and human rights programme that involved provision of humanitarian assistance to the internally displaced persons (IDPs) and training church leaders and students about human rights. It was during the launching of the Peace and Human Rights Programme in Apac district in Lango sub-region, which involved a retreat and meditation of the Anglican bishops that I became convinced that the military option to end the LRA conflict being pursued by government was not the only solution that would end the suffering of the people. At the time an estimated 1.6 million people were living as IDPs.

The bishops' retreat was concluded by a massive public rally where two bishops from rival ethnic groups embraced each other as a sign of forgiveness and reconciliation, which was punctuated by personal testimonies. From that day, I was convinced that national reconciliation

16

could bring an end to the brutal rebellion that had exploited ethnic differences prevalent in Uganda. It also made me realize the need to make a contribution to reconciliation and peacebuilding in the region. At this time, I was still significantly limited in my analytical understanding of this conflict and also lacked theoretical grounding in conflict resolution. The opportunity to do a Master's degree in Peace Studies at the University of Bradford in 2000 - 2001, and subsequently a PhD in 2005 - 2010, provided an opportunity for me to expand my knowledge and skills in the subject area, and further equipped me to participate in the peace process in Northern Uganda.

Since 2001, I have been involved in different peace initiatives aimed at contributing to the resolution of the conflict in Northern Uganda. These initiatives include: conducting research, organizing public dialogues and provision of technical backstopping to the Government and LRA peace negotiating teams. In 2003, while working as a Civil Society Fellow with the International Peace Institute (IPI), a New York-based think tank; I organized two high-level policy dialogues in New York focusing on the war in Northern Uganda. The main objective for the public dialogues was to draw the attention of the policy community at the United Nations (UN) to the suffering of the people in Northern Uganda. One such public dialogue was organized for the Acholi religious and traditional leaders to interact with the United Nations policy community. The religious leaders were drumming up support for the resumption of peace talks between the LRA and the Government of Uganda.

In 2004, I participated in a study that detailed the peace processes in Northern Uganda and why they repeatedly fail. The policy research report that came out of the study titled: 'The Torturous Peace Process in Northern Uganda' greatly helped me to understand that the 24 year conflict in Northern Uganda is complex and deep-rooted, with multiple actors and interests. These issues combined to make the conflict difficult to resolve. The study greatly influenced my interest in later undertaking a more scholarly work on the conflict in Northern Uganda.

It is my hope that this book on the rehabilitation of former child soldiers based on traditional and indigenous resources will extend the frontiers of knowledge in the area conflict transformation, post-conflict peacebuilding and the search for durable peace in Northern Uganda.

Book Structure

This book is organized into eight chapters. Chapter one focuses on the Introduction which details the background and context of the book, and also provides some anecdotal note about how my conflict intervention policy engagements in Northern Uganda stimulated my interest in undertaking research for this work.

Chapter Two examines the child soldier phenomenon from diverse intellectual perspectives at the global and continental (Africa) levels. The chapter also defines and conceptualizes key concepts such as: who is a child, Childhood, and who is a child soldier. The methods of recruitment, use of child soldiers and why children are preferred by armed groups and government forces are also discussed. Finally, Chapter Two evaluates the existing international legal mechanisms for protection of child soldiers in armed conflicts, including their effectiveness and limitations.

In Chapter Three, I discuss disarmament, demobilization, reintegration and rehabilitation (DDRR) of child soldiers as elements of peacebuilding. The Chapter also examines DDRR in the context of the neglected psychosocial support aspect of post-conflict peacebuilding.

Chapter Four examines the child soldier phenomenon in the context of Uganda, which is the key focus of the book. The chapter traces the child soldier problem from the country's political history and political economy. The chapter also analyses the causes of conflicts in Uganda which gave birth to the violent conflict in Northern Uganda. The chapter traces the genesis of the LRA rebellion, the recruitment and use of child soldiers, and its consequences on the people of Northern Uganda and the country as a whole. Furthermore, the chapter examines the available national legal mechanisms for protection of children's rights in Uganda.

Chapter Five focuses on peacebuilding interventions in the RR of former child soldiers in Northern Uganda. The chapter specifically examines the official government and United Nations agencies top-down approaches of peacebuilding interventions which in most cases do not consider local resources and local participation in the planning and programming of interventions. Non-official peacebuilding interventions implemented mainly by local Non-Governmental Organizations (NGOs), Community Based Organizations (CBOs) and International

18

Non-Governmental Organizations (INGOs) are also examined in this chapter.

In Chapter Six, I discuss the importance of psychosocial resources in the RR of former child soldiers. Emphasis is put on the neglected African traditional and indigenous resources and approaches in contrast with Western approaches of psychosocial support. Specific focus is placed on the traditional and indigenous resources used in the RR of former child soldiers in Northern Uganda, which is the main focus of this book. Chapter Six also explores the challenges and limitations of reliance on traditional and indigenous resources.

Chapter Seven focuses on the Ugandan national legal framework for the RR of former child soldiers. It also examines the necessary conditions for effective RR of former child soldiers and proposes key agendas for future research.

Chapter Eight summarises the key findings of this book and more significantly expounds a new framework for post-conflict peacebuilding in Northern Uganda in the light of the empirical and policy intervention gaps identified in the study.

Part 1

Conceptualization of the Child Soldier Phenomenon

CHAPTER TWO

Understanding the Child Soldier Problem

If there is any lesson that we can learn from the experience of the past decade, it is that the use of child soldiers is far more than a humanitarian concern; that its impact lasts far beyond the time of actual fighting; and that the scope of the problem vastly exceeds the number of children directly involved—Kofi Annan (Singer, 2006:94).

The practice of children's involvement and participation in armed conflicts in many war-torn societies around the world is not a new phenomenon. Historically young people are known to have been at the forefront of political conflicts in several parts of the world (Rosen, 2005). However, modern warfare where numerous children have been recruited and used to fight kills, maims and exploits them more callously and systematically as a deliberate and well crafted war strategy (Machel, 2001:1). The plight of children's involvement in these civil wars has grown in magnitude such that it has alarmed the international community. The level of destruction and suffering endured by children in several civil wars, that have occurred in most of the Third World, both as victims and perpetrators of violence is shocking (Machel, 1996). Images of boys and girls carrying guns and ammunition flash across television screens and appear on the front pages of the newspapers.

Many children are abducted and coerced into fighting; while others are pushed into it by poverty and crisis in their societies. Others are motivated by promises of glory or excitement. Consequently, armed conflicts have transformed children into merciless killers, committing the most horrendous atrocities with apparent indifference and even pride (Francis, 2007). The plight of children and other non-combatants in armed conflicts has prompted some analysts to describe contemporary civil wars as a total societal crisis since social order is almost entirely disrupted (Honwana, 2006).

This chapter critically examines the child soldier phenomenon from diverse intellectual perspectives at the global and continental (Africa) levels. Particular emphasis is placed on Uganda since it is the main focus of this book. The book explores the 'reintegration and rehabilitation of former child soldiers by providing psychosocial support based on traditional and indigenous resources may have contributed to conditions of peace and stability in Northern Uganda.'

It should be noted from the onset that the child soldiering phenomenon poses a serious challenge to international peace and security. Consequently, this book on the RR of former child soldiers in Northern Uganda concurs with the views of scholars who argue that unless the RR of former child soldiers is effectively handled, they could pose a security threat and undermine efforts for peacebuilding (Singer, 2006:40).

Child Soldiers: Global and African Perspectives

This section critically examines the child soldiers' phenomenon at the global and African levels. The section examines the historical perspectives of the child soldiering phenomenon across various civilizations especially within Western civilization and African traditional societies. The intention here is not to try to justify the child soldiering phenomenon, but to demonstrate that the practice has long been part of human society which in recent times has gone out of control and poses a serious threat to international peace and security in many different ways, including refugee generation and serving as a breeding infrastructure for terrorist organizations (Singer, 2006).

In recent decades; children have featured more prominently in the various armed conflicts going on in various war zones around the world as both targets and perpetrators of violence. However, for one to understand the current child soldier phenomenon, it is important to analyse the contemporary developments from a historical perspective. The participation of children in armed conflict is a historical phenomenon and is rooted in the history of civilizations and traditions. According to Honwana (2006:26), in Europe during the Middle Ages, the upper-class young boys who wanted to become knights would be required to serve as Squires. Thirteen year old boys would be attached to knights who taught them skills with the sword, lance, and the duties and responsibilities of knighthood. The Squires were required to serve their mentors, look after their master's horses, polish their weapons and armour and serve them at meals. When the Squires grew older, they were expected to follow their mentors to the battle to protect them in case the knight fell in combat.

Singer (2006:11) and Cohn et al (2003:13) concur with Honwana that historically, children have always been involved in warfare. Singer (2006) for instance, points out that while in European history, the exclusion of children from war was a general rule; some male children did play military roles. He notes that page boys helped arm and maintain the knights of medieval Europe while drummer boys and 'powder monkeys' were a requisite part of any army and navy in the seventeenth and eighteenth centuries.

It is also observed that while historically across most of Europe, children were used in the military; the children who were recruited into the armed forces were required to serve under a few adult commanders. The children's Crusades of 1212 for instance included thousands of boys and girls between the ages of 10 and 18 years who joined together, believing that God would deliver Jerusalem into their hands. As it turned out, most of these child soldiers died on their long march due to exhaustion and harsh climatic conditions (Honwana, 2006). Further, it is noted that much of Napoleon's army was comprised of boys as young as 12 years old. Also, the British navy under Admiral Nelson, who fought Napoleon's army to ensure that Napoleon did not step on British soil, is known to have included many naval cadets and midshipmen of fifteen as well as younger cabin boys (Honwana, 2006).

Rosen (2005:4) further points out that until recently, the armies of Western Europe and the United States were filled with 'boy soldiers.' In Britain, the Royal Hibernian Military School was founded in 1765 for the children of the so-called rank and file soldiers. Among the earliest recruits were twelve and thirteen year-olds, who were placed in regiments and served under General Thomas Gage in 1774 to suppress the American Revolution. Rosen (2005) further notes that available data indicate the presence of young soldiers on the side of the American Revolutionary War. To Rosen, the Civil War in the United States was largely a war of boy soldiers since, throughout the war, thousands of youngsters followed brothers, fathers and teachers into the war. While the actual number of boy soldiers in the American Civil War is not well known, some writers estimate that out of the total 2.7 million soldiers, more than a million were eighteen or under; about eight hundred thousand were seventeen or under; two hundred thousand were sixteen or under; about one hundred thousand were fifteen or under; three hundred were thirteen or under (Rosen, 2005:5).

Rosen (2005) and Singer (2006) observe that during World War 1, many children were recruited into armed forces and participated in battles where many of them lost their lives. Worth noting for example is that during World War 1, the first child soldier to die: Private James Martin had enlisted at Melbourne in 1915 at the age of 14 years. On the other hand, Albert Cohen of Memphis, Tennessee, reputed to be the youngest American soldier to participate in combat in World War 1, joined the army at the age of thirteen and died at the age of 14 years (Rosen, 2005).

It is also observed that during World War 11, Hitler deployed young boys who were ill-trained but had received quasi military training as part of a political programme to maintain the Nazi rule in power. These youths who were lightly armed were mostly sent out in small ambush squads and many of them were killed by the allied forces (Singer, 2006:15). In China, it is also noted that during the Chinese Cultural Revolution, the Red Guards aged between eight and fifteen carried out some of the more violent acts.

Some scholars (Obote-Odora, 1999) have observed that historically across most of Africa, especially in sub-Saharan Africa, young children would be organized in age sets and trained into military techniques as a transition from childhood to adulthood. After the training which was usually crowned with rituals, these children were expected to defend their societies which meant participation in battles. Commenting about child soldiering in Africa from a historical perspective, Obote-Odora (1999:12) observed that:

> ...the political, social and military situation in Africa......is very complex.
> ....In some parts of Africa, 16 and 17-year-old children especially from pastoral cultures are expected to bear arms and fight....that being the only way to be initiated into adulthood.[2]

---

[2] Obote-Odora, A. (1999). 'Legal Problems with the Protection of Children in Armed Conflict,' *Murdoch University Electronic Journal of Law*, Volume 6, Number 2, June.
Available at: http://www.murdoch.edu.au/elaw/issues/v6n2/obote-odora62_text.html
Accessed on 25/9/2009.

Furthermore, Francis Deng observes that among the Dinka of the Sudan, traditionally boys were initiated into adulthood between the ages of sixteen and eighteen, and would be immediately given gifts of well designed spears symbolizing the military function of the youth (Rosen, 2005:4). The story of Francis Deng is not different from other traditional societies in most parts of pre-colonial Africa. Among the Karimajong and Pokot of Kenya and Banyankole in Uganda, young boys had to learn at an early age to fend off lions and cattle rustlers that threatened the cattle. President Museveni of Uganda who himself used child soldiers during the guerrilla war which brought his government to power in 1986 points out that children in traditional Africa especially among the Banyankole used to train in military skills. In an interview in 1985 concerning the young soldiers that were part of his victorious National Resistance Army (NRA), popularly called the *Kadogos* or young soldiers, President Museveni justified the use of child soldiers based on the African tradition. Museveni noted that traditionally in most African societies, children as young as four years would be trained in the art of warfare but would not be allowed to participate in battles until they were mature enough to fight[3]. However, the Government of Uganda under his leadership has since outlawed the recruitment and use of children in armed conflicts. The 1995 Ugandan Constitution and the Children Act, 1997, outlaws the recruitment and use of children in armed conflicts as discussed in Chapter Four of this study.

Suffice to say that while child soldiering is as old as warfare and has been going on for centuries across most civilizations, the nature of warfare and political violence has changed over the past decades. As Machel (2001) and Honwana (2006:27) have observed, the world has witnessed a shift from conventional warfare between states, in which soldiers fight soldiers, to civil wars within states. Most of these civil wars are fought mainly by proxy means, use of guerrillas and other irregular fighters, and target defenceless civilians. Children are frequently abducted and forcefully recruited into armed groups, which was not the case before. What is also clear from the analyses of several scholars cited in the foregoing analysis is that prevention or complete stoppage of child soldiering has not been possible simply because the vice is rooted in

---

[3]BBC interview with Uganda's President Museveni on the involvement of children in armed conflicts in Uganda. Available at: www.youtube.com/watch?.v=up1tvcxw_gk. Accessed on 28/6/2010.

cultures and traditions across the world. This is also evidenced by the protracted discussions that went on before the Convention on the Rights of the Child 1989 could be passed. But even then, the failure of the Optional Protocol to the Convention to generate a global consensus on 18 years of age as an age for recruitment into armed groups demonstrates how the practice of child soldiering is deeply embedded in human history (Wessells, 2006).

While historically child soldiering was practiced across most human societies and cultures it was for the most part systematically controlled and regulated, compared to contemporary time where the practice has degenerated into anarchy and destruction of whole communities caught up in war zones. Worth mentioning also is that historically most armed conflicts in which children participated seemed to have had clear starting and ending points and strategic military and political objectives as compared to contemporary civil wars which lack any of these (Ramsbotham et al, 2005).

Contemporary Child Soldiering

Today's warfare is often marked by appalling levels of violence and brutality, from systematic rape and destruction of crops to the poisoning of wells and outright genocide. Ferocious assaults are unleashed against children and their communities. Children themselves are drawn in war as fighters, caught up in a general maelstrom in which they are not just targets of warfare but even the perpetrators of atrocities (Machel, 2001:1).

The end of the Cold War has seen tens of thousands of children taking part in armed conflicts in Asia, Latin America, Africa and the Middle East (Cohn et al, 1994:24). In the early 1990s, the world witnessed a new threat to global security in a manner that political and policy analysts had not anticipated. This period saw an upsurge of civil wars taking place mostly in the developing world, which accounted for 94% of all armed conflicts fought in the 1990s. Of particular interest is that from a humanitarian standpoint, these civil wars inflicted appalling losses on civilian non-combatants rather than the combatants. As Paris (2004:1) points out, attacks and atrocities against non-combatants, including abduction and forced recruitment of children into armed groups became widely employed as deliberate strategies of warfare.

Scholars point out how presently, more children and youth bear arms in internal violent conflicts than ever before. These civil wars where children are key participants as combatants are characterized by guerrilla-style warfare conducted largely by part-time participants, which inevitably results in excessive civilian deaths and injuries, extensive damage to health and education systems and massive movements of refugees (Summerfield, 1998:9).

Kaldor (2001) has described these civil wars as 'new wars' to distinguish them from prevailing perceptions of war drawn from an earlier era. To Kaldor, the new wars involve a blurring of the distinctions between war usually defined as violence between states or organized political groups for political motives, organized crime which is violence undertaken by privately organized groups for private purposes and large-scale violations of human rights. Kaldor (2001:2) also observes that although most of these new wars are localized, they involve a myriad of transnational connections so that the distinction between internal and external, between aggression (attacks from abroad) and repression (attacks from inside the country), or even between local and global, are difficult to sustain. Cohn et al (1994) and Machel (2001:7) also point out that young people have always been trained for battle throughout history, but the weight of the weapons often limited their involvement. These analysts observe that today arms technology is so advanced that even small boys and girls can handle common weapons like M16 and AK47 assault rifles. Consequently, children can be useful in battle with less training than ever before.

The United Nations report titled *"The Impact of Armed Conflict on Children"* by Machel (1996:5) captures the alarming global picture of children caught up in armed conflicts. The report reveals how millions of children are caught up in conflicts in which they are not mere bystanders, but targets. Most children fall victim to a general onslaught against civilians while others die as part of the calculated design to eliminate them. Other children suffer the effects of sexual violence and the multiple deprivations of armed conflicts that expose them to hunger or disease. The Machel report further observes that during the 1990's more than 2 million children died as a result of armed conflicts and most times these children were deliberately targeted and murdered. The report describes the callousness of modern warfare resulting from the breakdown of traditional societies, brought about by globalization and social revolutions. The societal breakdown has led to loss of distinction between combatants and civilians, horrible levels of brutality including systematic rape, scorched-earth policies and ethnic cleansing.

According to Collins (2007:373), currently over forty five countries are known to use approximately 300,000 child soldiers in on-going civil wars. Collins, who notes that the lives of these child soldiers are highly expendable further observes that the majority of children are active in government armed forces and the youngest are often to be found in the armed groups. Harvey (2003:25) concurs with Collins and notes that while most of these children are recruited as adolescents, the majority of the children at a very young age are being recruited for direct and indirect participation in armed conflicts.

Despite the near-universal condemnation of child soldiering by the international community, hundreds of thousands of children have continued to fight and to die in almost every armed conflict in the World. The former Secretary-General of the United Nations, Kofi Annan, condemned child soldiering as a damaging and despicable practice. Pope Paul 11 called the use of child soldiers a 'horrible form of violence' (Global Report, 2004:13). All these international endeavours have not been able to stamp out the practice of child soldiering.

Suffice it to say that children from well-to-do families in war zones are usually at a lesser risk of being recruited by armed groups because their parents can afford to buy their freedom or challenge their recruitment through legal means or political influence. On the other hand, children from poorer families are most vulnerable and at risk of being recruited into government forces or armed groups. Children in large cities who are living on the streets face a great risk of recruitment as well as those children who are internally displaced or are living in refugee camps (Singer, 2006). According to the International Labour Organization (ILO) Commission of Inquiry, children as young as ten years in Myanmar have been used as porters or to sweep roads for landmines using brooms and branches (Machel, 2001:8). Underpinning the increased recruitment and use of child soldiers in armed hostilities is the increased availability and proliferation of small arms and light weapons. It is observed that unlike older weapons which used to be too heavy and difficult to operate modern weapons are so light that children can use them and so simple to be dismantled and reassembled by a child as young as 10 years of age (Harvey, 2003; Machel, 2001:13).

In Asia, the Khmer Rouge of Cambodia and the Tamil Tigers in Sri Lanka are known for their record of using child soldiers. Children also play a critical role in conflicts in Kashmir, the Philippines, Burma and Afghanistan (Honwana, 2006: 30). In the Middle East, children are active participants in the conflict between the state of Israel and the Palestinians. The Coalition Global Report (2004:19) noted that in Israel security forces shoot the Palestinian children if they threw stones and participated in demonstrations. The Report accuses Israel of denying Palestinian children protection rights in detention which are accorded to Israeli children. A study supported by the Coalition to Stop the Use of Child Soldiers established that Palestinian children were tortured by Israel in attempts to coerce them and recruit them as spies.

On the other hand, the Palestinian militants recruit, indoctrinate and deploy children against the Israeli forces so that when they are killed, it attracts international sympathy and condemnation of Israel as merciless killers of innocent children (Global Report, 2004). In Indonesia, it is reported that government was using children as informants in counter-intelligence activities. In Europe, the conflicts in the Balkans and Northern Ireland exposed many young people to violence and war. In the Middle East, armed conflicts have drawn in children in fighting largely as part of rebel groups fighting against several regimes (Singer, 2006:21). Children as young as 15 years are reported to be serving in armed groups in Algeria, Egypt, Iran, Azerbaijan, Iraq, Lebanon, Tajikistan and Yemen. Iran is identified as the first country in the Middle East in modern times to have used children on a large scale, during the Iran-Iraq war in the 1980s (Honwana, 2006). Iran's use of child soldiers at the time went against the Koranic Sharia law that forbids recruitment of children below sixteen into armed conflicts (Singer, 2006).

Child Soldiering: The African Context

Commenting on civil wars in Africa where many of children are active participants as victims and perpetrators, Hutchful has observed that:

> Over the last decade, Africans have been subjected to an extraordinary variety of sources and forms of violence: civil wars, ethnic pogroms, religious conflicts, political repression, forced migrations and upheaval associated with structural adjustment. The end of the Cold War has thus sharply undermined existing security paradigms, intensifying the

security dilemma of some African states, and giving rise in the process to complex new forms and permutations of force within and beyond the state (Hutchful, 2000:210).

While child soldiering is a universal phenomenon in the sense that the practice has historically been found to have taken place in most human societies (Collins, 2007:368), its manifestation in contemporary Africa, has become endemic, complex and devastating. Most analysts point out that in the 1990's most of the regions on the African continent experienced violent civil wars, which greatly affected the lives of civilians, mostly children and women (Summerfield, 1998:9). The distinguishing feature of the violent civil wars in Africa has been the use of child soldiers. In almost all the countries where civil wars have been fought, are still going on, or have ended such as Sudan, the Democratic Republic of Congo (RDC), Congo-Brazzaville, Sierra Leone, Liberia, Mozambique, Angola, Burundi, Rwanda, Uganda, Somalia and Cote d'Ivoire, children under the age of 18 have been abducted, recruited, coerced and manipulated into joining either government forces or rebel groups and militias (Francis, 2007:208).

The magnitude of the child soldiering phenomenon in Africa is also evidenced by the fact that, currently, Africa alone accounts for more than 120,000 child soldiers who are spread across the war zones. This figure is about 40% of the global figure of about 300,000 child soldiers (Dudenhoeffer, 2016; Sesay, 2003:9). While this figure may be reducing based on the fact that the number of conflicts has also been decreasing and due to a universal consensus against the use of children in hostilities; according to the Global Report 2008, the level of child soldiering in Africa is a cause for worry and continues to pose a threat to international peace and security (Dudenhoeffer, 2016).

Both the 2004 and 2008 Coalition Global Reports indicate that most governments in Africa involved in armed conflicts, recruit children directly into the official armed forces and indirectly recruit children into proxy forces backing the government army. The Global Report (2004) revealed that most armed groups involved in peace processes in Africa recruited children to back up their bargaining power during the negotiations. In Burundi for example, Burundian armed political groups recruited children into their ranks and this was also the case in neighbouring Democratic Republic of Congo (DRC). In Sudan, the Global Report 2004 found out that in March 2004, there were an estimated 17,000 children in government forces, allied militias and opposition armed groups in the north, east and south of the country. However, Sudan has since taken significant steps to stop recruitment and use of child soldiers. During the recent visit to Sudan in early 2018, the Special Representative of the Secretary-General for Children and Armed Conflict witnessed progress in the implementation of the Government's Action Plan to end and prevent the recruitment and use of children and initiation of a process to create a national plan of prevention of violations against children (United Nations, 2018).

The Coalition Global Report 2008 also found out that while the Interim Constitution of Sudan adopted in December 2005 defines a child as anyone under the age 18, government continued to recruit children into the armed forces. The Global Report observed that military officials within the Sudan Armed Forces (SAF) acknowledged that children from various armed groups were integrated into SAF during the unification process. The report also found in the case of South Sudan, where the Child Bill 2006 which prohibits the recruitment and use of children in armed forces had passed its first reading in parliament in June 2007, child soldiers were still within its forces. The United Nations in September 2007 confirmed the presence of children associated with South Sudan People's Liberation Army (SPLA)[4].

Furthermore, in South Sudan, UNICEF has estimated that between 15,000 to 16,000 children may have been recruited and used by both the Government army and armed opposition groups during the fresh violent conflict that erupted in December, 2013 when soldiers loyal to President Salva Kiir and his former Vice President Riek Machar fought in Juba, the capital (Human Rights Watch, 2015).

The situation in the Democratic Republic of Congo (DRC) has not improved substantively in spite of the arrest and prosecution of former warlords: Timothy Lubanga and Jean-Pierre Bemba. The Global Report 2008 estimates that there are about 7,000 child soldiers in government forces and armed groups, including foreign armed groups, which are

---

[4] Child Soldiers Global Report, 2008. Available at:
http://childsoldiersglobalreport.org/contents/sudan-0. Accessed on 29/4/2010.

mostly found in the eastern provinces of Equatoria, Ituri, Katanga, North and South Kivu and Maniema.[5]

In West Africa, specifically Sierra Leone and Liberia, both theatres of conflict in Africa in the 1990s generated thousands of child soldiers. The conflict in Liberia alone is estimated to have generated 20,000 child soldiers while Sierra Leone produced about 10,000 (Sesay, 2003:12). Sesay (2003), commenting on the plight of child soldiers in Liberia and Sierra Leone, observed that while child soldiers in Liberia became cannibals, those in Sierra Leone became associated with highly unusual atrocities of hacking limbs and cutting off ears and buttocks. The Global Report 2004 also found out that sometimes, the armed groups from Liberia and Sierra Leone recruited children from refugee camps in neighbouring Burkina Faso, Cote d'Ivoire and Guinea. In Chad, over 600 children were found to be still serving in government and opposition forces. In the case of Somalia, due to a complete state collapse, the level of weapons proliferation boosted the numbers of child soldiers. It is estimated that about 200,000 children in Somalia have carried a gun or have been involved with any of the armed groups since 1991 when the central government collapsed (Global Report, 2004:32).

In much of Africa, the Machel Report (1996) observed, "strong martial cultures" no longer have rules that prohibit attacks on women and children. The report further points out that modern war does not match the traditional conceptions of two opposed armies; or even of an internal conflict pitting an armed opposition force against the established government, in which each side generally abides by the rules of the game, respecting the basic inviolability of civilian non-combatants and the special protection due to the young.

In Angola, a survey conducted in 1995 found that 36% of children had accompanied or supported soldiers, and 7% of Angolan children had fired at somebody (Honwana, 2006:29). Equally important to note is that as a result of poor border controls, during the civil wars in most of Africa, especially in West Africa and the Great Lakes Region, conflicts have been spilling over to other countries through contagion effect where they have produced and reproduced child soldiers. Consequently,

---

[5] Child Soldiers Global Report 2008. Available at:
http://www.childsoldiersglobalreport-org/content/congo-democratic-republic.
Accessed on 29/4/2010.

child soldiers have become a regional security dilemma with some of them hiring their services to various war lords who pay better, thereby making civil wars more violent and protracted (Sesay, 2003:18). Sesay points out that in the case of West Africa; the war in Sierra Leone was augmented through contagion effect by the use of child soldiers from neighbouring Liberia where close logistical and strategic linkages between the National Patriotic Front of Liberia (NPFL) and the Revolutionary United Front (RUF) were enhanced by the geographical proximity with Liberia.

The regional security dilemma created by child soldiers is further collaborated by Wessells (2006) who points out that even when the civil war in one country has ended, child soldiers who see no future for themselves in civilian life cross the boarders and become soldiers in neighbouring countries. The regional problem of soldiers for hire applies to adults, too, but most adults can fight for only a few years. Analysts such as Wessells (2006:3) note that children who grow up having learned fighting as their only means of livelihood and survival are likely to continue fighting for more years than adults. Child soldiering damages societies, threatens regional stability, and should be a high-priority issue in building peace, which is indivisible from human rights (Wessells, 2006).

It is noteworthy that in spite of the state of affairs which show that children's rights have been grossly violated across much of Africa's war zones, Africa has also hosted significant events aimed at ending the impunity of violators of children's rights. In March 2004, the Special Court of Sierra Leone indicted 11 people for war crimes and crimes against humanity, including the recruitment of children below 15 years of age. In 2004, the International Criminal Court (ICC) announced investigations into child recruitment and use in the DRC and Uganda (Global Report, 2004:33). However, the conviction of Thomas Lubanga, one of the notorious rebel leaders, the founder and President of Union of the Congolese Patriots (UPC) for enlisting and use of child soldiers was a landmark verdict by ICC. Lubanga was a first person to be arrested by an arrest warrant on 17th March 2006. Commenting about the verdict, Michael Bochenek, Director of Amnesty International's Law and Policy Program observed that,

Today's verdict will give pause to those around the world who commit the horrific crime of using and abusing children both on and off the battlefield (Amnesty International, 2012)

Unfortunately, the arrest and prosecution of Lubanga has not completely recruitment and use of child soldiers in DRC. Amnesty International revealed that recruitment of children into armed conflict has continued in DRC by Congolese armed groups and foreign armed groups. This is largely attributed to the lengthy trials of alleged perpetrators by ICC and lack of corporation by some of the governments.

By March 2004; only 11 out of 46 countries in Africa had ratified the Optional Protocol to the UN Convention on the Rights of the Child on the Involvement of Children in armed conflict. The DRC signed and ratified the Optional Protocol in 2001, Uganda in 2002 while Burundi also signed and ratified in 2001. Ironically, in spite of this level of endorsement of the international law, none of these countries stopped the recruitment and use of children in armed conflicts (Global Report, 2004). One wonders what could be the missing link. How can the very people who sign and ratify legal instruments for protection of children, governments that are mandated to protect the rights of their citizens be the ones to violate them with impunity? This question is discussed extensively in succeeding sections of this chapter.

Definition and Conceptualization of a Child, Childhood and Child Soldier

In order to understand the phenomenon of child soldiering, it is important to understand the legal and international definitions of a child, childhood and a child soldier and how these relate to socio-cultural construction and conceptualization of a child and childhood in the African and Ugandan contexts.

Who is a Child?

A number of challenges arise when defining a child. The challenges arise because notions of childhood in most societies are socially and culturally constructed. According to the United Nations Convention on the Rights of the Child; a child 'means every human being below the age of 18 years

36

unless, under the law applicable to the child, majority is attained earlier' (Cohn et al, 1994:6). This international definition is also upheld by the African Charter on the Rights and Welfare of the Child. Article 2 of the Charter states that, 'For the purposes of this Charter, a child means every human being below the age of 18 years (Human Rights Watch, 1997:120).

While the definition of the child by the Convention on the Rights of the Child has been set at 18, its limitation in the protection of children's rights is that a child is defined differently across various cultures and the convention simply adopted the Western notion of a child and childhood. Commenting on the international definition of a child and childhood, Honwana (2006:41) has observed that ". . . Although this notion of childhood is often generalized and even universalized, it derives from a Western and middle-class view of childhood that is not categorically shared around the globe".

Faced with the contradictions and challenges of the definition of childhood based on age, Cohn et al (1994) have settled for the Inter-Parliamentary Union's recent decision after reviewing 150 of the world's 186 sovereign States. It states that: ". . . The right to vote supposes that electors should have an age at which they are able to express an opinion on political matters, as a rule coinciding with the age of legal majority...".The norm today is eighteen years; an overwhelming majority of 109 States has opted for this minimum age limit, with most other States having a slightly higher limit (19-21 years). The lowest limit -16 years is practiced in four countries: Brazil, Cuba, Iran and Nicaragua (Cohn, 2003:7).

The Inter-Parliamentary Union's definition of the age of the majority is in conformity with other internationally accepted standards such as the Convention on the Rights and Welfare of the Child (Article 2), and the International Labour Organization (ILO) Convention on the Worst Forms of Child Labour (Article 2) No 182 (Francis, 2007: 211).

Cohn et al (1994) agree with Honwana (2006) and observe that the universal definition of a child is limited and conflicts with culturally and religiously constructed definitions. And yet it is this universal and rather Western-centric construction of a child and childhood that has been applied to Africa and other parts of the world. In most of Africa, the age of maturity is a social and cultural device by which societies acknowledge the transition from childhood to adulthood. For the purpose of participating in religious rituals, for example, a child may become an adult at age 13 (Cohn et al, 1994). This is collaborated by both Wessells (2006:5) and Honwana (2006:53) who observe that in non-Western societies such as those in sub-Saharan Africa, particularly in rural areas where traditional ways remain strong, a person is regarded as an adult once he or she has completed the culturally scripted initiation ceremony or rite of passage into manhood or womanhood. Normally such rites occur when a person is around 14 years of age. Also, many developing societies define childhood and adulthood in terms of labour and social roles, arguing that people become adults when they do adult work.

In Uganda, like most other African societies, the definition of the child and childhood has little to do with chronological age. Rather, the age of children is socially constructed and defined based on social responsibilities being performed by such a person in society. It is very common in Uganda to find households headed by 13 year olds or parents marrying away 13 or 14 year old daughters to older men especially those poor families that cannot afford to support their daughters through secondary education. More so, in Uganda as in most African societies, a boy child of even four years could become a man upon being made an heir of his father in case of sudden death. The situation has been compounded by HIV/Aids and civil war related deaths which have increased the numbers of child headed households in Uganda which automatically changes children's status in society.

Article 34 of the Ugandan Constitution defines children as persons under the age of 16. However, the Children's Act 1997 defines a child as a person below the age of eighteen years. This apparent inconsistence between the Constitution and the Children's Act makes children vulnerable. In any case, both the Government of Uganda and the LRA rebels have been known to recruit and use children in armed conflicts even when both parties know this is against the constitution and other pieces of legislation. It can be argued that the cultural construction of the child and childhood may be the contradiction that makes it difficult to uphold the rule of law. However, this is a subject that begs further inquiry in the quest to establish a robust legal protection mechanism for children's rights in armed conflicts.

Who is a Child Soldier?

Regarding the definition of a child soldier, there is no generally agreed international definition. However, Coalition to Stop the Use of Child Soldiers defines a child soldier as any person under the age of 18 who is a member of or attached to government armed forces or any other regular or irregular armed force or armed group, whether or not an armed conflict exists (Global Report, 2004:15). Wessells (2006:7) agrees with the above definition but makes some additions. To Wessells, a child soldier is 'any person under 18 years of age who is part of any kind of regular or irregular armed force in any capacity, including but not limited to cooks, porters, messengers and those accompanying such groups, other than purely as family members. Wessells further observes that girls recruited for sexual purposes and forced marriages are included in the above definition.

Rosen (2005) who observes that the term soldier connotes men or women who are skilled warriors, defines a child soldier as a person below eighteen years of age. However Rosen does not believe that eighteen years represents the idea of who is a child. Rosen observes that it is a fact the world over; historically young people have always been on or near the battle field. He for example concurs with Francis Deng who notes that traditionally among the Dinka of Sudan, boys were initiated into adulthood between the ages of sixteen and eighteen and they immediately received gifts of well-designed spears that symbolized the military function of youths. Rosen also notes that among the Cheyenne-Native Americans, boys joined war parties at 14 years; while among the Samburu and Masai of Kenya, adolescents are initiated into military rituals at an early age.

Machel (1996:7), on the other hand, defines a child soldier as any child-boy or girl under the age of 18, who is compulsorily, forcibly or voluntarily recruited or used in hostilities by armed forces, paramilitaries, civil defence units or other armed forces.

It is worth noting that the definitions of child soldiers by most analysts and scholars are useful in providing a deeper understanding about who child soldiers are in terms of age, which is under 18 years, the international legal age, whether compulsorily or voluntarily recruited; whether in government, civil defence, paramilitary or in armed or rebel groups. However, as Francis (2007:215) has observed, the definitions by most of the scholars fail to distinguish between the different types of child soldiering. Instead all child soldiers are uniformly categorized. Failure to distinguish child soldiers makes it difficult to design relevant reintegration and rehabilitation programmes suited to different categories of child soldiers.

Most observers point out that the universal definition of childhood which goes against culturally constructed childhood across different cultures could be behind the failure of the legal protection of children's rights in armed conflicts. The analysis that the conflicting definition and conceptualization of a child and childhood is responsible for the failure by the international community to protect children in armed conflicts does not complete the picture. There are quite a number of other factors that make it difficult to protect children's rights in armed conflicts including failure to enforce the existing legal instruments, international political calculations, double standards, and the fact that there is always a war to fight. Consequently, it is noted that there is a need that the existing legal instruments are comprehensively enforced. There is also a need to support conflict resolution and peacebuilding frameworks that address the root causes of conflicts in a comprehensive manner. It is worth noting that as long as there are on-going civil wars; children will always be recruited into armed groups. A testimony by a former child soldier from Sierra Leone who was with the Revolutionary United Front confirms this argument as follows: ". . . People blame all the bad things that have happened on the soldiers or the commanders. But I can tell you, the problem is the war itself. You... You will never stop children from fighting unless you stop the war" (Wessells, 2006:240).

Recruitment and Use of Child Soldiers in Armed Conflicts: A General Perspective

This section focuses on the methods of recruitment of children into armed conflict by either the government forces or armed groups fighting against government forces. There are two main methods by which children are recruited into armed groups or government forces: forced recruitment and voluntary recruitment. Voluntary recruitment has however been challenged based on the fact that what most violators of children's rights- government and rebel groups alike - call voluntary recruitment is simply manipulative. They create an environment where children find that they have no choice but to join the armed groups or

40

government forces if they are going to survive. The conflict creates an environment of death and deprivation that children find it impossible to survive outside the armed groups. When children decide to join either side as a survival strategy armed groups or government forces call it voluntary recruitment.

Motivations for Children's Recruitment into Armed Conflicts

This section discusses the motivations for children's involvement in armed conflicts -what some analysts consider to be voluntary recruitment in spite of the risks involved in the practice. This is part of the debate which postulates that in spite of the condemnation levelled at warlords in war zones, children acting on their own initiative join the armed groups or government forces.

According to Singer (2006:61), available information shows that 40% of the FARC's child soldiers are forced into soldiering while 60%joined of their own volition. Another study in East Asia found that 57% of child soldiers had volunteered. Singer (2006) further notes that another study carried out in four African countries found that 64 per cent of child soldiers joined armed groups voluntarily. Also, Cohn et al (1994:23) have argued that not all children are necessarily driven into conflicts. He points out that in Liberia and in the Palestinian intifada in the Israel occupied territories for example, young people are the catalysts of violence. To Cohn et al (1994) the motivation of these young people in joining violent armed conflicts lies in the very roots of the conflicts, in the predominant macro social, economic and political issues defining their lives. Consequently, Cohn et al. suggest that confronting these larger concerns may be the only plausible option to prevent children's involvement in armed conflicts.

While there is evidence that some children voluntarily join armed conflicts, it is imperative to note that what appears to be voluntary recruitment sometimes is manipulated to look as such. A deeper analysis of voluntary recruitment provides a picture of a carefully crafted system of forced recruitment disguised by the violators of children's rights to look like voluntary recruitment. For example, in a war situation where parents have been killed or are away fighting, neighbours have been displaced, crops and schools destroyed, most children find no alternative but to join the armed groups not because of self will but as a way of survival. Consequently, it is argued here that a majority of children are driven to make decisions to join armed groups by factors that are far beyond their control. These motivational factors include; the fact that war comes home; personal and situational influences, push and pull factors, family matters, the desire for revenge, education and power, excitement and glamour. Other factors include political socialization, poverty and a myriad of other causes. These motivating factors are discussed in detail below.

War Environment: War Comes Home

Some analysts have pointed out that most young people become involved in armed conflicts because there is a war and the war environment has become part of their lives. The situation is well captured by Cohn et al (2003:30) and Bracken et al (1998:62) who observe that vast majority of young soldiers are not directly forced or coerced into participating in conflicts; but are subject to many subtly manipulative motivations including economic hardships and other pressures that are more difficult to eliminate than blatant forced recruitment. The story of a former child soldier from the DRC captures the picture of how 'war comes home' influences the decision of children to join the armed groups. As the DRC ex-child soldier observed:

> "I joined (President Kabira) Kabira's army when I was 13 because my home had been looted and my parents were gone. As I was then on my own, I decided to become a soldier" (Singer, 2006:62).

Brett et al (2004:9) who interviewed young people, found their testimonies about why they took part in armed conflicts complex and diverse. Most of those who become involved in warfare do so because there is war. War creates the environment for child soldiering in different ways. First, for young people, war rapidly becomes the normal everyday background for their lives. Second, the war comes to them, rather than them going to look for a war to fight. Third, living in a violent situation creates the need for self-protection and to use violence to do so. Fourth, war causes many other conditions that drive children to participate in war including closing of schools and family break ups. The testimony by Hassan below, an Afghanistan child soldier, is a case in point:

42

I entered in war very early, when I was about 12 or less. . . I came to Mazarsharif for schooling and I became involved in war. I never wanted to use a gun and I never wanted to fight in my country. . . We had to defend and fight; there was no way but war (Brett et al, 2004:11).

Hassan's testimony demonstrates that when war comes to children, even those who did not want to join the armed groups end up joining as a way of survival. However, the war environment is not the only explanation since even in a war environment there are children who never join. This means there are other motivating factors.

Poverty and Economic Agendas

Brett et al (2004) and Singer (2006:63) have argued that poverty is perhaps the most obvious common feature of child soldiering, which is one of the reasons why it is frequently identified as the cause of child soldiering. According to these analysts, poverty applies to both peaceful and war situations where armies recruit young people. Their study on demobilized soldiers in the DRC found that 61% of 300 surveyed said that their families had no income and more than half had at least six siblings at home. The poverty motivation factor is also supported by Bracken et al (1998:61) and Wessells (2006:23) who argue that poverty, which often contributes to the outbreak of war, intensifies during war as it damages well-being and societies slide into economic collapse. Poverty pushes children to drop out of schools hence creating a pool of poor people who view joining armed groups as the only way of accessing economic resources.

Commenting on poverty and economic hardships as a motivating factor for child soldiering, Machel (2001:9) observes that: "As conflicts drag on, recruits tend to get younger. This is partly because deteriorating economic and social conditions drive families deeper into poverty. But also conflicts shut down schools. And the longer a conflict continues, the more likely it is that armed forces, having exhausted the supplies of available adults, will turn to children to fill their ranks".

A testimony by a boy from Colombia who was part of the paramilitaries captures how poverty drives children to join armed groups. The Colombian boy joined the paramilitaries when he was 14 years old. He pointed out that:

After school I was a baker's assistant. It was hard work and paid badly. I went to work on a farm but the work was hard too, so finally I joined the paras. I had friends inside. It paid 300,000 (US$ 100) a month. It seemed like an easier life (Wessells, 2006:54).

War normally exacerbates poverty as it destroys other alternative livelihoods leaving soldiering as the only choice for children to make a living and support themselves and their families. Poverty and war are self-reinforcing and interconnected which ultimately leads to protractedness of civil wars. Consequently, one can safely deduce that as long as war and poverty persists, it will always constrain measures for prevention of recruitment and use of children in armed conflicts. It should be noted however that poverty alone may not be a decisive factor for children's decisions to take a risk and join the armed conflict. This is so because in most conflicts not all poor children decide to join the armed groups or government forces. In most cases a combination of factors work together to compel children from poverty stricken families to join the armed conflict.

Education and Employment

Most observers have pointed out that lack of education is a crucial factor that motivates children to join armed conflicts. It is observed that for most young people, access to education is a critical factor for preparing them for future employment and modern life (Peters et al, 1998:82). However, during civil wars, many schools and other educational institutions are destroyed and teachers flee for their dear lives leading to the closure of schools and other educational institutions. Also, during civil wars, public resources are diverted to finance the war effort at the expense of social sectors such as education and health. With the education institutions closed down, destroyed or malfunctioning, most children who had viewed education as the only hope for a bright future become disillusioned. Consequently, children turn to military life as an alternative livelihood.

Additionally, not being at school or employed is a critical risk factor for young people. If they are not involved in either education or employment, what are young people going to do to fill their time, to support themselves or their families? This point is supported by Machel's

Report (1996:12) which points out that as conflict persists, socio-economic conditions suffer and educational opportunities become limited making soldiering the most viable opportunity.

Education has another side of influence or motivation for young people to join armed groups. This has to do with the fact that education shapes the understanding, attitudes, and behaviour of individuals. In a politically charged environment, sometimes the military and political forces use the school curriculum as a tool to influence students to support their cause. For example, the practice of segregated education that existed in Apartheid South Africa motivated the youths who knew their education was poor quality to join the armed and political struggle to bring it down. Elements in the educational situation in South Africa were major factors in the political mobilization of the youth, particularly in the townships (Brett et al, 2004:18).

In some schools, teachers have a great influence in motivating the children to join the armed groups. A case in point is the Madrassah schools in Pakistan, which teach radical Islam and have become breeding grounds for recruitment of jihad martyrs. In Pakistan, Madrassahs are private Islamic religious schools where tuition, room and board are provided free. Accordingly, most of these students are from poor backgrounds (Brett et al, 2004). Brett et al (2004:19) quotes the testimony of one of the pupils, who noted that: "We were taught in the maddrassah that one who sacrifices his life in jihad, is a martyr and will be rewarded generously. Besides he will recommend other people for Paradise in addition to rewarding him Paradise without judgement".

It should be noted that even after the war, provision of educational opportunities to former child soldiers is critical in prevention of re-enlisting into other rebellions. The interviews that were conducted by Krijn Peters and Paul Richards (1998:82) among the former child soldiers in Sierra Leone, found that these former combatants stressed that it makes little sense to stand down voluntarily without a real promise of social reintegration, education or training. Former child soldiers noted that failure to address these aspirations 'first caused and now prolongs' the conflict. In fact, it is noted that when most former combatants in Sierra Leone became frustrated by the failure of the demobilization process, several of them who had been informants in the study by Peters and Richards, re-enlisted after the military coup of 1997. The link between education and child soldiering is convincing such that the provision of education, especially technical education, to former child soldiers becomes imperative in their RR processes. During the fieldwork in Northern Uganda, it was established that most child soldiers want to go back to school to better their future.

Orphaning and Separation of Children

Wessells (2006:25) observe that orphaning and separation from parents motivates children to voluntarily join armed conflicts. He notes that of all the losses children suffer in war zones, none is more painful than the death of their parents, their primary sources of love and protection. The loss of parents not only creates heavy emotional burdens but can also begin a downward spiral into increased poverty and vulnerability. Failing to meet their basic needs and desperate to survive, orphans and separated children decide to join armed groups, or perform dangerous functions such as labourers or in prostitution. Wessells' point is collaborated by stories told about the former child soldiers in Uganda. During the guerrilla war that brought Uganda's current President Museveni to power in 1986, government forces used scorched earth policy in their offensive against the NRA rebels. These offensives involved destruction of property and indiscriminate killings of suspected rebel collaborators which left many children orphaned.

Commenting on how child soldiers came to be recruited into the National Resistance Army (NRA) which after capturing power was renamed: Uganda Peoples Defence Forces (UPDF), Kaihura observed that:

> When the National Resistance Movement (NRM) came to power in Uganda in 1986, there were as many as 300 child soldiers in the National Resistance Army (NRA). However, these child soldiers, some of them as young as five years old, had not been deliberately recruited by the NRA to fight its bush war, as was widely alleged in 1986. Rather, they were orphaned or abandoned children, victims of the *'scorched earth'* policy of the then government army the Uganda National Liberation Army (UNLA). They were children who had either fled to the nearest NRA camp or been found in the bushes by NRA patrols or fighting units (Kaihura, 2000:11)[6]

---

[6] Kaihura, K. (2000). Uganda: The Integration of Child Soldiers into the School System. Association for the Development of Education in Africa (ADEA) International

Consequently, it is evident that for many children who become orphaned or separated as a result of the war joining either side of the opposing sides has a lot to do with the search for protection, love and care which children at a tender age badly need. In the case of the child soldiers or the *Kadogos* (Swahili word for small children) in the Uganda's NRA, the army became their surrogate mother and their commanders to whom most of them were attached effectively their guardians.

Joining in order to Revenge

> I joined the Army when I was fourteen because, one, I was persuaded that the only way to get my parents back or to stop that from happening was to be a part of the Army and kill those people who were responsible for killing my parents. But you see, the thing that is very disturbing is that once I joined the Army and started fighting, I was also killing other people's parents and so I was creating a circle of revenge where I killed somebody else's parents, he's going to be persuaded by a different group, either the RUF or the Army, saying, 'Okay join the Army and kill this person who killed your parents'. So, it's a circle of revenge. And the disturbing thing about it is that its kids that were killing kids (Voice of a boy child aged 14 years) (Singer, 2006:57).

War creates lawlessness and powerlessness especially among innocent civilians. Armed groups including the unruly government forces abuse human rights including wanton killings, rape and sexual slavery. Children who hopelessly witness the murder of their parents, rape of their sisters by armed gangs, summary executions and torture may be motivated to join armed groups or the government army in order to find an opportunity to revenge (Cohn et al, 1998:32). The above testimony from a child soldier from Sierra Leone is a clear example about how some children join the armed groups to avenge the death of their defenceless parents at the hands of either the government army or the rebels.

Institute for Educational Planning. Available at: http://www.adeanet.org. Accessed on 8/10/2009.
It should also be noted that there have been conflicting reports about the number of child soldiers that participated in the NRA struggle. While the official figure by government is 300, international agencies and human rights groups put the figure as high as 3,000 child soldiers.

Power, Excitement and Glamour

The situation in most war zones is characterized by lawlessness with armed gangs brutalizing innocent people. Because of the suffering and powerlessness, children in war zones are exposed to at the hands of armed groups or sometimes government forces, most of them decide to join armed groups to regain their freedom. The freedom comes about because of the gun which joining the armed group accords to children. Besides the protection that accrues to children because of being members of armed groups, the gun gives them a sense of power and prestige. A combination of re-humanization from humiliation and the pride of being able to be respected and also providing security to others become positive appeals to children for joining the armed groups.

Political Socialization

Most observers point out that the conditions in which children live determine their future outlook of the world (Wessells, 2006). For children whose whole life has been lived in a militarized environment, they also become militarized or politicized. Living in war torn societies under military occupation, children often learn to define themselves as part of the opposition to the enemy. In such circumstances, through political socialization, many children acquire a strong desire to serve and willingness to sacrifice their lives, which motivates them into joining armed groups. The example of a former child soldier from the Philippines provides a vivid explanation in the following narrative:

> I joined to serve the people in the mountains. We protected them from violence and harm, from the government soldiers. These soldiers, they were abusive; that is why we kept watch (Wessells, 2006:53).

The above point is true in respect to child soldiers in Uganda during the rebellion that was led by President Museveni (1981-86). Museveni's rebel forces: the National Resistance Army developed a 10 Point Programme which articulated the reasons for the rebellion which included restoration of democracy and rule of law, protection of human rights and human dignity and conducted political education in the areas under their control. The former child soldiers who were interviewed observe that they were convinced that they needed to fight and liberate the country from dictatorship (Interview with Okello).[7]

Multiple Causation

One of the motivating factors that has been identified with regard to why young people join armed groups or government forces is when many factors combine together. It is noted that children from abusive families may decide to join armed groups or the military because they are beaten at home, they earn less marks in class and teachers harass them or they are subjected to hard work at home. In the United States and the United Kingdom, young people of around 16 years mostly from poor backgrounds and marginalized groups are attracted to join the military in order to get free education and jobs so as to advance their careers and standards of living as well as a good image in the future (Wessells, 2006:56). In this case a combination of all these social needs and the possibility that all of them can be achieved in the armed forces may compel young people to join armed groups.

Family, Friends and Peer Pressure

The family environment has also been identified as an important determinant of children's involvement or non-involvement in armed conflict (Wessells, 2006:47). It is noted that the nature of the family and family situation into which children are born or grow in; has a great bearing on their decisions in life. In a normal family environment one finds children wanting to take on the professions of their parents since they are shaped and inspired by parents. In situations where parents are involved in the military it is normal for their children to join the military forces.

On the other hand, the lack of a family may become a push factor for some young people to join the armed forces. Without a family, children become vulnerable to both forced and voluntary recruitment.

---

[7] Okello, J., a former child soldier under the National Resistance Army (NRA) that brought President Museveni to power in 1986 after toppling the Obote 11 Government and the Okello Military Junta in 1986. Okello is currently working as a Senoir Resettlement Officer with the Amnesty Commission. He was interviewed in February 2010.

Cohn and Goodwin-Gill (1998) have observed that 'peer pressure can be very persuasive' in influencing the child to join armed groups as can the child's desire to win the approval of family or religious leaders. A good example is how the Palestinian children throwing a stone at the Israel army is said to be 'one of the guys' and this act confers on the child heroism among his/her peers.

Politics and Ideological Influence

It is argued that the nature of the political environment in which people grow influences their decisions and course of action. For example children, who are born in families that oppose the authorities, become distinctive and different from those who are from the ruling elites. In the event that the nature of political opposition changes to armed opposition, children from opposing families are likely to join the armed groups with conviction and strong ideological motivation. As Brett et al (2004:27) observe, to children with ideological orientation, there is a sense of need to overturn an oppressive regime. In this context, one child from the DRC remarked that:

> Mobutu and his soldiers, they were mean, they oppressed us, tortured us, we were always mistreated. . . He and his men! Once they had beaten me because of my boots! Till this day, I have hated them. When I was small, I had fashionable clothes, and I had boots like military boots; it was fashionable in Congo. But not everyone could have some because they were expensive. Once, my mother bought me some of it. Once I left for school with my boots, I was proud. A soldier called me over and said to me to come to him, and he asked me, 'who gave you a soldier's boots?' . . . The soldier told me to remove them . . . I told them that it was my mom who had bought these for me. They didn't care. The guy started to strike my back with a cord that hurts. I bled. – Germain (DRC).

Adolescent Pressure/ Influence

Scholars (Brett et al, 2004) note adolescence as a critical factor that motivates voluntary recruitment of young people into armed groups. The adolescence stage in human development is always a very challenging stage. During adolescence young people are transiting from childhood to adulthood and it is at this stage that human beings become too excited and hard to control across all cultures. According to Brett et al (2004:29), adolescence can be a difficult time for young persons and the family as well as other adults who have to deal with them. It is noted that during this stage adolescents may become perpetrators of physical and sexual violence as well as its victims. They may challenge authority and rebel against instructions, while at the same time they need support and encouragement, and moral and emotional guidance. Since adolescence inspires feelings of power and ambition in young people, it makes them think that all things can be overcome, which could influence them to find armed conflicts attractive. In this stage of human development, the real dangers that the armed conflict could bring to an individual are rarely considered as the following testimony by a former child soldier reveals:

> It was my friends that encouraged me to become a cobra. They told me that it was not dangerous. I could hold a weapon, they said. Above all, there was a good ambience, it's not complicated. When they return with money; you want to have some too! – Albert, Congo Brazzaville (Brett et al, 2004).

Forced Recruitment of Children in Armed Conflicts

This section discusses the methods of forced recruitment and the use of child soldiers in armed conflicts either by government forces or opposition armed groups.

> My parents refused to give me to the LTTE so about fifteen of them came to my house ... it was both men and women, in uniforms, with rifles, and guns in holsters... I was fast asleep when they came to get me at one in the morning...These people dragged me out of the house. My father shouted at them, saying, 'What is going on?' but some of the LTTE soldiers took my father towards the woods and beat him... They also pushed my mother onto the ground when she tried to stop them (HRW 2004b, 2).

It should be noted that forced recruitment entails the threat of or actual violation of the physical integrity of the youth or some people who are closely related to the child being forcefully recruited. In practice forced recruitment is practiced by both the government forces and armed opposition groups in war-torn societies (Cohn et al,1998:24). Forced recruitment has several faces: abduction, press ganging and the quota method. These forms of forced recruitment are explained in detail below.

Abduction

Most rebel groups use abduction as the most viable method of recruitment of children into armed conflicts. According to Singer (2006:61) abduction is by definition an act of violence that rips terrified children from the security of their families and homes. Killings, rapes and severe beatings often accompany it. Children who are abducted normally have two choices available to them – cooperate with the kidnapers and live or resist and you are dead. Abduction is an illegal practice that perpetrators seek to hide which makes it difficult to estimate the percentage of children who have entered armed groups through abduction. Usually, recruiting groups are given targets that may change according to the groups' needs and objectives.

It is observed that UPC/RP, a militia group led by Timothy Lubanga based in the eastern region of the Democratic Republic of Congo (DRC), had a military strategy in the area he controlled where each family was forced to provide a cow, money or a child to the group (Singer, 2006:59). On the other hand, LTTE is reported to have maintained sophisticated computerised population databases to direct its recruitment efforts while the Sudan People's Liberation Army (SPLA) used the presence of two molar teeth to determine whether the child is ready to serve. There are a number of children's testimonies from the various war zones, which confirm the abduction method of recruitment as a preferred choice of most armed groups. One of the child soldiers from South Sudan pointed out that:

> I was abducted during 'operation pay yourself', in 1998. I was 9 years old. Six rebels came through our yard. They went to loot for food. It's called *'jaja'*…'get food.' They said, We want to bring a small boy like you—we like you. My mother didn't comment; she just cried. My father objected. They threatened to kill him..... I heard a gunshot. One of them told me, Let's go, they have killed your father'. A woman rebel grabbed my hand roughly. .... I saw my father lying dead as we passed.- A., age fourteen (Singer, 2006:60)

Accordingly, camps for refugees and internally displaced persons (IDPs), street children, secondary schools or orphanages and market places are the most favoured areas for recruitment of children by the armed groups (Singer, 2006:59). The reason for targeting such places, is that there are always many children in one place and normally these places especially IDP camps lack security protection. Consequently, armed groups always have a field day to do whatever they want without being detected or prevented. In some situations such as in Afghanistan abduction takes the form of a mixture of organized abduction and positive inducements. In Afghanistan, child recruitment is carried out through house-to-house abductions mixed with felt loyalties and a sense of dignity. During the post-9/11 fight against the Taliban in Northern Afghanistan, Northern Alliance commanders frequently recruited by going from house to house. One Afghan child solider pointed out that:

> The commanders came to my house and told me to come with them.... If I had not gone with him, I would have been beaten or bad things could have happened to my family (Wessells, 2006:39).

In Northern Uganda, the Lord's Resistance Army (LRA) recruitment method has always been by child abductions, which involve house to house hunt or rounding up of school children as they sleep in their dormitories at night. Abducted children are then made to carry looted food and other supplies to safety. Most of the fighters of the LRA are child soldiers. Estimates indicate that between 70% and 80% of the LRA are child combatants (MacKay et al, 1999:26). The child abduction methods of the LRA are characterised by brutality and wanton killings of the children who fail to carry their heavy loads of the loot or get wounded and are unable to walk. A 13 year old boy told his story of abduction by the LRA as follows:

> Early on when my brothers and I were captured, the LRA explained to us that all the five brothers couldn't serve in the LRA because we would not perform well. So they tied up my two younger brothers and invited us to watch. Then they beat them with sticks until two of them died. They told us it would give us strength to fight. My youngest brother was nine years old (HRW 2003d).

Briggs (2005:116) observes that since 1987, the LRA has waged a bloody war targeting civilians, mostly the Acholi community who they accuse of betrayal for supporting the government. With limited support from the local population, the LRA resorted to abduction of children and indiscriminate killings of suspected government allies. Briggs notes that behind child abduction lies a carefully crafted element of war. Abducted children are trained to use weapons and how to fight. This is supported by the Human Rights Watch report which observes that girl child soldiers besides fighting and providing labour are also meant to provide sex to the rebel commanders (Human Rights Watch, 1997).

During the Angolan civil war, about 3,000 child soldiers were reported to have been forcibly recruited from the neighbouring countries. According to Machel (2001:9) in 1997 UNITA forcibly recruited an estimated 200 Rwandan refugee children who had been living along the border between Angola and the Democratic Republic of Congo. Also, in 1998, Rwandan boys and girls aged about 13 years were forcibly recruited by the Angolan Armed Forces.

In Sierra Leone, the Revolutionary United Front (RUF) which launched their armed struggle in 1991 with the backing of Liberia's President Charles Taylor after failing to attract widespread local support resorted to forced conscription and abduction of both boys and girls in its ranks (MacKay et al, 1999:30). MacKay further observes that children's rights in Sierra Leone were not violated by RUF alone. The Sierra Leone Government forces organized local militias who became known as Civil Defence Forces which recruited young people to support the government army in the fight against the rebels.

The situation was not different in Mozambique where the civil war raged on from 1976 to 1992 between the FRELIMO government and the Apartheid South Africa backed RENAMO rebels. The civil war in Mozambique, which left one million people dead,45% of whom were children, was fought by children forcibly recruited by both sides in the conflict (MacKay et al. 1999:107). Commenting on the devastation of the war in Mozambique MacKay et al(1999:32) observed that:

The war devastated the infrastructure, with schools and medical facilities systematically targeted by RENAMO. Both sides recruited and press-ganged girls and boys into their forces throughout the conflict. These children were used as combatants, spies, slaves, 'wives' intelligence agents and porters. Families were torn apart and physical and sexual violence, including murder, amputation, rape, forced cannibalism and torture, were widespread.

According to Cohn et al (1998: 24) in El Salvador and Guatemala, the armed forces use round ups to fill their ranks which involve taking children out of buses and cars, away from market places and churches. Neither Guatemala nor El Salvador maintains a formal conscription process, and with many peasants unable to obtain identification cards documenting their birth dates, since births are not registered, it is difficult for anyone to argue the case of being under age for conscription.

Press Ganging

Another form of forced recruitment is press ganging. Press ganging involves group recruitment where armed groups conduct massive sweeps through streets or market places, schools or orphanages rounding up young people. A case in point is the LRA rebels' raid of Aboke Girls Secondary School in Northern Uganda in 1996 where 139 girls were abducted. In Burundi, the armed groups are also known to have frequently abducted children from schools and forced them to carry military equipment or assist the injured soldiers.

Recruitment by Quota

Recruitment by quota is another method of forced recruitment. In order to subjugate and control people, armed groups seek to co-opt local authorities and force them to work as their agents. In the case of the Angolan civil war the rebel, UNITA directed the village leaders to recruit a certain number of children if the villages were not to be attacked. Fearing the possibility of being attacked and the destruction of whole villages; village leaders would turn up with the young people as was directed by UNITA (Wessells, 2006). Consequently, the practice of leaders recruiting the quotas for UNITA greatly undermined the credibility and prestige of local leaders who instead of offering protection to the children simply became violators of their rights. Quota recruitment was also practiced by the Taliban in Afghanistan. It is noted that the Taliban used the quota system in the North-Eastern provinces where the Northern Alliance fought against them. Wessells (2006) notes that the Taliban commanders used to move from village to village ordering parents to hand over a certain number of youths of six to 10 years to enlist as soldiers for three to six months. This quota system of recruitment would be repeated from time to time by commanders. A village which failed to deliver its quota would be attacked.

56

In order to protect their children from forced recruitment under this quota system, wealthy families in Afghanistan used to send their sons to Pakistan or pay poor families to send their sons to fight in their place. This emphasises the role of poverty as a motivating factor for poor children's involvement in armed conflicts. War creates a war economy and aggravates poverty situation compelling children mostly from poorer families to join the armed groups to contribute to the welfare of their families.

Preference for Child Soldiers by Armed Groups and Government Forces: Why?

Several reasons have been advanced to explain why children are preferred for recruitment into armed groups and government forces. First, it is noted that under-age children are highly rated by the commanders since they fight without a mind or any inhibition and kill without compunction; and sometimes as an extension of play (Peters et al. (1998:82). It is also observed that children are convenient to recruit. Most field commanders argue that they recruit children because they cannot replenish their troop losses by recruiting adults. In most areas that are experiencing civil wars, there is always a steady supply of children who in almost all cases form the majority of the population. In this case, rebels find it militarily expedient to recruit children who are readily available and in large supply.

Second, it is observed that children are cheap to get and sustain in armed conflicts. Most recruits are promised money by their adult recruiters, promises which are never honoured. In this case, as Brett et al (2004:34) point out, the promise of money to poor children, acts as a 'pull' factor. Most important to note is that once these children have joined the armed groups they may feel timid to demand for their pay as opposed to the adults who are confident to demand payment.

The third reason why commanders recruit children is that children have shock value. The argument here is that while on the battlefield, child soldiers sow disarray and confusion by confronting the opposing troops without fear, since the other troops may be reluctant to kill children. Examples are the wars in Sierra Leone and Liberia where small-boys units were used to spearhead assaults and sometimes could be sent forward naked as a means of causing confusion and terror among the opposing forces (Singer, 2006).

The fourth reason for recruitment of children, especially teenagers, is because of their ability to carry heavy loads of goods and to perform labour, and fight with an efficacy that rivals that of adults (Brett et al, 2004). It is noted that teenagers can be effective planners of war and can even lead attacks successfully, develop strategies for avoiding capture in equal manner as the adult soldiers. Most importantly, culture places teenagers at a high risk of recruitment since in some cultures teenagers of 14 years are considered adults and fit to do the work of a man or a woman.

Fifth, it has also been observed that while children make up the frequent shortfall in manpower suffered by both the government armed forces and armed groups in war zones some commanders deliberately look out for children in preference to adults simply because children are obedient and highly motivated. More so, children are said to be easily manipulated as they have not fully developed a sense of right and wrong and can therefore be trained to be brutal soldiers (Harvey, 2003). Indoctrination has been used in the conflict in Northern Uganda where rebels would smear young recruits with shear butter and tell them to fight without taking cover since sheer butter would repel enemy bullets (Human Rights Watch, 1997).

Sixth, youths are pliable which means that they are easily manipulated and controllable. The rebel commanders do this through brutality and spreading terror among child soldiers. Through use of violence and threat of violence, children can be trained to obey commands that adults would otherwise question or contest. Wessells (2006:35) observes that children in an armed group in 'a new world characterized by danger and recognizing their ignorance of the group rules and lack of survival skills, use obedience as a 'survival strategy'. Recruiters are also known to play on the children's cognitive and moral development. Teenagers are at a stage in their lives in which they are forming their own identity, achieving autonomy, and defining their wider beliefs and worldview. Teenagers are often more receptive to new ideologies and systems of thought than adults are. Most importantly, children tend to be more idealistic than adults. Consequently, recruiters play on this idealism and openness by promising opportunities and to solve some of the problems that young people may have, in exchange for 'overthrowing an unjust regime and building a better social order based on justice and equality' which appeals to children.

Seventh, children are also easily exploitable and expendable in civil wars. Most rebel leaders or commanders regard children as cheap resources that can be exploitable in many ways. The small size of children makes them unable to defend or protect themselves from sexual exploitation by the commanders and adult soldiers. More so, children have enormous capacity to learn new things, which allows them to be deployed to perform multiple roles such as porters, cooks, body guards, sex slaves and spies. This was the situation in Angola where UNITA rebels always preferred young children as labourers since they could carry heavy loads of materials that could not be carried by vehicles. In Northern Uganda, the LRA rebels never recruit adults at all. They abduct children who they use as labourers, sex slaves and as killing machines as well as human shields as they are sent on the frontline while adults remain behind in safety (Green, 2009).

Besides their tender age which makes children easy to manipulate, armed groups are known to provide children with drugs to regularly make them fearless and senseless in undertaking suicide missions. Most studies that have been conducted on these armed conflicts where children are being used found that marijuana was being frequently used as well as crack cocaine or a cocktail of local substances and gunpowder. Most crimes are committed under the influence of drugs. Girl combatants were found to experience regular rapes by fellow combatants sometimes as 'punishment' for losing ground (Peters et al, 1998:82).

It is important to note that in most civil wars and civilian based conflicts, children become perfect cover and military assets to be used to infiltrate the enemy camps either as spies or on suicide missions unnoticed. Consequently, most armed groups and government forces prefer children who because of their less developed intellect are fearless, less sensitive and cheap military assets to exploit. In the guerrilla war that brought President Museveni to power child soldiers, popularly known as *Kadogos*, played a crucial role in dislodging the government army by undertaking daring missions for which they would be cheered upon successful completion.

How Child Soldiers are used in Armed Conflicts

Machel (2001) observed that children once recruited are treated the same way as the adults. They begin with induction ceremonies, which include burial, killing of their friends and relatives in the case of the LRA in Uganda, RUF in Sierra Leone and RENAMO in Mozambique. The induction is supposed to make them brave, loosen relational ties with their families and communities and instil fear and royalty to the commanders.

Collins (2007:375) points out that in Mozambique children abducted by the rebel RENAMO were forced to return to their villages and attack them. The intention was that this barbaric and shameful action would prevent children from ever thinking of returning home and thus guarantee the rebels' allegiance to their cause. Consequently, these acts would alienate child soldiers from their families and communities which makes post-conflict RR very challenging.

Children within the LRA, the main focus of this book, are used to perform several roles or tasks. The first and most crucial task for children under the LRA is participation in combat operations against the government forces or Sudan Peoples' Liberation Army (SPLA). It is noted that almost 80% of the LRA rank and file are children and children are deployed on frontlines while the adults in command positions always remain safely in the rear (World Vision International, 2005:17). Other common tasks assigned to children under the LRA are to serve as porters, often carrying very heavy loads of looted food, ammunition and wounded combatants. Children who are too weak to carry heavy loads are often savagely beaten or killed. Mckay et al (1999), who conducted a study on the gender dimension of the LRA conflict in Northern Uganda which focused on former young women captives within the LRA, observe that the three primary roles girls reported were porters (41%), food producers (22%) and fighters (12%). They also note that although discussions regarding the roles of girls within the LRA focus on them as captive 'wives' only half (51%) reported serving as wives in either their primary or secondary roles.

Machel (2001) notes that both girls and boys are often compelled to provide sexual services. In the case of girls, those abducted into armed groups are usually forced into sexual slavery where they are distributed to rebel commanders as a payment or motivation. Unfortunately, most of the children who have been forced to provide sexual services end up contracting HIV/Aids and other sexually transmitted diseases. Machel (2001:13) observed that:

> Abducted girls as young as 10 have been kept as sex slaves by rebel leaders. Once the leader dies, the girl is typically put aside for ritual cleansing and then given to another rebel.

Machel's observation is collaborated by Mazurana (MacKay, 1999:72) who, commenting about the gender roles of girls among the LRA, found that 51 percent of the girl captives served as wives besides working as porters, labourers and fighters. However, the most distressing role of children is being used as human shields by rebel commanders whenever the rebels are attacked. In case of an attack by government soldiers, child soldiers are usually instructed to make a ring around senior rebel commanders to protect them from bullets. In such encounters many child soldiers are killed.

The children, besides being used as combatants, sex slaves and labourers, are deployed to loot food from civilians. A number of former child soldiers' testimonies under the LRA confirm this role. During the field work, one former child soldier narrated a story how he was almost killed for looting little food by the LRA commander who accused him of laziness. Another formerly abducted child soldier remembers how he collapsed under a fifty kilogram bag of looted maize floor he was forced to carry non-stop by the rebels after his abduction while chained on a rope with other abductees.[8]

By and large, it is evident that child soldiers in all civil wars are exploited, dehumanized and abused while serving with armed groups or government soldiers. Child soldiers serve multiple critical roles within the armed groups, which to a large extent explain why they are always preferred and why prevention of recruitment and use of child soldiers is difficult to eradicate (Francis, 2007:6).Children's potential, coupled with the lack of adult manpower as civil wars drag on compels rebel groups and government forces to recruit children into their forces where they are indoctrinated or drugged to fight without thinking. It is against this background, that the debate about voluntary and involuntary recruitment of child soldiers does not hold water.

---

[8] Interview with one of the formerly abducted child soldiers conducted in February, 2010 in northern Uganda.

A critical analysis of the methods of recruitment of children into armed groups finds that the claims that some children voluntarily enlist is nothing but a sham. Armed groups and governments create conditions that leave children with no choice but to join in the fighting. It is this disguised forced recruitment that is presented by armed groups and government forces as voluntary recruitment. Consequently, there is a need for the international community to craft a robust legal mechanism to protect children's rights in armed conflicts.

International Mechanisms for the Protection of Children in Armed Conflicts

> Throughout history, war has exacted a horrific toll on children. But modern warfare kills, maims and exploits children more callously and more systematically than ever before. Caught up in complex conflicts that have multiple causes and little prospect of early resolution, children are being sucked into seemingly endless endemic struggles for power and resources. During the 1990s, more than 2 million children died as a result of armed conflicts, often deliberately targeted and murdered (Machel, 2001:1).

The suffering of children in armed conflicts going on around the world is well documented. The use of child soldiers violates widely accepted principles of international humanitarian law about proper behaviour in the conduct of war. The human rights abuses involved, which range from abduction, forced conscription and rape, to torture and murder have shocked the conscience of the international community. Consequently, the twentieth century witnessed attempts by the international community to protect the rights of children in armed conflicts by developing a range of international conventions, protocols and resolutions aimed at preventing the use of children in armed conflicts. Most of these international legal instruments have been ratified and domesticated by national governments into their domestic law. However, as Wessells (2006:233) has noted, in spite of the tremendous progress by the international community in developing international legal mechanisms for the protection of children in armed conflicts, not much progress has been achieved in enforcing them.

This section examines the international legal mechanisms that have been developed for the protection of children in armed conflicts at the global and continental (Africa) levels. The section also discusses the reasons, why in spite of the existence of a substantive body of legal mechanisms, recruitment and use of child soldiers continues to be the common practice.

In order to deal with the alarming levels of negative impact armed conflicts were having on children, the international community throughout the twentieth century engaged in developing a number of international legal instruments for protection of children's rights. The international legal mechanisms for protection of children's rights in armed conflicts can be broadly categorised into: international humanitarian law, international human rights law, international customary law and national constitutions and legislations. Singer (2006:140) observes that regardless of where one stands in the debate about the protection of children in armed conflicts, there is no doubt that the practice of using child soldiers violates widely accepted international beliefs and norms about proper behaviour.

The legal mechanisms include the 1924 League of Nations Declaration on the Rights of the Child; 1948 UN Universal Declaration of Human Rights; 1949 Geneva Conventions; 1950 European Conventions; 1951 Convention and 1967 Protocol Relating to the Status of Refugees; 1966 UN Covenants on Civil and Political Rights and Economic, Social and Cultural Rights; 1969 American Convention on Human Rights; 1977 Additional Protocols to the 1949 Geneva Conventions; the 1981 African Charter on Human and Peoples' Rights; 1984 Convention Against Torture and Other Cruel, Inhuman or Degrading Treatment or Punishment; 1989 UN Convention on the Rights of the Child and 1990 OAU African Charter on the Rights and Welfare of the Child (Singer, 2006:141).

It should be mentioned from the outset, that the most influential international legal protection for children in armed conflicts is contained in two bodies of international law: International Humanitarian Law and International Human Rights Law (Harvey, 1997:6). To this end, the section below critically analyzes the main international humanitarian law and international human rights law instruments that have been designed for the protection of children's rights in armed conflicts.

International Humanitarian Law

International Humanitarian Law is one of the bodies of legal instruments that have been developed by the international community to protect civilians in armed conflicts. International humanitarian law, also known as the law of armed conflict, is the body of law that seeks to regulate the methods and means of warfare, and the treatment of people in times of war, who are not, or who are no longer, participating in the hostilities. Such people include prisoners of war, injured soldiers and non-combatants[9].

The Geneva Conventions of 1949

The Geneva Conventions of 1949 form one of the international legal instruments that provide for the protection of children in armed conflicts, in spite of their inadequacies. The main aim of all the four Geneva Conventions is the protection of the victims of international conflicts. Out of the four Geneva Conventions, Geneva Convention 1V was the first international treaty that sought exclusively to provide protection to civilians caught up in armed conflicts. It prohibits not only murder, torture or mutilation of a protected person, but also any other measures of brutality whether applied by civilians or military agents (Machel, 1996). It should be noted however, that the Geneva Convention 1V is mainly concerned with the treatment of civilians who are in the hands of an opposing party or who are victims of war rather than regulating the conduct of parties to a conflict in order to protect civilians.

The Geneva Conventions of 1949 impose a limited number of obligations on parties to a particular conflict to provide special protection to children, including allowing free passage of food, clothing and medicine destined for children and to assist children who are separated or orphaned (Harvey, 2001:8). The Convention also requires State Parties to establish hospitals and safety zones to protect children among other vulnerable groups.

---

[9]International Committee of the Red Cross (ICRC). Available at: http://www.ehl.icrc.org/images/resources/pdf/what_isihl.pdf. Accessed on 29/6/2010.

It should be noted that in respect of the Geneva Convention 1V, the majority of the provisions do not provide protection to all children who are below 18 years of age. The reason for this is that at the time the Geneva Conventions 1949 came into force after the Second World War, the concept that all persons below 18 years of age are children and therefore entitled to protection did not exist. Suffice to say that, while the Geneva Convention 1V only provides for limited protection for children, its provisions are applicable to every international conflict. This is so because of the fact that over 190 states are parties to the convention, and also the fact that the 1949 Geneva Conventions are now considered to be part of the Customary International Law. The consequence of this is that the few state parties that may not have ratified the Geneva Conventions are also bound to uphold its obligations (Harvey, 2001:8).

One of the weaknesses with the Geneva Conventions is that they were largely designed to protect children in interstate wars that were prevalent at the time. Most of the conflicts going on around the world today where most of the children are actively involved either as child soldiers, sex slaves, porters, labourers or spies are intra-state conflicts, which makes it difficult to apply the Geneva Conventions. This is in spite of the existence of Common Article 3 of the Geneva Conventions, which in a restricted sense, provides for protection of civilians and by extension to children's rights in internal conflicts (Machel, 1996). The utility of the Geneva Conventions though is that they provided a bedrock upon which future international agreements for the protection of children in armed conflicts are built.

The United Nations Declaration on the Protection of Women and Children in Emergency and Armed Conflict 1974

Another important, none-legally binding international legal instrument for the protection of children's rights in armed conflict is the United Nations Declaration for the Protection of Women and Children in Emergency and Armed Conflict of 1974. This Declaration was passed by the United Nations (UN) General Assembly Resolution 3318 (XXIX) of 14 December 1974.[10] Most observers note that even if this declaration is

---

[10] The UN Declaration on the Protection of Women and Children in Emergency and Armed Conflict was proclaimed by the United Nations General Assembly under the United Nations Resolution 3318 (XX1X) on the 14 December 1974. Available at:

not legally binding to the State Parties, it managed to raise awareness about the situation of women and children within the international community. For example the declaration expressed its deep concern over the suffering of women and children belonging to the civilian population who in periods of emergency and armed conflict, in the struggle for peace, self-determination, national liberation and independence are too often the victims of inhuman acts and suffer serious harm.

The declaration prohibits attacks and bombings on the civilian population, inflicting incalculable suffering especially on women and children who are the most vulnerable members of the population. The declaration was able to draw the attention of the international community to the plight of children and women and the need to offer them special protection during armed conflicts.

The 1977 Additional Protocols to the Geneva Conventions

In an attempt to address the inadequacies of the Geneva Conventions, the international community in 1977 adopted the Additional Protocols to the Geneva Conventions. The Additional Protocols of 1977 were developed as a result of an initiative of the International Committee of the Red Cross which sought to update the laws governing the conduct of war and to specifically encourage States to recognize and accept the reality of changed warfare based on the several wars of liberation and the guerrilla tactics that were being used (Cohn et al, 1994:57). Consequently, the Additional Protocols included provisions that limit the permissible means and methods of warfare and strengthen protection for civilians and extend the applicability of international humanitarian law. The experience of the war in Vietnam and the use of new weapons of war and the extent of suffering of innocent civilians mobilized the international community's resolve to strengthen international humanitarian law to protect innocent civilians in most of the wars of liberation (Hamilton et al, 2001:13). Both Additional Protocols 1&11 have special provisions for the protection of children in armed conflicts as articulated below.

---

http://www.cidh.org/Ninez/pdf%20files/Declaration%20on%20Protection. Accessed on 25/9/2009.

Protocol 1 Additional to the Geneva Conventions

Analysts such as Honwana (2006:35) have observed that the Additional Protocol 1 to the Geneva Conventions is an important international instrument that was developed by the international community for the protection of children in armed conflicts. The Additional Protocol 1 was able to widen the protection afforded to children in international conflict. Article 77 of the protocol states that:

> Children shall be the object of special respect and shall be protected against any form of indirect assault. The Parties to the conflict shall provide them with the care and aid they require, whether because of their age or for any other reason (Hamilton et al, 2001:15).[11]

The Protocol further sets 15 years as a minimum age for children's recruitment and involvement in armed conflicts. According to Harvey (2001:9), the setting of 15 years as a minimum age for children's involvement in armed conflicts marked the first time the issue of child soldiers was being addressed by a binding international agreement. The Protocol also provides that involved parties shall take 'all feasible measures in order that children who have not attained 15 years do not take a direct part in hostilities and in particular they shall refrain from recruiting them into their armed forces'. Additional Protocol 1 has been criticised in that 'protection' as provided in the protocol is, in the end, a compromise between humanitarian ideals and military necessity.

Hamilton et al(2001:16) observe that any provision which allows for loss of civilian life, provided that the loss is not excessive in relation to the concrete military advantage anticipated, is essentially incompatible with the right to life provisions of the United Nations Convention on the Rights of the Child. Both Hamilton and Abu El-Haj (2001) point out that the 'right' has the nature of an intransgressible norm (jus cognes) which is not reflected in the definition of 'protection' under Protocol 1, meaning that it does not uphold a child's fundamental right to life or their survival.

---

[11] Hamilton, C. & Tabatha, Abu El-Haj. 'Armed Conflict: The Protection of Children under International Law.' Available at:
http://www.essex.ac.uk/armedcon/story_id/000577.html. Accessed on 25/9/2009.

Protocol 11 Additional to the Geneva Conventions

While Additional Protocol 11 contains similar versions of the children protection provisions, like Protocol 1, Article 4 (3) (c) of the protocol recognizes that children need protection from the possible recruitment by both the government and the armed groups. One of the important aspects of the Additional Protocols to the Geneva Conventions is that all the four Conventions contain an identical Article 3, which extends general coverage to non-international conflicts.[12]The weakness of the Additional Protocols is that they set a minimum age of 15 for recruitment and participation of children in armed conflicts considered by most International Non-Governmental Organizations and child advocacy groups to be too young for a person to be involved in armed conflicts.

Furthermore, the challenge with both Additional Protocols is their applicability in view of the fact that not many states have ratified these protocols (Hamilton et al, 2001). Noteworthy also, is the fact that few countries experiencing internal armed conflicts have been willing to abandon their presumptive claim to a free hand in dealing with local threats, so that the applicability of Additional Protocol 11 is resisted, even where the objective criteria are satisfied (Cohn et al, 1994:60).

International Human Rights Law

Human rights law establishes rights that every individual should enjoy at all times, during peace and war. The obligations to ensure that these rights are protected have been placed on the State and are based on the Charter of the United Nations and are also reflected in the Universal Declaration of Human Rights. It should be noted that human rights law also has quite a number of specialized treaties that provide for the protection of children's rights in armed conflicts. These include; The International Covenant on Civil and Political Rights which covers several rights including the right to life, and the right to freedom from slavery, torture and arbitrary arrest; The International Covenant on Economic,

---

[12]A Summary of Geneva Conventions and Additional Protocols. Available at: http://supportgenevaconventions.info/library/geneva_conventions_summary.pdf: Accessed on 29/5/2010.

Social and Cultural Rights which recognizes the right to food, clothing, housing health and education. The Covenant on the Elimination of All Forms of Discrimination against Women (CEDAW) of 1979 is also an important agreement of particular relevance in the protection of children's rights in armed conflicts that fits in this category of legal standards (Machel, 2001).

Convention relating to the Status of Refugees

The Convention relating to the Status of Refugees of 1951 and its 1967 Protocol is one of the important international legal protections of children in armed conflicts. The convention that was adopted on 28 July 1951 by the United Nations General Assembly seeks to protect the rights of refugees and stateless persons who include children. One of the consequences of armed conflicts is the generation of large numbers of refugees who flee their countries due to fear of persecution on the basis of their ethnicity, religion, social or political grounds. Consequently, both the convention and the protocol provide standards for protecting refugees. The preamble of the convention emphasizes the commitment by the United Nations and the Universal Declaration of Human Rights approved on 10 December 1948 and affirmed by the General Assembly, which affirmed the Principle that human beings shall enjoy fundamental rights and freedoms without discrimination.

The recognition that all human beings shall enjoy fundamental rights and freedoms without discrimination is crucial for protection of refugees especially children. The Convention and the Protocol have been complemented by regional agreements such as the Organization of African Unity (OAU) (now African Union) Convention Governing the Specific Aspects of Refugee Problems in Africa of 1969 and the Cartagena Declaration of Refugees 1984.[13]

---

[13] Convention relating to the Status of Refugees was adopted on 28 July 1951 by the UN Conference of Plenipotentiaries on the Status of Refugees and Stateless Persons Convened Under the General Assembly resolution 429 (V) of 14 December 1950 and entered into force on 22 April 1954 in accordance with article 43. To date the Convention has been ratified by 147 countries around the world. Available at: http://www.tamilnation.org/refuges/51 convention.htm. Accessed on 29/6/2010.

The Convention on the Rights of the Child (CRC) 1989

Most scholars observe that the Convention on the Rights of the Child (CRC) is instrumental and a landmark legal protection for children in armed conflicts (Cohn et al, 1994; Honwana, 2006:35; Wesselles, 2006: 233) Singer, 2006:141). Singer (2006) points out that the 1989 Convention on the Rights of the Child is the most comprehensive, explicit and most representative legal instrument for the protection of children in armed conflicts. Singer further notes that the Convention was the most quickly and widely ratified internationally by more than 190 state signatories. In ratifying the Convention on the Rights of the Child, the international community proclaimed its political, legal and moral commitment to safeguarding children's rights and to ensure their protection as 'zones of peace'. As Machel (2001:139) observed, the Convention obliges States to protect children at all times, including in situations of armed conflict and to ensure that children have no direct part in hostilities.

Honwana (2006) concurs with Machel and observes that the Convention on the Rights of the Child of 1989 is a landmark agreement particularly the fact that all the Convention's 54 articles reaffirm the fundamental place of the family in society and sets global precepts for a child's inherent right to life, survival, development, and freedom of thought, regardless of race, religion, or gender. To date, only two countries- United States and Somalia have not yet ratified the treaty (Obote-Odora, 1999:12)[14].

Article 38 of the Convention on the Rights of the Child states that:

1. States Parties undertake to respect and to ensure respect for rules of international humanitarian law applicable to them in armed conflicts which are relevant to the child;
2. States Parties shall take all feasible measures to ensure that persons who have not attained the age of fifteen years do not take a direct part in hostilities;
3. States Parties shall refrain from recruiting any person who has not attained the age of fifteen years into their armed forces. In

---

[14] Obote-Odora, A. (1999) Legal Problems with the Protection of Children in Armed Conflict, Murdoch University Electronic Journal of Law, Volume 6, Number 2 (June). Available at: http://www.murdoch.edu.au/elaw/issues/v6n2/obote-odora62_text.html. Accessed on 29/6/2010.

recruiting among those persons who have attained the age of fifteen years but who have not attained the age of eighteen years States shall endeavour to give priority to those who are oldest;

4. In accordance with their obligations under international humanitarian law to protect the civilian population in armed conflicts, States Parties shall take all feasible measures to ensure protection and care of children who are affected by armed conflict (Human Rights Watch, 1997:111).

Article 39 of CRC focuses on rehabilitation of child victims of armed conflict. The Article states that:

States Parties shall take all appropriate measures to promote physical and psychological recovery and social reintegration of a child victim of…..armed conflicts. Such recovery and reintegration shall take place in an environment, which fosters health, self respect and dignity of the child (Harvey, 2001:22).

The CRC also contains a comprehensive set of socio-economic, cultural, civil and political rights all of which are considered indivisible and interdependent. The indivisibility and interdependence nature of these rights demands that there should not be any hierarchy in their implementation. Further, as Harvey (2001) observes, four general principles underpin the CRC. First, is non-discrimination (Article 2); Second is best interests of the child (Article 3); Third is the right to life, survival and development (Article 6); and Fourth, the right for the children to have their views heard and given due weight in all decisions affecting them (Article 12). These principles must be taken into account at all times during the implementation of the CRC.

The weakness of the CRC is that it generated a lot of controversy by its decision to make 15 years a minimum age for recruitment and participation of children in armed conflicts. It is this limitation that prompted several humanitarian organizations and pressure groups around the world, which considered 15 years of age too young for children's participation in armed conflicts to push for another international legal instrument that would raise the age limit to 18 years. It is against this background that the Optional Protocol to CRC was born.

As Wessells (2006) has noted in most countries 15 year olds are not allowed to vote. So the issue is how do you subject 15 year olds in wars they would not have had any say in through voting a government into power that declares a war. Consequently, in 1994, the United Nations (UN) constituted a working group to examine the issue and the debates on the need to increase the minimum age of military enrolment to 18 years. The debate which lasted for a period of six years led to the adoption of the Optional Protocol to the Convention on the Rights of Child on involvement in armed conflicts.

Some scholars have observed that while the CRC has been widely acclaimed as a vital legal mechanism for the protection of children in armed conflicts; in reality it has been found lacking. For example, the monitoring mechanism for the CRC - the Committee on the Rights of the Child - is not able to respond in situations of emergency; cannot make ad hoc recommendations or comment on situations in countries outside its concluding comments on State reports; cannot hear individual complaints; impose sanctions on offenders or order compensation (Harvey, 2001:12).

The Optional Protocol of May 2000

The Optional Protocol to the Convention on the Rights of the Child was adopted by the UN General Assembly in May 2000 (Honwana, 2006:36).The protocol which applies to both national armies and non-state armed groups requires nations to rehabilitate former child soldiers. While the Protocol prohibits compulsory recruitment below the age of 18, voluntary recruitment at sixteen years of age is permitted. This compromise was reached to cater for the interests of the United States, United Kingdom and Australia which insisted that 16 years for voluntary recruitment be permitted. The protocol however provides that while recruitment and training of 16 year olds can take place, such children are not supposed to serve in combat operations before they turn eighteen years.

Most humanitarian organizations and advocates for children's rights have not been comfortable with this compromise. In fact, this compromise is largely viewed as failure on the part of the international community to reach a consensus of 18 years. International organizations and pressure groups observe that by failing to reach the consensus of 18 years as the right age, governments continue to base their positions primarily on their narrow military interests rather than on what is best for the children (Honwana, 2006). The Optional Protocol also has been criticized for creating double standards by prohibiting all recruitment of children under 18 but allowing the recruitment of volunteers below eighteen years.

The double standard also raises the problem of trying to define the difference between voluntary and involuntary recruitment, which is hard to determine. The concern here for most advocates against recruitment of children in armed conflicts is that this window can give a chance to errant governments and armed groups to recruit underage children under the guise of voluntary recruitment. For example indirect and coercive measures such as deliberately creating unemployment in civilian jobs and creating job opportunities in the army could influence young people to join the military or armed groups. Indirect and coercive measures that persuade young people to join the military include intimidation and physical protection, access to food and shelter and opportunity for revenge. This was the case in Mozambique and Angola where boys were encouraged to join armed forces through intimidation and social pressure (Honwana, 2006:37).

International Labour Organization Convention 182 on the Worst Forms of Child Labour 1999

The International Labour Organization Convention (ILO) 182 on the Worst Forms of Child Labour which was adopted in 1999 is considered a big boost in the quest for higher international standards to protect children in armed conflicts (Singer, 2006; Honwana, 2006:38). The ILO Convention lists 'forced or compulsory recruitment of children for use in armed conflict' among the worst forms of child labour. Accordingly, the ILO Convention on the 'Worst Forms of Child Labour Convention' was the most rapidly endorsed labour convention in history, with 147 states ratifying by November 2003 (Honwana, 2006).

The linkage between child soldiering and exploitative labour is critical in the sense that children in most societies are expected to work and support their families. The Convention draws a line between moderate, acceptable forms of labour in which children do chores to help their families, and extreme dangerous forms of labour that jeopardize children's health and violate their rights (Singer, 2006:134). The criminalization of child labour in armed conflict is critical for the protection of children. The LRA rebels in Northern Uganda are known to abduct children who are forcefully conscripted into their ranks. The

LRA then deploys the children against the government army as well as using them as labourersby carrying looted goods and ammunitions as well as growing food in the camps in southern Sudan. The girls are used as sex slaves for the rebel commanders. The government army has also been castigated for recruiting and re-deploying rescued children against the LRA rebels, which is a violation of their rights (Global Report 2004).[15]

The Rome Statute of the International Criminal Court 1998

One of the most prominent international legal mechanisms that criminalizes the recruitment and use of children in armed conflicts is the 1998 Rome Statute of the International Criminal Court (ICC). The ICC was established to become a permanent court for investigating and prosecuting genocide, war crimes and crimes against humanity which national courts or governments are unable or unwilling to prosecute (Wessells, 2006:237). One of the most important achievements in the global efforts to protect children in armed conflicts associated with the ICC is that the Rome Statute defined as a war crime the recruitment and use of children under the age of 15 in armed conflicts. From the onset, the negotiators of the Rome Statute agreed that it is a war crime to use children, not only in combat but also in military activities such as spying, scouting, or serving as decoys or as guards.

Article 8 (1) of the Rome Statute of the International Criminal Court, states that:

> The Court shall have jurisdiction in respect of war crimes in particular when committed as part of a plan or policy or as part of a large-scale commission of such crimes. Article 8 (2) (e) (VII) considers the 'Conscripting or enlisting children under the age of fifteen years into armed forces or groups or using them to participate actively in hostilities' to constitute a war crime.[16]

---

[15] Child Soldiers Global Report (2004). Available at:
http://www.unhcr.org/refworld/country,,CSCOAL,,UGA,456d621e2,49880620c,0.html. Accessed on 29/6/2010.

[16] The Rome Statute of the International Criminal Court available at:
http://en.wikipedia.org/wiki/Rome_Statute_of _the_International_Criminal_Court. Accessed on 29/6/2010.

Most crucially, according to the principle of complementarity, the ICC has jurisdiction in situations where the State is unable or unwilling to prosecute persons accused of committing offences. The ICC is an important development in the sense that some governments, especially those guilty of recruitment and use of child soldiers, may not be able or willing to prosecute criminals. At the same time, the court comes in handy to assist weak States lacking capacity to apprehend and prosecute strong personalities including Heads of States. One of the test cases for the ICC is the indictment of General Bashir, the President of Sudan accused committing war crimes by government forces in the on-going civil war in the Darfur region of Sudan.[17] While the ICC has not been successful in apprehending General Bashir largely due to the uncorporative governments especially in Africa and the Arab world, the case has given him sleepless nights and has forced his government to make serious progress on the prevention of recruitment and use of child soldiers (United Nations, Office of the Special Representative of the Secretary-General for Children and Armed Conflict (2018).

Since the establishment of the ICC in 1998, the idea of prosecuting individuals involved in the recruitment and use of children as a war crime has taken root in the UN Special Courts established by the United Nations. An example is the UN Special Court in Sierra Leone established in June 2002 which indicted Charles Taylor, former President of Liberia, for recruitment and use of child soldiers. The ICC has also handed down indictments to the rebel leader of the Lord's Resistance Army Joseph Kony and four other rebel commanders for child abduction, forced recruitment and use of child soldiers in Northern Uganda (Wessells, 2006:238). The arrest and prosecution of LRA's top commander Dominic Ongwen is a major breakthrough in bringing the leadership of the rebel force to justice for the very first time. Commenting on the pending trial at the Hague, Elise Keppler, Associate Director International Justice at Human Right Watch observed that: The LRA leadership is reviled worldwide for its brutality against Africans, but never before as an LRA commander faced trail (HRW, 2016).

The ICC can be credited for a number of achievements in the struggle to stop the recruitment and use of child soldiers. First, the ICC criminalizes and exposes the abusers of children's rights at the

---

[17] See *World Politics Review* (2008). The ICC's Bashir Indictment: Law against Peace, 23 July. Available at: http://www.worldpoliticsreview.com/articles/2471/the-iccs-bashir-indictment-law-against-peace Accessed on 29/6/2010.

international level which leads to their sponsors in the diaspora to distance themselves which limits funding for the criminals. This specifically affects armed groups that recruit and use child soldiers. The result is that this could scale down armed conflicts with both the government and the armed groups seeking to use peaceful means of resolving the conflict. In the case of the LRA in Northern Uganda, the ICC indictments had two implications. First is that the ICC indictments dragged the LRA to the negotiating table in order for the indictments to be lifted. The second implication of the ICC indictments is that once they remained hanging around the necks of rebel leaders, the LRA refused to sign the Final Peace Agreement (FPA).

The weakness of the ICC is what some observers have called pursuit of victors' justice. In the case of the war in Northern Uganda, the ICC indictments generated resentment among the Acholi people who have suffered most under the LRA brutality. The Acholi people point out that they have their own traditional and cultural ways of handling conflict which have been ignored by the ICC. Also, the ICC's decision to leave out the government soldiers who are implicated in children's rights abuses and focus solely on the LRA angered the Acholi people who think the ICC court was biased against the rebels (World Vision, 2005:42). Commenting about the objectivity of the ICC, the World Vision Report noted that:

> ... the ICC has inevitably had to have a close relationship with the Ugandan Government, which calls into question their ability to conduct an objective and balanced investigation of all combatants. This has been reinforced by the way in which the Ugandan investigation was launched through a high profile press conference with President Museveni in January 2004 (World Vision, 2005:42).

By and large, while some people hail the efforts of the ICC in the protection of children's rights in armed conflicts, others see it as being one sided and biased. However, it is certain that the ICC indictments of various warlords have sent a serious warning that the days of violation of children's rights with impunity could be coming to an end.

United Nations Security Council Resolutions on the Rights of Children in Armed Conflicts

It is worth noting that United Nations Security Council has passed a number of resolutions designed to protect children in armed conflicts. While these UN Security Council Resolutions are not legally binding on States, they provide a framework of standards for protection of children in armed conflicts upon which child protection in country-specific situations can be assessed by the international community. Further, as some scholars (Harvey, 2001:16) have observed, the yearly open debates of children and armed conflict in the UN Security Council, the resolutions and subsequent reports of the UN Secretary-General on the progress recorded in the implementation of the recommendations are indications that the issue of children in armed conflict remains high on the UN agenda.

UN Security Council Resolution 1261

Security Council Resolution 1261 of 2000 stresses the responsibility of all states to prosecute those responsible for grave breaches of the Geneva Conventions. Security Council Resolution 1261 formally affirmed that the protection and security of children affected by armed conflict is an international peace and security issue and is therefore firmly within the remit of the Security Council. The resolution also highlights the harmful and widespread impact that armed conflict has on children and the long-term consequences that this has on durable peace, security and development. The resolution also contains a list of calls on states to take action on issues including the recruitment and use of children, small arms proliferation and access to humanitarian and UN staff.[18]

UN Security Council Resolution 1314

The UN Security Council Resolution 1314 was adopted in 1999. This resolution essentially reiterated and expanded its list of concerns and calls for action. The resolution also noted that in situations where there were systematic and widespread violations of International Humanitarian and

---

[18] UN Security Council Resolution 1261 available at:
http://www.un.org.News/Press/docs/1999/199990825.sc6716.html. Accessed on 29/6/2010.

Human Rights Law, including those related to children in situations of armed conflict, deemed to constitute a threat to peace and security, the Security Council could consider such situations and adopt necessary measures (Child Rights Information Network, 2010).[19]

UN Security Council Resolution 1379

The UN Security Council Resolution 1379 of 2001 urges member states 'to prosecute those responsible for egregious crimes perpetuated against children' (Honwana, 2006:39). This resolution also focused on critical areas of concern that were not previously catered for. For example, the resolution focused on the link between HIV/Aids and armed conflict. Consequently, the HIV/Aids link was acknowledged and HIV training recommended for peacekeeping personnel. Further, the resolution recognized the role played by the corporate sector in starting and sustaining conflicts. The resolution urges the corporate actors to refrain from doing business that does not protect children's rights in armed conflicts.

UN Security Council Resolution 1460

The UN Security Council Resolution 1460 which was adopted on 30th January 2003 endorsed the UN Era of Application Campaign which was spearheaded by the Special Representative of the Secretary-General for Children and Armed Conflict. This resolution was aimed at ensuring a more robust and systematic monitoring and reporting on the recruitment and use of children in armed conflict and other types of abuses and violations against children's rights in armed conflicts.

---

[19] UN Security Council Resolution 1314 available at:
http://www.crin.org/law/instrument.asp?Inst1D=1056 Accessed on 29/6/2010.

African Mechanisms for Protection of Children's Rights in Armed Conflicts

The African Charter on the Rights and Welfare of the Child of 1990

The African Charter on the Rights and Welfare of the Child promulgated in 1990 is an important international agreement for the protection of children in armed conflicts. The Charter defines a child simply as a person younger than eighteen years of age. Article 22 relates to children and armed conflicts; Article 15 prohibits child labour and Article 16 relates to protection against child abuse and torture. All these articles of the Charter are very instructive in the protection of children in armed conflicts.

The African Charter is important because it sets the upper limit of a child's age. Its definition at the age of 18 years without exception and prohibition of recruitment and use of children in armed conflicts, have been hailed as instrumental and progressive.

Article 22, which focuses on armed conflicts, states that:

1.   States Parties to this Charter shall undertake to respect and ensure respect for rule of international humanitarian law applicable in armed conflicts which affect the child.
2.   States Parties to the present Charter shall take all necessary measures to ensure that no child shall take a direct part in hostilities and refrain in particular, from recruiting any child.
3.   States Parties to the present Charter shall, in accordance with their obligations under international law, protect the civilian population in armed conflicts and shall take all feasible measures to ensure the protection and care of children who are affected by armed conflicts. Such rules shall also apply to children in situations of internal armed conflicts, tension and strife.

Article 22(2) of the African Charter has been found to be stronger on State Parties as it states that involved parties shall take 'all necessary measures to ensure that no child shall take a direct part in hostilities and refrain in particular from recruiting any child'. Honwana (2006) has observed that the language in the African Charter is even stronger than the one in the 1989 Convention on the Rights of the Child as it requires states to take 'all necessary measures' rather than just 'feasible' ones.

79

Article 15 of the African Charter on the Rights and Welfare of the Child on child labour is also crucial in the protection of children in armed conflicts especially on the African continent. Article 14 provides that;

1. Every child shall be protected from all forms of economic exploitation and from performing any work that is likely to be hazardous or interfere with the child's physical, mental, spiritual, moral, or social development.
2. States Parties to the present Charter take all appropriate legislative and administrative measures to ensure the full implementation of this article which covers both the formal and informal sectors of employment and having regard to the relevant provisions of the International Labour Organization's instruments relating to children.

Article 16 (1) states that:

> States Parties to the present Charter shall take specific legislative, administrative, social and educational measures to protect the children from all forms of torture, inhuman or degrading treatment and especially physical or mental injury or abuse, neglect or maltreatment including sexual abuse, while in the care of a parent, legal guardian or school authority or any other person who has the care of the child.

In spite of its pragmatism by defining a child as a person below the age of 18 years, the African Charter has not prevented the recruitment and use of children in armed conflicts going on in much of Africa. The charter in its quest to protect children's rights faces several challenges. First, its restrictive definition and construction of the meaning of a 'child' and of 'childhood' is at odds with the context-specific socio-cultural construction of childhood in Africa. The different perceptions and understandings of childhood undermine the practical implementation of the charter and other international mechanisms. For example, the preamble of the African Charter of the Rights and Welfare of the Child states that it is informed by the historical background and values of the African civilization. However, this is contradicted by the Charter's definition of a child as a person below 18 years. This rather Western-centric definition contradicts the perception of a 'child' and 'childhood' across much of Africa (Francis, 2007:13). To this end, one wonders how the Charter can accommodate or work for people who do not perceive

80

themselves as belonging to the under 18 years category, in particular when communities treat them as adults.

Apart from the African Charter on the Rights and Welfare of the Child of 1990 there have been other regional agreements designed to protect children in armed conflicts on the African continent. Critical among the regional legal instruments include: Cape Town Principles; Maputo Declaration on the Use of Children as Soldiers and the Lome Accord.

Cape Town Principles 1997

The Cape Town Principles and Best Practices on the Prevention of Recruitment of Children into the Armed Forces and Demobilization and Social Integration adopted in April 1997 set standards for the protection, demobilization and reintegration of child soldiers.[20] These principles re-affirm the correct age for children's recruitment and participation to be 18 years of age. The Cape Town initiative is credited for re-affirming the age limit of 18 years as the minimum age for any participation in armed conflicts. However, some analysts have noted, this high standard is at odds with the cultural and sociological construction of childhood across much of Africa which renders the Principles of limited practical effect(Francis (2007). For example, in most of Africa the age of maturity is determined by when one begins to take on the responsibilities of an adult.

Moreso, although the Cape Town Principles were developed in Africa, and are claimed to be based on African experiences, the elitist and Western-based composition of the participants at the 1997 Symposium limits the potential input of any 'authentic' and only normative standards, with no binding legal obligations. It is against this background that in October 2005 attempts were made to update the Cape Town Principles in order to take into account the lessons learned, the advances in international customery law and legal standards relating to the protection of children's rights in armed conflicts and how to mobilize a broader political and geographical endorsement. It is worth noting though that

---

[20]UNICEF (1997). Cape Town Principles and Best Practices on the Prevention of Recruitment of Children into Armed Forces and on Demobilization and Social Reintegration of Child Soldiers in Africa, April 27-30. Available at: http://www.unicef.org/emerg/files/Cape_Town_Principles(1).pdf. Accessed on 10/9/2010.

the Cape Town Principles have had a positive impact of raising awareness of the international community about the suffering of children in Africa's conflict zones.

Maputo Declaration on the Use of Children as Soldiers 1999

In the context of Africa, the Maputo Declaration on the Use of Children as Soldiers of 22 April 1999 is an important instrument for protecting children in armed conflict. The declaration builds on the Cape Town Principles and Best Practices on the Prevention of Recruitment of Children into the Armed Forces and on Demobilization and Social Reintegration of Child Soldiers in Africa of 1997, the Organization of African Unity/ Africa Network for Prevention and Protection Against Child Abuse and Neglect Continental Conference on Children in Situations of Armed Conflict of June 1997, the Resolution 1659 (LX1V) on the Plight of African Children adopted by the Council of Ministers of the OAU in July 1996 Yaoundé, Cameroon.

The Maputo declaration, among other issues, observes that the use of any child under 18 years of age by any armed force or armed group is wholly unacceptable, even where that child claims to be or is a volunteer. It calls upon the African States, to promote an environment that favours the safe and healthy development of children and to take all necessary measures to ensure that no child under 18 years of age takes part in armed conflicts. The declaration requires states to bring to justice those who continue to recruit or use children as soldiers; establish thorough recruitment procedures in particular for determining age, ensuring the physical and psychosocial rehabilitation and effective reintegration into society of demobilized child soldiers, and ratifying without delay the Convention on the Rights of the Child and the African Charter on the Rights and Welfare of the Child[21].

---

[21] Maputo Declaration on the Use of Children as Soldiers of 22 April 1999. Maputo Declaration is available at: http://chora.virtualave.net/Maputo-declaration.htm. Accessed on 15/5/2010.

Lome Peace Accord of 1999

The Lome Peace Accord of 1999 was signed between the Government and the rebels in Sierra Leone to bring to an end the nine year torturous civil war. The violent conflict in Sierra Leone had indiscriminately killed innocent civilians including children. Over 10,000 children were forcefully recruited by the government pro-militia groups and the Revolutionary United Front (RUF) to take part in the armed conflict (Sesay, 2003). In the Sierra Leone conflict, children were both victims and violators of human rights. The Rome Accord became the first peace agreement in Africa that paid attention to the special needs of former child soldiers in disarmament, demobilization and reintegration processes.

The Lome Peace Agreement was however undermined by the fact that it traded peace for impunity by granting a blanket amnesty to the perpetrators - members of the armed groups who had presided over the campaign of terror in full view of the international community. As Machel has observed:

> Founded on a false peace, the Lome Peace Accord proved unstable. The terms of the agreement were broken repeatedly and finally discarded when in May 2000; the RUF took 500 UN peace-keepers hostage. The failure of the Lome Accord was failure of accountability (Machel, 2001:145).

The failure of the Lome Accord, paved the way for United Nations together with the Government of Sierra Leone to establish a Special Court for Sierra Leone to prosecute persons accused of committing serious international crimes. The United Nations Special Court for Sierra Leone since its establishment in 2000 can be credited for issuing arrest warrants for Charles Taylor former President of Liberia who was subsequently apprehended and is currently being tried for war crimes and crimes against humanity at the ICC in The Hague.

Reasons Why Legal Mechanisms have not prevented Recruitment and Use of Child Soldiers

This section discuses the reasons why in spite of the international condemnation of the practice of recruitment and use of child soldiers and the existing body of conventions, declarations, treaties and protocols, child soldiering continues to be the order of the day. Singer (2006:143) observes that there is evidence that while there are more than one hundred signatories to the various conventions for the protection of children in armed conflicts, child soldiers are still present in roughly 85 countries around the world. The subsequent section discusses challenges of legal mechanisms.

National Interests Override Children's Rights

One of the major challenges facing the international legal mechanisms in the protection of children's rights in armed conflicts relate to the fact that most States Parties' interests override the interests of children's rights. An example to illustrate this point is the Optional Protocol to the Convention on the Rights of the Child on involvement in armed conflicts adopted by the UN General Assembly in May 2000. Several advocates for the protection of children's rights in armed conflicts have expressed discomfort with the protocol maintaining sixteen years as minimum age for military enrolment, a position that was pushed by the United States, United Kingdom and Australia. Over a period of six years (since 1994) international NGOs and humanitarian organizations had campaigned and lobbied the UN without success to increase the age of recruitment to 18 years (Wessells:234).

While the campaign resulted in the adoption of the Optional Protocol to the Convention on the Rights of the Child which sets the minimum age at 18 years, the protocol was watered down by state interests. A provision in the Optional Protocol was made to the effect that while compulsory recruitment below the age eighteen is prohibited, voluntary recruitment at sixteen years of age is permitted. The insistence by the United States, United Kingdom and Australia on sixteen years for voluntary non-combatant recruits significantly weakened the protocol (Singer, 2006:36). Interestingly, the United States which has not signed and ratified the Convention on the Rights of the Child is evidently instrumental in watering down the Optional Protocol which was supposed to be an improvement to the Convention on the Rights of the Child (Obote-Odora, 1999:12).

The danger with the compromise to accommodate the interests of the United States, United Kingdom and Australia, is that it provides an

84

opportunity for other governments to continue to base their positions primarily on narrow military interests rather than on the best interests of children. More so, as Singer (2006) observes, the protocol created a double standard by prohibiting all recruitment of children under 18 years of age, but allowing the enlisting of volunteers at 16 years. The exception raises the problem of how one can draw a distinction between voluntary and involuntary recruitment. An observation has been made that although many young people do volunteer to join the military forces, not all of them truly volunteer in the correct sense. In many cases, indirect coercive mechanisms have been used to motivate young people to join the military (Singer, 2006:37). The point being made here is that such an international legal instrument can be easily exploited by errant governments and armed groups to recruit and use children in armed conflicts.

Conceptualization of a Child and Childhood: Challenge for International Legal Mechanisms

The discrepancy between the restrictive definition and construction of the meaning of a child and of childhood undermines the practical implementation of international protection mechanisms (Francis, 2007:222). Cohn et al. (1994) observes that the universal definition of a child is limited and conflicts with culturally and religiously constructed definitions. It is the universal and rather Western-centric construction of a child and childhood that has been applied to the rest of the world. In most of Africa for example, the age of maturity is a social and cultural device by which societies acknowledge the transition to adulthood. For the purpose of participating in religious rituals, for example, a child may become an adult at age 13 (Cohn, et al, 1994).

The example of this contradiction in the definition and conceptualization of a child and childhood in respect of Africa is evident in the Preamble to the African Charter of the Rights and Welfare of the Child which states that it is informed by the 'historical background and values of the African civilizations.' Ironically, the same Charter defines a child in Article 2 as any person under 18 years, which contradicts the perception of a child and childhood across much of Africa (Honwana, 2006:52). Honwana (2006) observes that the notions of childhood are culturally and socially constructed and vary across societies. While in the West a person below 18 years of age is viewed as a child, in most of sub-

Saharan Africa, particularly in rural areas, where traditions remain strong, a person is regarded an adult once he or she has completed the culturally scripted initiation ceremony marking the rite of passage into manhood or womanhood. This contradiction makes it difficult to implement the African Charter on the Rights and Welfare of the Child and other legal instruments for the protection of children's rights in armed conflicts.

The failure by the international community to adopt a mandatory internationally acceptable definition of the term 'child' partly explains the failure of compliance by the States Parties to international legal mechanisms. Consequently, this failure provides latitude to States Parties not to comply and to hide behind such a contradiction. This also allows States Parties discretionary powers to determine when to comply with the legal protection mechanisms for protection of children's rights in armed conflicts. Most critically, the contradiction over the definition of who is a child makes it problematic to guarantee the protection of human rights of children and effective enforcement of the law (Obote-Odora, 1999).

Domestication of International Law in National Legislations and its Applicability

Another reason why international legal instruments have become ineffective especially in Africa has to do with failure by some countries to ratify and domesticate international treaties into domestic law. During the negotiations of international legal instruments for the protection of children's rights in armed conflicts, it is generally believed that when states ratify these international agreements they agree to implement them. Unfortunately, the ratification of the international agreements has not led to their immediate enforcement in contracting countries. Five reasons have been advanced why States Parties, especially in Africa, have been reluctant to incorporate international customary rules into domestic laws and also for those that have ratified and domesticated but do not enforce the laws.

The first relates to failure by many states to enact national legislations to implement duly ratified international treaties due to state capacity limitation especially after the civil war that could have destroyed most of the state institutions. In this situation, domestication of the international

86

treaties to protect children's rights in armed conflict may not be the first priority for a country emerging from a destructive civil war.

The second reason is that some states enter reservations at the time of ratification of the treaty such as the Optional Protocol to the Convention on the Rights of the Child. These reservations render the ratified treaty meaningless and inconsequential in a practical legal sense. The third reason is that some governments evade international obligations by passing a national legislation that restricts or waters down the scope or grounds of jurisdiction provided in the international treaties. The fourth reason is that national courts have developed in their judicial practice a tendency to limit as much as possible the impact of international rules. As some scholars have pointed out, the issue of national sovereignty has been found to be a major challenge in the implementation of international treaties. This is most common in Africa with a background of colonial struggles for independence which makes most countries sensitive about how much power they are ceding to international law.

The fifth reason is that most of the countries, especially the conflict prone ones, even when they have ratified and domesticated international treaties, do it to satisfy the international community. Most of these countries fear to implement the treaties because they are also culpable of child abuses. Most governments recruit and deploy child soldiers in combat. An example is Uganda, which is the focus for this book. Government has ratified and domesticated almost all the international agreements for the protection of children's rights in armed conflicts including the ICC. Surprisingly, the government of Uganda has been accused by the Coalition to Stop Use of Child Soldiers for recruiting and use of child soldiers (Global Report, 2008).

Lack of Respect or Knowledge of International Law Relating to Laws of Armed Conflict

Another challenge in the implementation of international legal standards for the protection of children's rights in armed conflict relates to the nature of the State being engaged and the nature of the armed groups. Most of the armed groups and governments, especially in Africa, are outlaws, which do not observe rule of law (Wessells, 2006). It should be noted that most of the armed groups do not even understand international humanitarian law and international human rights laws governing the conduct of war since their forces are not professional soldiers. Rebel groups such as the Revolutionary United Front (RUF), former UNITA and the LRA are examples of rebel groups that operated, and some still operate, based on the law of the jungle-'survival for the fittest'. In such circumstances, most armed groups behave as if they are above the law. As Wessells (2006) has observed, the world over, non-state actors or armed groups never pay serious attention to issues of child soldiering, even when they are under obligation to do so under international law.

Commenting about the inadequacy of the international humanitarian law, Honwana (2006:39) has observed that:

> The central challenge is how to make international humanitarian law understood, recognized, and enforced in places where children are recruited into armed conflicts on a daily basis. Even the current international laws and agreements requiring nation-states to prevent children under eighteen from military involvement are not widely known or observed. Beyond strengthening international laws, it is vital to reinforce local understandings and norms about notions of childhood and child protection from war…

Lack of Adequate Resources and Moral Support

Additionally, for the legal mechanisms to succeed, they need moral support and adequate resources from all the State Parties to these instruments. International politics has not allowed the ICC and other UN Special Courts to get the support they deserve in order to enforce international law. In respect to the ICC, a number of influential countries have followed the only super power: United States to water down the international instrument. The United States that should have otherwise offered international leadership has refused to sign the Rome Statute and has gone ahead to sign agreements with some countries which undermine the effectiveness of the ICC. Commenting on the position of the United States towards the Convention on the Rights of the Child, Wessells (2006:253) observed that:

> The failure of the United States to ratify and accede to the CRC is a highly visible and noteworthy gap, since progress in protecting children's rights requires the support of the world's most powerful

nation for the foundational child's rights instrument. The refusal of the U.S. Congress to ratify the CRC reflects deep mistrust of international law and a wider belief of U.S. citizens that U.S. law trumps international law.

Also, the Special Courts, such as the UN Special Court in Sierra Leone are known to be faced with many cases to handle and without adequate resources leading to delayed justice, which ordinarily amounts to justice denied. For the legal system to succeed and contribute to lasting peace, UN Specialized Courts such as the one for Sierra Leone and for Rwanda must demonstrate competence in delivering timely justice. The Rwandan Criminal Tribunal in Arusha was criticised for being slow and biased in delivering justice to the victims of the genocide. The international community needs to unwaveringly support these courts to succeed and therefore send a firm message to the offenders against children's rights that they have no hiding place in the world.

Double Standards of the International Legal Mechanisms

Another challenge for the international law in the protection of children in armed conflicts relates to double standards, and selective justice that is largely seen as the pursuit of victors' justice. Particular criticism has been levelled at the International Criminal Tribunal for Rwanda (ICTR) based on the way it handled the prosecution of the people alleged to have been involved in the 1994 Rwandan genocide. It is noted that ever since the ICTR was established in November 1994, it has tried only leading figures responsible for Rwanda's 1994 Genocide in the previous regime and has failed to bring cases against the Rwandan Patriotic Front (ruling government) army officers despite having jurisdiction to pursue these crimes. In a letter to the Chief Prosecutor for the ICTR of 1 June, 2009, Human Rights Watch observed that, 'The tribunal's failure to address the war crimes committed by the Rwandan Patriotic Front risks leaving the impression that it is delivering only victors' justice'.[22]

A similar accusation has been levelled at the ICC by the Acholi leaders in Northern Uganda who would have wanted the crimes

---

[22]The Letter from the Executive Director of Human Rights Watch to the International Criminal Tribunal for Rwanda. Available at:
http://www.globalpolicy.org/component/content/article/163-general/47873-rwandans-tribunal-risks-supporting victors justice.html. Accessed on 21/9/09.

committed by the government army: Uganda Peoples Defence Forces (UPDF) to be investigated and prosecuted. The ICC simply chose to focus on the LRA atrocities. It is argued here that the legitimacy of any legal system is derived from its fairness and its wide acceptance of those affected by it. Consequently, unless the international, regional and national legal mechanisms are seen to be fair to all and not one sided, they will not be accepted and they will not offer the protection of children in armed conflicts that they seek to achieve.

Failure by International Mechanisms to Address Root Causes of Conflicts

Another challenge to international law in the protection of children in armed conflicts arises because it fails to address the root causes of conflicts. In situations where civil war has become the only way of life, children will inevitably find soldiering the best option for their survival. The African situation perhaps provides the best illustration for this legal challenge to prevent children from participation in armed conflict. In Somalia and the Democratic Republic of Congo where the states have collapsed or are too weak to protect children, the gun is the best option for self-protection or protection for one's family (Obote-Odora, 1999). The argument here is that the international law for protection of children's rights in permanent war situations becomes unenforceable.

The international community needs to do more beyond developing international legal mechanisms to protect children in armed conflicts. Significant investment by the international community should be devoted to prevention of conflicts and peacebuilding of war-torn societies where children's rights are being violated.

Conclusion

This chapter has specifically discussed the issue of child soldiering at the global and continental (Africa) levels. The chapter examined the child soldier phenomenon from the historical context to try and establish the genesis of the practice. Evidence from the analysis shows that child soldiering is a historical practice and is as old as warfare itself but has always been culturally controlled and regulated to avoid harming children in wars that were usually taken to be the domain of the adult men

(Singer, 2006:3). This is contrasted with 'new wars' which are not regulated and do not respect the rights of children and non-combatants especially children.

The chapter also focused on the definition and conceptualization of a child, childhood and a child soldier in the context of child soldiering. It is argued that the universalization of the concept of a child and childhood from the Western perspective conflicts with other cultures such as African cultures where the conceptualization of the child and childhood is culturally and socially constructed. Consequently, the apparent differences in the conceptualization of a child and childhood, makes the international legal protection of children's rights in armed conflicts difficult. This chapter also discussed the methods of children's recruitment and involvements in armed conflicts; why they are preferred by armed groups and government forces and how they are used. The chapter further analysed the international legal mechanisms for the protection of children in armed conflicts and reasons why in spite of the existence of an elaborate body of legal protection, child soldiering has continued to thrive in most war zones.

In the final analysis, it is worth noting that whether children have historically participated in warfare, the contemporary civil wars in the last two decades have crossed the known limits in terms of destruction of innocent lives of civilians the majority of whom are children. The experience of Serb snipers during the Sarajevo siege who deliberately shot at children walking between their parents, to Rwanda where radio broadcasts before and during the genocide advised the Hutu Interahamwe militias to be sure not to forget the little ones (Singer 2006), to Mozambique and Angola and Sierra Leone, DRC, Liberia and Northern Uganda where children were indoctrinated and trained to become killing machines should compel the international community to act and protect children's rights. The protection should not only focus on putting into place global, continental and national legal mechanisms, but should also focus on identifying and dealing with the root causes of the conflicts in the deepest sense where children have become the pawns.

CHAPTER THREE

—————————●—————————

Child Soldiers in the Context of Disarmament, Demobilization, Reintegration and Rehabilitation as Peacebuilding

Introduction

> When the war ended, people said we should come out of the bush. But I was not going to come out with no shirt on my back and people looking down on me because I have no shoes… If there was no job and no money, no way would we come out … we would go back to the bush and fight again (Wessells, 2004:185)
> *-Former Child Soldier in Sierra Leone with RUF.*

Disarmament, demobilization, reintegration and rehabilitation (DDRR) programmes are considered standard features of post-conflict peacebuilding interventions. The main objective of DDRR is to remove and dispose of the guns and other means of violence, disperse the fighters and facilitate their transition and transformation into socially and economically useful citizens (Jennings, 2008:157). Disarmament, demobilization, reintegration and rehabilitation (DDRR) programmes intended to assist former child soldiers in their transition to civilian life are often designed for the immediate containment, disarmament and demobilization of rebel forces (Honwana, 2006:136). However, the RR of child soldiers, which forms the last stages in the processes of attempting to return their childhood is always the toughest undertaking.

As Singer (2006:97) points out in the case of reintegration; reunifications with families often face the challenge of acceptance and willingness even after completing the hardest task of tracing and relocation. Rehabilitation of child soldiers is a difficult process due to the added psychological and physical scars that these children carry. Yet empirical evidence shows that without effective RR, former child soldiers could pose a security risk of more and longer wars since they can be re-recruited to fight fresh rebellions (Singer, 2006). Dzinesa (2007:77) concurs with Singer's analysis and observes that poorly organized and managed DDRR processes always result into increased violence, banditry and criminality as was the case in Angola and Mozambique.

This book contends that the RR of child soldiers based on psychosocial support that relies on traditional and indigenous resources has been a neglected and marginalized field by the development interveners, the policy makers and scholars. Yet experience in war-torn societies such as Northern Uganda, Mozambique and Angola shows that traditional and indigenous resources have played a crucial role in the RR of former child soldiers as the discussions in Chapter Six will reveal. The book is premised on the hypothesis that the promotion of RR of former child soldiers by providing psychosocial support based on traditional and indigenous resources may contribute to conditions of peace and stability in Northern Uganda. It should be noted however, that by no means does this book argue that other aspects of peacebuilding are not important. Rather, it is observed that the provision of psychosocial support is very crucial in the RR of former child soldiers. Most crucially, psychosocial support is effective if it is based on traditional and indigenous resources rather than the Western approaches that have cultural and context limitations (Kostelny, 2006:19).

This chapter explores how effective disarmament, demobilization, reintegration and rehabilitation (DDRR) of former child soldiers is critical for their successful transition into civilian life and peacebuilding. However, for the purpose of this book, the emphasis will be placed on reintegration and rehabilitation of former child soldiers. The chapter is organized in three main sections. Section one focuses on the DDRR of former child soldiers as integral elements of peacebuilding; the second section focuses on the conceptualization of peacebuilding while the third section analyses the link between DDRR of child soldiers and the neglected psychosocial dimension of peacebuilding followed by a conclusion.

In this chapter, it is noted that failure to effectively reintegrate and rehabilitate former child soldiers is likely to constrain peacebuilding processes (Singer, 2006:183) and as such any attempts to build durable peace in Northern Uganda would require systematic planning and programming for the RR of former child soldiers. Secondly, it is worth noting that effective RR of former child soldiers is not an end in itself but a means to an end, which is sustainable peace. Finally, it is also observed that most peacebuilding processes neglect the traditional and indigenous psychosocial supports to former combatants and instead focus on provision of the official top-down United Nations standardized one-off material supports that are normally short term; yet successful RR requires long term and committed support which resides in the local traditional and indigenous resources.

It is currently understood by most analysts and scholars that effective implementation of DDRR of former combatants including child soldiers is crucial for successful peacebuilding of war torn societies (Singer, 2006). However, most literature on DDRR shows that these programmes often exclude soldiers under the legal age of 18 for military recruitment. What is also surprising is that normally these programmes exclusively focus on males, leaving out girls and young women who had been held captive in service of military forces (MacKay et al, 1999:111). The argument being made here is that unless former child soldiers and other ex-combatants are well reintegrated, rehabilitated and provided for by the DDRR processes, they are likely to constrain peacebuilding of societies emerging from violent conflicts.

Disarmament, Demobilization, Reintegration and Rehabilitation of Child Soldiers as Peacebuilding

As Jennings (2008:157) observes, disarmament, demobilization, reintegration and rehabilitation (DDRR) programmes are now standard features of post-conflict peacebuilding interventions in war-torn societies. However, in order to best understand the reintegration and rehabilitation of former child soldiers as integral elements of peacebuilding, it is important to define and conceptualize key terminologies within the context of DDRR and peacebuilding. Due to the rapid proliferation of DDRR activities around the world and the high level of importance attached to DDRR, a bewildering array of expressions and concepts have emerged used in the policy and practice of DDRR. As Muggah (2004:28) observes, some of these concepts are vague, abstract and lack robust conceptual or normative foundations. Some of these terminologies include disarmament, demobilization, reintegration, repatriation, resettlement, reinsertion and reconstruction which are sometimes used by UN agencies, World Bank and donors synonymously even where these expressions have different meanings. According to Muggah (2004) definitions matter and unambiguous definitions allow for a clear and transparent understanding of the problem, the elaboration of measurable standards and benchmarks and determination of success. Consequently, for the purpose of this book, concepts of disarmament, demobilization, reintegration and rehabilitation are defined and conceptualized in the context of peacebuilding.

Defining and Conceptualizing Disarmament and Demobilization

According to Spear (2002:142), there are two types of disarmament: cooperative and coercive disarmament. Coercive disarmament is the form commonly practised by the victor or the intervention forces. Examples of coercive disarmament include India in Sri Lanka and the US forces intervention in Iraq. Cooperative disarmament on the other hand is commonly associated with peace agreements where there has not been a clear winner of the war. The success stories of cooperative disarmament include El Salvador and Mozambique led by the United Nations. Porto et al. (2007) point out that disarmament involves the collection, documentation and disposal of weapons, ammunitions and explosives. These analysts also note that disarmament is often regarded as an activity, which follows the assembly of combatants in demobilization centres. They note that disarmament is central to any DDRR programme since the control of the quantity and type of weapons in circulation in the immediate post-conflict environment plays a crucial role in increasing security in the short-term, as well as contributing to confidence building of all the stakeholders in the peace process and ultimately reduces the possibility of reoccurrence of future conflicts.

Disarmament fulfils two interactive roles in civil war termination: a) the removal of the means by which civil wars have been prosecuted leading to prevention of reigniting of conflict; and, b) the creation of a stable environment thereby strengthening confidence and security building among the parties at conflict (Spear, 2002). Accordingly, there are five key elements that underpin successful disarmament and demobilization. These are; the viability and feasibility of the peace process and its aims, the implementation environment, the warring parties and verification.

In terms of viability and feasibility, Spear (2002) observes that a crucial aspect of any peace settlement concerns the degree of detail provided to guide implementation. In regard to the implementing environment, Spear observes that in many ways the levels –individual, local, national, regional and international levels in which the DDRR are being implemented determine the success of the process because of their interconnectedness. By implementers, Spear notes that there is a need for the different stakeholders involved in the implementation of the peace agreement to cooperate for its effective implementation. The point here is that the degree of involvement of all stakeholders in the conflict in the implementation of DDRR programmes is crucial to the success of the peace agreement.

Dzinesa (2007), on the other hand, defines disarmament as a military operation concerned with the management of arms and ammunition-the tools of violence- in order to create secure and stable frameworks out of the usually volatile immediate post-conflict situations. According to Dzinesa, disarmament involves the collection, control, and disposal of small arms, light, and heavy weapons of combatants and often also of the civilian population. Commenting on the danger of ineffective DDR Dzinesa (2007:76) observes that:

> Angola represents how ineffective DDR can easily cause antagonistic armies to recidivate. Failed attempts at DDR twice contributed to the resumption of armed conflict between the Movement for the Liberation of Angola (MPLA) and National Union for the Total Liberation of Angola (UNITA).

In the case of the disarmament process in Angola, Dzinesa concurs with Virginia Gamba (1999) that without proper disarmament and only partial demobilization, any possibility of creating a unified national army or of reaching elections under secure conditions was precluded. The enormity of the task and the international pressure to hold free and fair elections as soon as possible without implementing prior obligations, which related mostly to disarmament and demobilization chores, was a time bomb for the disaster that ensued in Angola (Dzinesa, 2007:76).

Vines (1998:191) points out how the United Nations failure to carry out meaningful disarmament during its ONUMOZ operation in Mozambique has had serious security consequences to both Mozambique and South Africa. He notes that while it would have been impossible for ONUMOZ to disarm all armed individuals, it should have efficiently destroyed those weapons it did obtain, especially when it became apparent that the new integrated FADM army would be far smaller than anticipated. In Mozambique, the ONUMOZ's failure was tied to its weak mandate regarding disarmament, which failed to spell out clearly what disarmament should entail and the criteria for its success. Accordingly, the mandate did not distinguish between disarmament and demobilization. Most crucially, the operation lacked resources to deal with disarmament issues of arms collection and decommissioning. As a result, Mozambique witnessed increased violence and criminality in the post-conflict stage, while South Africa up to this day still suffers a high crime rate and gun related violence as a result of the proliferation of small arms and light weapons from neighbouring Mozambique (Vines, 1998:205).

The analysis by Spear and others is very crucial in the DDRR of ex-combatants in war torn societies. The point that successful DDRR depends on the implementation environment is critical to the DDRR of former child soldiers in Northern Uganda in several ways. For example, the observation that success in the implementation of DDRR is dependent on different levels: individual, local, national, regional and international levels is critical in respect to the conflict in Northern Uganda where the rebel LRA has largely survived on military and financial support from the Government of Sudan which has been fighting a proxy war against the Government of Uganda.

Sudan accuses the Government of Uganda of supporting the rebels of the Sudan People's Liberation Army/Movement (SPLA/M) fighting against political domination and imposition of Islamic Sharia law on south Sudanese who are largely Christians and animists (ICG Report, 2008:13). At a regional level, Sudan's continued rearmament and financial support to LRA is likely to dissuade them from pursuing peace negotiations to end the 24 year old violent conflict. Also, without political commitment to end the LRA rebellion through peaceful means on the part of the Ugandan government as well as the continued involvement and support by the international community, the conflict is likely to continue. More so, small and light weapons continue to flow into Northern Uganda from war-torn regional countries: Somalia, DRC, Burundi and South Sudan which fuel and sustain the LRA rebellion.

Suffice to say that most of the above analyses by scholars are based on the United Nations' formal and structured DDRR that normally takes place following the United Nations brokered peace agreement (Gamba, 1999; Spear, 2002; Dzines, 2007). In the case of Northern Uganda, which is the focus of this book, DDRR programmes are being implemented without a formal peace agreement between the LRA rebels and the Government of Uganda. The peace process between Government of Uganda and the LRA mediated by the Government of South Sudan broke down when rebel leader refused to show up for the official signing in Juba South Sudan. The government unilaterally set up the Amnesty Commission which is mandated to implement DDRR of former combatants who surrender or rescued abducted child soldiers. With support of the international agencies including the United Nations and development partners; the Amnesty Commission has been engaged in the DDRR of former combatants including formerly abducted child soldiers. Consequently, Spears' five aspects of disarmament and demobilization do not apply generally in the Ugandan context.

Porto et al (2007) observation that disarmament is central to DDRR since the control of weapons in circulation in post-conflict environments increases security and reduces the possibility of future wars is relevant to peacebuilding processes generally. However, this analysis is most valid when subjected to the usual United Nations sponsored processes of DDRR which involve peace negotiations leading to a peace agreement. It is not applicable to the DDRR going on in Northern Uganda, the focus of this book. In Northern Uganda, the DDRR is taking place with no peace agreement, no international observers and the majority of the ex-combatants are formerly abducted children who have either been rescued by the government army or have escaped from LRA captivity. Most importantly, the war between the government and the LRA is still going on although presently it is being fought on foreign soil: the DRC, Central African Republic and South Sudan where the LRA relocated in July 2006 at the start of the now collapsed Juba peace negotiations in Southern Sudan.

Ozerdem (2002:961), drawing on the experience of DDR in Afghanistan, points out that disarmament does not ensure a total collection and disposal of arms which in most cases is the expectation. To Ozerdem, the real importance of disarmament is perhaps more at a symbolic level and the task of disarmament in war to peace transitions tends to be sensitive, testing the commitment of all the parties in the peace process. This sensitivity arises partly from its significant relationship with security. He argues that while disarmament is the first step in establishing a secure environment, there is no automatic or inherent relationship between the process of disarmament and the creation of a secure environment. Consequently, Ozerdem notes that as the cases of Liberia and El Salvador and Haiti show disarmament, whether voluntary or coercive, on its own is not sufficient to eradicate or permanently remove the means of violence in the short to medium term.

Accordingly, porous borders with countries with active weapon markets; lack of capacity to enforce regulations; criminal use of weapons; political, economic or security climates which enhance the security and economic value of owning and using a weapon make disarmament a difficult undertaking. Ozerdem (2002) advises that since peace agreements are vehicles for initiating disarmament, it is important that peace agreements specify the timing and scope of disarmament as well as procedural issues such as the sequence of disarmament and the extent to which it can be inspected, the ratio or proportion of forces to be disarmed at each stage and the disposal of weapons and its supervision (Ozerdem, 2002:966). Ozerdem makes a convincing analysis that disarmament alone cannot ensure a secure environment in war-torn societies. Based on this analysis, it becomes evident that other factors must be taken into consideration including the economic, political and regional security environment in which disarmament is taking place. Consequently, disarmament must be done within the holistic context of DDRR that takes care of all the necessary conditions.

The problem with Ozerdem's views on disarmament in the context of a peace agreement is that they are not relevant to the conflict in Northern Uganda, which is the focus of this study. As already noted above, DDRR processes are being implemented unilaterally by the Government of Uganda without a peace agreement with the rebel LRA. Nevertheless, the issue of porous borders with active arms markets in neighbouring countries which are also experiencing civil wars, such as Burundi and DRC and prevailing economic and political environments in which disarmament is taking place are both found to be critical factors to consider in respect to DDRR of ex-combatants including former child soldiers in Northern Uganda.

It is should also be noted that achieving a stable peace in the post-war torn society is dependent on how well the former combatants have been demobilized. According to Verhey (2001:6), demobilization refers to a formal exercise or a variety of informal occasions. Formal demobilization, including child soldiers, usually follows a peace agreement but may also occur as part of a military restructuring or military victory after the conflict. Informal demobilization may include situations where child soldiers escape from or are released by their armed group either spontaneously or because of advocacy pressure. In the case of demobilization of child soldiers, Verhey notes that the exercise may be involuntary for many child soldiers may fear the transition from military to civilian life and an unknown future. Consequently, he observes, that during the demobilization process, it is imperative to gain support and encouragement of military and civilian officials as well as families and communities.

Noteworthy, is that former child soldiers themselves can play a variable role of counselling their peers (Verhey, 2001). Verhey's point is valid in respect of the demobilized former child soldiers in Northern Uganda where former child soldiers associations are providing counselling to their peers and members of the community who are traumatized (Focus Group discussion with members of KICA Ber Youth Group). Some of the former child soldiers have been officially demobilized by the Amnesty Commission which provides to them a one-off, inadequate subsistence as part of the reintegration package which includes transport to their homes. During the fieldwork, it was established that most of the former child soldiers are surviving by belonging to self-help associations which are providing counselling services and soft loans to start income generating activities.[23]

Muggah (2004:31), on the other hand, defines demobilization as the formal and usually controlled identification, registration and discharge of active combatants from regular or irregular forces. Regular forces are used here to mean soldiers serving in the government army, while irregular forces refer to forces such as guerrilla or militia groups. Accordingly, the objectives of demobilization include efficient massing of ex-combatants together in encampment sites designed for this purpose and their registration. Demobilization sometimes includes

---

[23]During the fieldwork in northern Uganda, it was found out that several former child soldiers have formed associations where they are engaged in income generating activities. The associations also provide counselling services to their members who are experiencing psychological problems. Fieldwork was conducted in northern Uganda from December 2008 to March 2009.

101

disarmament although it is primarily concerned with registration of former soldiers as part of a security sector reform initiative or ex-combatants in post-conflict situations. It involves distribution to ex-combatants of non-transferable identification cards, the collection of relevant demographic and socio-economic information into a database, and sometimes health screening, orientation and facilitation of transport to a new site (Muggah, 2004). Muggah's definition and conceptualization of demobilization is relevant to Uganda's situation except that in the case of Uganda, demobilization of child soldiers has not focused on their disarmament.

The United Nations Department of Peacekeeping Office (UNDPKO) observes that demobilization involves the assembly, quartering, disarmament, administration and discharge of former combatants, who may receive compensation and other assistance to support their transition to civilian life.[24] In the case of the war in Northern Uganda, the government, through the Amnesty Commission, provided resettlement packages and amnesty certifications to the ex-combatants who surrender (they do not necessarily assemble at any one particular place); hand in their guns and renounce violence. This means that demobilization can be context specific based on the prevailing realities on the ground in any particular conflict situation.

In respect to the DDRR of child soldiers, Singer (2006:188) observes that it is now believed that the process of turning a child soldier back into a child must take place in three main phases. Phase one is disarmament and demobilization; phase two is rehabilitation of both the physical and psychological realms and the third phase is reintegration with families and communities. According to Singer, reintegration must include a sustained follow-up support including self-capacity building and long term counselling. Analysts note that the time requirement for each phase varies although there is a general consensus that the overall process must be measured in terms of months rather than weeks or days as normally happens in most official DDRR processes due to lack of resources or improper attention to needs (Singer, 2006).

---

[24]United Nations, Department of Peacekeeping Operations (1999). 'Disarmament, Demobilization and Reintegration of Ex-Combatants in a Peacekeeping Environment: Principles and Guidelines.' Available at:
http://www.un.org/Depts/dpko/lessons/DD&R.pdf Accessed on 27/10/09.

Like Spear, Singer's analysis of DDRR is the one that is formally conducted based on the UN standard procedures, which is not the case in Northern Uganda. In Northern Uganda some of the former child soldiers escaped from the rebel LRA and simply walked directly home and reintegrated themselves with their families and communities. Other children are captured in combat and are taken to the military barracks from where they are taken to reception centres for initial rehabilitation and finally reintegrated with their families. This means that demobilization does not necessary follow a particular procedure, which calls for flexibility and being context specific by the interveners in different situations.

Defining and Conceptualizing Reintegration and Rehabilitation

UNDPKO defines reintegration as measures provided to former combatants that would increase the potential for them, and their families, economic and social reintegration into civil society.[25] Accordingly, reintegration programmes include cash assistance or compensation in kind, as well as vocational training and income generation. On the other hand, Singer (2006:160) defines reintegration as a reciprocal process that includes not only the adoption of former soldiers but also the rebuilding of healthy families and communities, without which former soldiers have few positive roles and options (Singer, 2006:160). Singer further observes that the reintegration of child soldiers is the final stage in the process of attempting to return childhood to young soldiers. As such, reintegration of child soldiers involves a process of re-introducing the children back to their homes or communities, so that they can rejoin society on positive terms.

According to Jareg (2005:1) rehabilitation of child soldiers means to restore the child's functioning 'as it was' before their experiences-but this will be a well-nigh impossible task in the case of those who have been with armed forces for many years. Rehabilitation is supposed to be an organized process, which follows children's demobilization, escape, or capture and then release by another armed force. It is a process of re-orientation with people who have received special training to facilitate the re-adjustment processes.

---

[25] Ibid.

Jennings (2008:157) defines reintegration as 'the process by which ex-combatants acquire civilian status and gain sustainable empowerment and income ... social and economic process... primarily taking place in communities at local level ... part of the general development of a country (that) often necessitates long-term external assistance.' Jennings notes that although reintegration programming tends to vary little from place to place, there is no such uniformity on what reintegration actually means and implies. Jennings, who critically analyzes reintegration process in Liberia, points out that in the absence of critical thinking on the social, economic and political project that the reintegration concept seems to promote, reintegration in Liberia essentially meant temporary removal of idleness. Reintegration of ex-combatants in Liberia involved the provision of education or vocational training, a small monthly stipend and a set of tools upon course completion (Jennings, 2008).

According to Berdal (Berdal, 1996:39), reintegration refers to medium- and long-term programmes, including 'cash compensation, training or income generation meant to increase the potential for economic and social reintegration of ex-combatants and their families.' Berdal further notes that in most cases there is an overlap of activities for reintegration and demobilization. He however, observers that the extent to which their interdependence is recognized and incorporated into funding and implementation is very critical for their long-term success.

Porto et al (2007) who conducted research on DDR in Angola, observe that there is a risk of seeing disarmament, demobilization and reintegration as separate processes subject to sequential implementation. They note however that increased international experience with DDR has exposed the limitations of an uncritical sequential approach to DDR, exposing the urgent need for a better understanding of all the components (disarmament, demobilization and reintegration) and especially of reintegration (Porto, 2007:17). These analysts pose the question that, 'If one's understanding of reintegration is that it is the 'process by which ex-combatants acquire civilian status and gain access to civilian forms of work and income,' a process considered primarily social and economic in nature and with an open time-frame. What could be the justification of including it as part of DDR processes? They advise that the long-term nature of the process and complexities involved should not be underestimated. They argue that reintegration is essentially determined by the economic situation in the country and by the extent of co-operation with other development programmes and that this long-term perspective should be reflected in the mandate of the institutions involved.

Kingma (1999) notes that while demobilization and resettlement might have to be implemented quickly; reintegration is by nature a slow, social, economic and psychological process. Consequently, Kingma observes that successful reintegration into civilian life depends to a large extent on the initiatives of ex-combatants and their families and on the support they receive from their communities, the government, NGOs, or foreign development corporation. Accordingly, in the longer term reintegration also depends on the process of democratization, including the recovery of a weak (or collapsed) state and the maturing of an independent civil society.

Kingma (1999), like Porto et al (2007), warns against enthusiasm normally expressed by policy makers about DDR, particularly reintegration, and calls for understanding the very conditions that pertain in many, war to peace transitions. These analysts concur and point out that in the majority of cases, DDR programmes have been implemented in places where devastated political, social and economic structures are all that have been left after the war. They also note that in many countries that are experiencing protracted armed conflicts, state weakness and decay, poverty and underdevelopment, discriminatory political institutions and lack of opportunities are at the core of violent conflicts in the first place. Consequently, it becomes confusing, they argue, to use the prefix (re) for reintegration.

Porto et al further observe that successful reintegration requires that particular attention be made to issues such as political participation, respect for human rights, equitable distribution of resources, security sector reform, democratization and rule of law which are at the core of most conflicts. This analysis is relevant to the RR of child soldiers in Northern Uganda which is the focus of this book. Even if most of the child soldiers were abducted and forcefully conscripted into the LRA rebellion, economic marginalization and livelihood issues have been cited as some of the major causes of the conflict. Consequently, reintegrating child soldiers into the same conditions that obtained before the conflict would not ensure sustainable peace.

The limitation of Porto et al.'s analysis in respect of the reintegration of former child soldiers in Northern Uganda is that they view reintegration from the usual official perspective and conducted within the framework of UN supported processes. There are situations in various war torn societies such as Northern Uganda where DDRR programmes can be implemented outside the framework of a peace agreement and without UN supervision. In the case of Northern Uganda, RR of ex-combatants the majority of who are children are being implemented without formal United Nations sponsored peace agreement.

It should be noted that the observations by the various analysts (Muggah, 2004; Kingma, 1999; Porto et al, 2007) about the need for proper conceptualization of reintegration within the framework of the DDRR are crucial for effective reintegration processes. This observation is relevant to the conflict in Northern Uganda. The DDR of ex-combatants is generally poorly articulated and conceptualized in the Peace, Recovery and Development Plan (PDRP) for Northern Uganda, the official government recovery programme. A closer look at the PRDP also one finds that the DDR component has not been fully explained in detail compared to other components. More so, the funding for the overall DDR is only USD 10 million, which is not enough considering the magnitude of the task at hand. The Minister in charge of the reconstruction of Northern Uganda agreed that the component on DDR in the Peace, Recovery and Development Plan (PRDP) of Northern Uganda is not well conceptualized since during the design stage government lacked expertise in that particular area (Interview with Minister Wakikhona).[26] The DDR component lumps together all ex-combatants as if they are a homogenous group without consideration for peculiar challenges and needs of former child soldiers. What this means is that former child soldiers are likely to be marginalized in the DDRR processes.

Honwana (2006) like Singer (2006) observes that in most post-conflict recovery programmes disarmament: demobilization, reintegration and rehabilitation of child soldiers are either forgotten or lumped together under general groupings of "ex-combatants." Honwana, who conducted a study on the DDR of former child soldiers in Mozambique, found that the process excluded girls and young women who had been held captive in the service of military forces. She noted that transitional aid programmes assumed that these demobilized soldiers

---

[26] Interview with Minister Wakikhona was conducted in his office in Kampala in December, 2009.

could simply re-enter intact families and communities although many had lost kin and their neighbours and communities were unable to absorb them. More so, boys and girls recruited at an early age had missed schooling and job training, which made their future livelihoods unpredictable.

In comparison to boys and young men, the situation of former girls/young women combatants in Mozambique was worse. Scholars note that during the reintegration process younger women faced gender related problems ranging from their sexual reputations to marital prospects which had been severely compromised by their captivity (Honwana, 2006:147). In spite of the neglect by the official reintegration, the families in Mozambique made concerted efforts to reintegrate the young women once they had been reunited with their relatives. The reunification of young women and boys was immediately followed by organizing traditional cleansing and purification rituals performed by traditional healers and by the priests from local Zionist Churches. Cleansing ceremonies reaffirmed family cohesion and support and tended to address the emotional and psychosocial problems experienced by child soldiers.

Commenting about the challenge of reintegration, Honwana (2006:138) observes that

Data provided by the technical unit of the UN Mission in Mozambique (ONUMOZ) indicates that 27% of the soldiers presented for demobilization were younger than eighteen at the time. Child combatants younger than fifteen, even after fighting the war for many years, could not be considered soldiers under international law, according to Geneva Conventions. Ironically, the same Geneva Conventions could not be enforced to preclude these young combatants from being recruited into the military in the first place.

Singer (2006) further observes that poorly reintegrated child soldiers are likely to join criminal gangs which could result in increased levels of crimes after the end of the war; they may also hire their services as mercenaries to on-going regional conflicts, ultimately threatening regional peace and security. In Sierra Leone for example, Singer (2006:185) points out that the United Nations earmarked $34 million to disarm, demobilize and reintegrate ex-combatants. A small portion of $965,000 of the already small figure was directed to thousands of child soldiers. Singer warns that the implications of neglecting child soldiers are long-lasting societal repercussions, including extremely high levels of banditry and crime as was the case in Mozambique in the decade following the end of war.

The observations by Singer (2006) and Honwana (2006) about marginalization of child soldiers in most DDRR programmes is critical and is relevant to the situation in Northern Uganda. In a situation where DDR does not specifically target former child soldiers, it becomes clear that this category is likely to be sidelined.[27] Moreover, since the LRA has not officially disbanded, and with the majority of the fighters still engaged in active combat operations, most of the ex-combatants to be demobilized are currently former child soldiers. Consequently, the RR of former child soldiers should have informed the design process of the PRDP. Further, Honwana's findings about the relevance of cultural and traditional practices in the reintegration of former child soldiers in Mozambique resembles the traditional practices that are being relied upon in the RR of former child soldiers in Northern Uganda. In Northern Uganda, while the RR of child soldiers is not well documented, when formerly abducted children leave the reception centres their families and communities, with support by the cultural institutions, organize traditional ceremonies and rituals to welcome them home.

Singer (2006:200) who observes that reintegration is the final stage of returning childhood to child soldiers argues that the ideal outcome for the reintegration process is to return them to their families. Singer further notes that the family helps former child soldiers to recover from Post Traumatic Stress Disorder (PTSD). He, however, points out that family reunification in most cases faces several challenges which include acceptance and willingness of some families to take these children in after a very difficult task of tracing families and relocation of children. A survey conducted in Africa shows that 80% of parents regarded former child soldiers a threat to society and did not want their children to mix with them(Singer, 2006:2001). Consequently, Singer advises that in order to ensure community acceptance which is critical for successful

---

[27] According to the PRDP, most of the reporters ('reporters' is a term that has been used to mean all ex-combatants in northern Uganda who are undergoing DDRR) were abducted against their will and forced to join the rebellion. Of the total number of reporters from the north, 5677 are children below 18 years of age. The PRDP further notes that in their captivity these children have been through a lot of indoctrination and violence including being forced to kill their own relatives (and neighbours), raping, and brutally cutting off lips and limbs of innocent civilians with the aim of creating public horror.

reintegration, a significant programme of sensitization should be put into place to prepare and educate the community on the challenges and difficulties that these children have gone through and the fact that they too are victims of the conflict. This is critical for acceptance especially in war-torn societies where children were forced to commit atrocities against their communities and families such as Northern Uganda.

Singer's analysis of the challenges of reintegration especially family acceptance is true to most war zones particularly in Northern Uganda. There have been reports in Northern Uganda which indicate that family reunifications often break down resulting in some of the children living on the streets (Liu Institute for Global Issues & Ker Kwaro Acholi, 2005). This has a lot to do with the behaviour that children acquired in the bush including the power that the gun used to bestow on them. When children come home they fail to cope with the authority of their parents who want to treat them like any other ordinary children. Two testimonies from Northern Uganda confirm the risk former child soldiers pose to their families and society generally. A story is told about how an old man was hacked to death by his grandson (a former child soldier) when he asked him to demonstrate how he used to kill people in the bush. To demonstrate how he used to kill, the child picked up a pestle and smashed the old man's head.[28]

Another story is about two sisters who were sent by their mother to harvest cassava from the garden. On their way back home the older sister told the younger sister who had recently been rescued from the rebels that she was tired and needed to rest first. The younger sister killed her with the hoe and proceeded home with the cassava and started peeling it for cooking as if nothing had happened. When their mother inquired where she had left the sister, the girl said that she had helped her to rest since she was tired. The girl was subsequently found dead some distance away from their home.[29] Consequently, Singer advises that aid workers should always ensure that both former child soldiers and parents are

---

[28] Key Note Address by Hon. Henry Oryem, Minister of State for International Cooperation and Deputy Leader of the Government Peace Team who himself comes from Gulu, northern Uganda. He said that unless former child soldiers are well reintegrated and rehabilitated into normal life, they are a time bomb for all Ugandans as they have capacity to harm anybody. Hon. Oryem was speaking at a National Prayer Breakfast for the peace process organized by civil society organizations before the collapse of the Juba Peace negotiations at Serena Hotel, Kampala in March, 2007.
[29] Ibid.

prepared for such challenges before reintegration by emphasizing reconciliation and healing. Another challenge for reintegration identified by Singer (2006) is when the children come home to find that they lost whole families during the war or they are not able to trace their families. In this case, he notes, arrangements should be designed to respond to such a scenario even before the need arises. Singer proposes that children's homes should be established where children live together under the supervision of a mentor while at the same time they are provided with educational and vocational training programmes.

Singer's proposal for the children's home should however be approached with caution and implemented as a temporary measure. Children whose parents have died have been found to do better if they are supported to stay with their close relatives than those brought up in institutionalized homes. Commenting on the dangers of institutionalized homes for separated children, Petty and Jareg (1998:150) observe that:

> ... whatever circumstances of separation, for the children themselves, removal from family, clan, and community can have serious long-term consequences. Besides developmental, psychological and child rights concerns, that are associated with institutional care, ...loss of a family name and place of origin deprives children of the links they need in many societies to establish a foothold in the adult world.

Singer also advises that in order to achieve successful reintegration, effort should be made to overcome the stigma and stereotypes that often surround ex-child soldiers. He advises that there is a need for society to acknowledge that the children were also the victims of the armed violence. Singer's observation is relevant to the situation in Northern Uganda, where the recent study found that name calling and abuses directed at former young women soldiers is stigmatizing them and making it difficult to reintegrate fully (Liu Institute for Global Issues, 2005:35).

Brett et al (2004:99) identify several challenges associated with demobilization and reintegration of former child soldiers, particularly of girls. They observe that problems arise for girls' demobilization and reintegration when the conflict ends. For example, most girl soldiers do not go through the official demobilization processes for a number of reasons including the fact that most armed groups do not consider girls part of their fighters. Also, most former girl combatants dodge official demobilization for fear of public opinion and shame that they were used as sexual slaves and concubines of commanders which could jeopardize future prospects for marriage.

Since most girls do not make it through the demobilization processes, there is always lack of accurate figures about their real numbers and of child soldiers generally which affects planning for their effective reintegration. Brett et al. cite the example of Sierra Leone where it is reported that 8% of demobilized soldiers were female with only 3% of demobilized child soldiers being girls in the most recent phase. As part of reintegration process in Sierra Leone, school fees was waived for child soldiers who had a demobilisation number and the schools which accepted these children received packages of materials accessed by all students. In this case, girl soldiers who did not formally demobilize did not receive school fees waiver nor did they bring any benefits to the schools.

The issue of marginalization of former girl soldiers raised by Brett et al. supported by Honwana (2006) and Singer (2006) is crucial and should always inform overall planning and programming by policy makers and international agencies involved in DDRR of former child soldiers. Former girl soldiers suffer a lot because of their gender by performing multiple roles during the armed conflicts. They are used as combatants, cooks, sex slaves and many of them end up having unwanted pregnancies and sometimes sexually transmitted diseases. It is imperative therefore that former girl soldiers are not marginalized during DDRR processes. This analysis is true in respect to Northern Uganda, the focus for this book, where most formerly abducted girls have not been successfully reintegrated forcing some of them to resort to prostitution in towns (Liu Institute for Global Issues, 2005:35).

During the field work in Northern Uganda, it was established that most parents are ready to receive back their abducted daughters without the babies they conceived and produced in the bush. Most of them are told to first take the children to their fathers and then come back. Faced with rejection of their families because of the children they came back with from the bush, most of these young women have ended up in towns such as Gulu and Kitgum doing petty jobs with some of them ending in prostitution (Allen et al, 2006:26).

Brett et al (2004) and McKay et al (1999:53) observe that during armed conflicts girl soldiers usually get involved in relationships, become pregnant and produce babies. After the war, most of these relationships break down due to the fact that husbands cannot afford to support their partners or lose interest. The presence of babies normally compounds the transition of girl soldiers due to economic hardships. One of such girls observed that:

> The last time when I asked him if that's the way to treat me, he only told me that now the war is over; we only got married while the war lasted---now that the war has ended the marriage should be ended too (Brett et al, 2004:100)

Worth noting also is that in most post-conflict societies, the job opportunities for former young women combatants are very limited than those of boys. Consequently, it is imperative that reintegration and rehabilitation programmes should take into account the special needs of this category of former child soldiers within the context of their culture.

Wessells (2006:180) advocates for provision of livelihoods as a key to successful RR of former child soldiers. He points out that there is a worrying linkage between poverty, conflict and child soldiering. Wessells notes that poverty destroys health services and the well-being of all the children and sometimes obstructs positive options including access to education as a means of earning future livelihoods. To Wessells, although poverty is not a cause of armed conflicts, its enabling role is visible in the disproportionate numbers of wars fought in developing countries, particularly those with failing economies. He further points out that available evidence shows that some children have been found to join armed groups with the hope of gaining the otherwise unattainable wealth and sending such money home to help their families. Wessells gives the example of Sierra Leone where a combination of stigma, fear, and lack of livelihoods left many former child soldiers in doubt about their ability to reintegrate into civilian society. One sixteen year old former child soldier remarked that:

> When the war ended, people said we should come out of the bush. But I was not going to come out with no shirt on my back and people looking down on me because I have no shoes…. If there was no job and no money, no way would we come out ….we would go back to the bush and fight again (Wessells, 2006:184).

112

After the end of war, Christian Children's Fund (CCF) implemented a DDR programme in Sierra Leone which aimed at supporting the reintegration of former child soldiers and peacebuilding. One of the testimonies of the beneficiaries of the programme emphasizes the relevance of the support provided by CCF on the livelihood and RR of child soldiers generally. A former girl soldier pointed out that:

> I was called *kolonko* (prostitute) before. Now I am respected and held in high regard in my village because of my business accomplishments. I can buy food. I save money in my cash box (Wessells, 2006:190).

The nexus between poverty, conflict and child soldiering is also collaborated by Boothby (2006:170) who conducted a study on RR in Mozambique. Boothby (2006:160) notes that Save the Children, which was instrumental in the RR of former child soldiers, among other activities organized apprenticeships with local carpenters, masons and other skilled labourers for older boys so that they could earn basic employment and business skills. CCF supplemented the training with provision of microcredit loans to former child soldiers who were selected based on their high levels of motivation and trust by their colleagues. Solidarity groups of 3 to 10 people who each agreed to be accountable to the others received an initial loan of USD 60 to be repaid over a period of six months. Loans were used to purchase farming tools, sewing machines, fabric for dyeing among others. CCF staff provided continuous training and follow up to the beneficiaries. Interestingly, the loan repayment rate was 99%, which contrasts starkly with the frequently heard comments in the field that ex-combatants are bad investment for microcredit programmes (Wessells, 2006:189).

The analysis by Boothby (2006) and Wessells (2006) is crucial in respect to RR of child soldiers in Northern Uganda. Most former child soldiers missed out on their education and now lack basic skills for the job market. During the fieldwork, it was established that most of them are struggling to survive since they missed out on schooling and have been integrated among equally poor communities that recently returned from IDP camps where they stayed for over 15 years. Consequently, as part of RR programming for former child soldiers, it is imperative to include provision for skills training including technical and business education to enable them acquire skills which can ensure sustainable livelihoods. It should be noted however, that economic livelihoods should not only target former child soldiers to avoid creating resentment from the community members, the majority of whom suffered greatly including loss of livelihoods during their displacement into camps. Creating an economic imbalance in favour of former child soldiers, would lead to community resentment which could further stigmatize the former child soldiers and constrain their reintegration[30]

Boothby (200:170) who conducted a longitudinal study on the reintegration of thirty-nine former child soldiers in Mozambique who were rehabilitated and reintegrated by Save the Children found out that all the boys were successfully re-united with their families or relatives. Underpinning the reintegration, Boothby found that traditional ceremonies organized for child soldiers upon return to the villages were paramount for acceptance by families, communities and individual children. In addition to traditional ceremonies, the study found out that sensitization campaigns that were carried out by government officials before the actual reunifications played a positive role in community acceptance of former child soldiers. Sensitization campaigns were designed to enable the community to understand that children too were victims of war (Boothby, 2006:173). Boothby's findings regarding the relevance of traditional rituals and ceremonies have been emphasized by several scholars and analysts including Machel (2001). In the case of Northern Uganda, the Acholi cultural institution Ker Kwaro and the elders have been supported by international agencies to conduct traditional ceremonies and rituals for the RR of former child soldiers across the entire Acholi sub-region. A number of cultural ceremonies including stepping on the egg and *Mato Oput* are being used to promote RR of children with families and communities.

In respect of rehabilitation of former child soldiers, Singer (2006) has observed that it is the most difficult task since it involves dealing with both the physical and emotional injuries of these persons. Commenting on the rehabilitation of former child soldiers, Jareg (2005:2) points out that:

> When talking with children undergoing 'rehabilitation' I often use the metaphor of crossing a bridge between the 'military life' to life in one's home and community to capture the process they are going through. This journey is not straight forward: there will be times of good

---

[30]Interview with a representative of Caritas in Northern Uganda, in 2007.

progress followed by periods of very slow movement. …. Indeed, sometimes there will be a complete halt and even active retreat. Fear, grief, anxiety, anger, guilt and shame, lack of confidence, diseases….. hamper progress. Determination, good health, the comfort, love and encouragement….. are the best companions on this journey, which in many cases will be life-long.

According to Jareg (2005), the children who need rehabilitation are those who participated in committing atrocities; children with severe physical and psychological health problems including those with disabilities. Other categories of children that need rehabilitation are those whose families have been destroyed or have rejected them for various reasons; including girls who have been severely abused and girls who have produced children while serving under the various armed groups. Jareg advises that rehabilitation requires that such children be given a period of intensive assistance from trained social, health workers and teachers in some form of interim care before being released to their communities.

Jareg further notes that children who have participated in committing atrocities are those most likely to be troubled with more serious post-traumatic manifestations and at the same time are the ones who are likely to face rejection or are at the risk of retaliation from community members. In the African situation, it is also noted that such children require some form of ritual cleansing to rid them of contaminating evil spirits before they can be accepted into the community again. The emotional implications are increased when children have been forced to kill, maim or rape family members. Jareg's observation is critical in respect to children who are traumatized due to atrocities committed during the war. In any case, the intention of the rebels in forcing children to kill their relatives or community members is to make children perpetually guilty and alienated from the community. Jareg rightly observes that rehabilitation using traditional ceremonies is crucial in the rehabilitation of former child soldiers. In Northern Uganda, traditional rituals have been performed to treat psychosocial trauma of former child soldiers as part of the RR.

Jareg suggests six programmatic areas when planning for rehabilitation and reintegration of former child soldiers. These include; restoring family relationships; relationships with the community; children's health-physical and psychological; organized learning opportunities; vocational training and income generation; recreation and play. Accordingly, these aspects of RR ought to be integrated in a holistic manner based on a child's rights and child development framework. It is also observed that during the rehabilitation process, children should be encouraged to take active roles in the planning and implementation of their own RR processes. The point being advanced here is that by children doing this is not only their right, but it can help to mitigate the feelings of helplessness, distrust and estrangement often associated with traumatic experiences. This is thought to be important in the RR of child soldiers since it gives them a sense of direction, shape, and goals to work for. Participation in the planning and implementation of their own RR is also thought to have an impact of completely turning around the ways children have been trained to behave in the military environment where they received orders that were not negotiable. In this case, children are asked to reflect, plan, explore, discuss and even protest. Most crucially, Jareg advises that different approaches to address various issues need to be developed according to the different cultural, social and political contexts one is working in and also the phase of the conflict.

By and large, Jareg's analysis is crucial for effective RR of child soldiers particularly of girl soldiers. Her advice of ensuring that children become part of the design, planning and implementation of their RR programme is very relevant since not only does it restore confidence, self esteem and self worth to the traumatized children, it also re-humanises them and ensures ownership of the RR processes which is critical for its success. Jareg advocates for an interim care of children in a particular place such as a reception centre for them to first undergo rehabilitation before they are reintegrated with their families or communities. While one would agree with the interim care of children undergoing rehabilitation before reintegrating them with their families, it is important to be careful about the kind of interim care that is being provided.

In Northern Uganda for example, most of the children's reception centres which proliferated during the conflict were using Western approaches of psychosocial support especially counselling by unqualified people which has been found to be contextually irrelevant and sometimes harmful to children (Bracken, 1998:4). Consequently, it is important to make sure that the interim rehabilitation given to children in the reception centres is context specific and conforms to socio-cultural settings (Machel, 2001).

Guyot (2007), commenting on the rehabilitation of former child soldiers, observes that the traditional DDR programmes have been limited by the concentration on their external aspects such as collection of arms and return of combatants to their original communities. She notes that the needs of children and youth who are subjects of larger narratives are always subsumed within other issues[31]. Guyot notes that shifting the attention to the children as potential implementers and partners in endeavours would place the issues that affect child soldiers at the centre of dialogue. She further notes that participatory exploration of young people's engagement in the processes of rehabilitation lends itself to a more comprehensive view of the whole situation and yields an understanding which may prove useful in crafting more effective and welcome programming.

Guyot further observes that the impact of the trauma brought about by the war is normally experienced not only by individual children and youth, but also impacts on social cohesion since it undermines the trust between community members formerly bound by complex extended networks that comprise traditional affiliations. Consequently, attempts to mend the social fabric bring the opportunity to address issues that are relevant to the community as a whole. Consequently, Guyot advises that RR of child soldiers must go hand in hand with other programmes for community recovery.

Guyot, like Wessells (2006), advocates for economic empowerment of former child soldiers as necessary for their successful rehabilitation. To Guyot, continued social and economic marginalization of these children can only make for a lingering risk of destabilization. She argues that community based strategies have the potential to empower communities to exercise control over their collective lives and to heal together. Facilitating community empowerment can counteract the destructive effects of wartime upon communities and the emotional lives of the extended families that populate them. She also notes that rehabilitation of former child soldiers should be mindful of the fact that recruitment and training of child soldiers is a process whereby children were conditioned to obey without question; desensitized to violence and indoctrinated. Consequently, the rehabilitation efforts need to be as

---

[31]Guyot, J. (2007). 'Suffer the Children: The Psychosocial Rehabilitation of Child Soldiers As a Function of Peace-building.' London. Coalition to Stop Child Soldiers. Available at: http://www.child-soldiers.org/psycho-social/Linked_Guyot_2007.pdf. Accessed on 27/10/09.

comprehensive and should provide new role models to replace the old ones for these children.

Guyot posits that in most cases traumatic experience in war torn society is not only experienced by former child soldiers who are being rehabilitated but the entire community among whom they are being reintegrated. Consequently she advises that it is important that planning and programming of the RR initiatives for child soldiers should be mindful of this fact. This observation is crucial in the RR of former child soldiers. Guyot's observation that war destroys people's socio-economic wellbeing and livelihoods of most societies emerging from civil wars making them dependent on relief aid is true in respect to Northern Uganda. The suffering endured during the years of internal displacement during the war, the disempowerment, hopelessness and shame as effects of the war often traumatize whole communities.

In the case of Northern Uganda, which is the focus of this book, particularly the Acholi sub-region, where over 80% of the entire population were internally displaced into camps, most people are still traumatized by over 15 years of internal displacement life subsisting in very poor living conditions (Liu Institute for Global Issues et al, 2005). Ironically, it is among these very poor and traumatized people that the former child soldier is always returned for RR. In such circumstances, as Guyot observes, RR programming should take into consideration the needs of former child soldiers as well as the needs of the entire society.

Conceptualizing Peacebuilding

This section focuses on the conceptualization of peacebuilding in the context of RR of child soldiers. As Jennings (2007:157) has noted, disarmament, demobilization and reintegration programmes are now standard features of post-conflict peacebuilding interventions whose aim is to take away the guns, disperse the fighters and facilitate their transformation into socially and economically productive citizens. While DDRR are standard features of peacebuilding, there has not been a standardized understanding of peacebuilding among policy makers, international donors and practitioners, which makes it difficult to achieve successful peacebuilding processes. Richmond (2007:287) has observed that though the importance of a social contract and civil peace has long been recognized, peacebuilding approaches have increasingly been co-opted by statebuilding agenda that reflect a predatory, neoliberal, ideological perspective aiming to justify and enhance the governance of unruly others. Richmond further observes that Lockean liberalism, which aimed at the social contract between subjects and rulers over the preservation of life, liberty and prosperity, is heavily reflected in the intellectual discourses of conflict resolution and liberal peacebuilding. To Richmond, societies, groups, identities, cultures and welfare are often only rhetorically part of this discourse.

Following from the above observation by Richmond, it is apparent that peacebuilding has been conceptualized differently by various practitioners who are involved in the reconstruction and recovery processes of war-torn societies. Yet, in order for the RR of former child soldiers to contribute to successful peacebuilding various stakeholders involved must have a common and clear understanding of what peacebuilding is all about. This section engages with the debate about peacebuilding as conceptualized by several scholars and analysts. It is hoped that this section will contribute to a better understanding of the concept of peacebuilding in the context of RR of child soldiers.

As already noted, analysts (Spear, 2002:141; Brett et al, 2004; Ramsbotham et al, 2005) concur that unless former combatants (including child soldiers) are successfully reintegrated and rehabilitated into civilian life, they could constrain the peacebuilding processes. In most war torn societies, peacebuilding processes overlook the RR of former child soldiers. The neglect of RR of child soldiers often leads to renewed insecurity and ultimately undermines the consolidation of peace (Singer, 2006:185).

It is noted here that in order to understand the relevance of effective RR of former child soldiers as part of peacebuilding, it is important to define what is meant by peacebuilding. There is not yet an agreed definition of peacebuilding. However, Pugh (2000:2) observes that peacebuilding can be construed as activities intended to strengthen structures and processes with the main aim of preventing a return to violent conflict. Pugh links peacebuilding with regeneration of war-torn societies. He defines regeneration as a process of social, political and economic adjustment to, and underpinning of, conditions of relative peace in which the participants, not least those who have been disempowered and impoverished by violence, can begin to prioritize future goals beyond their immediate survival. Within this linkage between peacebuilding and regeneration, Pugh points out that some organizations participate in peacebuilding because they have a dual mandate to adapt their operations by providing relief to lay the foundations for development. He notes that other organizations specializing in development programmes may design projects for longer-term economic and social development. Pugh observes that peacebuilding occurs alongside diplomatic initiatives that lead to a peace agreement. Consequently, Pugh argues that conditionalities for securing peace and its implementation have an impact on regeneration.

Pugh however cautions that an emphasis on regeneration during peacebuilding can restore the kind of neo-liberal development policies that perhaps contributed to the conflict in the first place. He therefore advises that the more meaningful difficulty may be in recognizing flaws in peacebuilding and adjusting accordingly which would include sometimes accepting defeat. He also notes that the conceptual baggage of peacebuilding is the assumption that external actors wield power and moral authority to bring about the peaceful change that communities have failed to achieve. To Pugh, external intervention in peacebuilding and regeneration of war-torn societies is based on technical fixes in the form of disarmament, law and order programmes, reconstruction projects, refugee returns and elections. Such approaches, he argues are less concerned to interact with local norms and dynamics at the grassroots than to produce inventories of measurable outputs at a strategic level to make way for regeneration of war-torn societies into the global economy. Consequently, this approach creates a pattern of development that is determined by dominant democratic and neo-liberal, capitalist ideology. Pugh's analysis is supported by Berdal (2009:19) who notes that approaches to peacebuilding by the United Nations and in parts of the peacebuilding literature have a tendency to abstract the tasks of peacebuilding from their political, cultural and historical context. Berdal (2009) observes that:

> All too often, the result has been an ahistorical and static view of the challenges posed to the outside intervention in war-torn societies and a consequent failure to take account of the variety of ways in which the past constrains, shapes and imposes limits on what outsiders can realistically achieve. This tendency has encouraged a social-engineering approach to the concept of peacebuilding. It also helps to explain why external actors have persistently failed to gauge the extent to which their own actions, policies and historical baggage necessarily contribute

to shaping the 'post-conflict environment', whether through the stirring of nationalisms or through the legitimization or delegitimisation of indigenous power structures, or by empowering or disempowering what are, for better or worse, key local actors.

Pugh and Berdal's analyses raise important issues to consider during peacebuilding processes, which include DDRR of child soldiers. For example, while external support in the regeneration and peacebuilding is useful for societies that are emerging from war, external prescriptions and assumed answers which often overlook local agency always cause more problems to such societies. Consequently it is imperative that external support should be directed to empowerment of local institutions and constituencies of peace within the affected societies and should allow the local people to be in charge of their future goals and destiny.

On the other hand, Cockell (2000:15) argues that peacebuilding remains subject to variance in definition, interpretation and execution. He observes that peacebuilding has been the least examined term in peace studies for almost two decades and has now entered the international policy lime light as a key plank of post-Cold War global security. Its jump into prominence has outpaced the development of its meaning in clearly understood policy and operational terms. Consequently, this has resulted in relative absence of consensus among governments on the question of appropriate implementation. Cockell observes that the difference between peacebuilding and other forms of international assistance such as humanitarian aid lies in its emphasis on addressing the root causes of the conflict within societies. Cockell agrees with Galtung who in 1976 argued that unlike other approaches to the management and resolution of conflict, peacebuilding is based on an associative approach: peace as the abolition of structural violence and not just of direct violence (Cockell, 2000:16).

Cockell advises that peacebuilding should not be confused with development as has been advocated by some practitioners. For to do that, he argues, would present conflict as a development issue and would suggest that the root causes of protracted violent conflicts are apolitical issues of poverty, resource scarcity and unemployment. He notes that human needs are perceived differently by different groups caught up in contemporary conflicts: intrastate conflicts which are fundamentally political in nature. He argues that the operational objective of peacebuilding should not be expressed in a way that can easily be expressed as regular development programming, neither should it be restricted to nor defined by a specific phase of conflict such as post-conflict. He agrees with the expanded definition of peacebuilding in the 1995 Supplement for Peace which is currently understood by the UN Department of Political Affairs to be 'a continuum of activities, which may be present in all phases of a conflict cycle'.[32]

By and large, Cockell's analysis provides clarity about peacebuilding. Cockell's analysis is relevant to the conflict in Northern Uganda especially about the clarification that development should not be confused with peacebuilding. In fact, in respect to Northern Uganda, the focus of this study, government's response to peacebuilding has tended to concentrate on development needs while ignoring the political underpinnings of the conflict. A deeper analysis of the root causes of the LRA conflict places political needs higher on the agenda. Consequently, to respond with development per say is to miss the point. However, the challenge with Cockell's analysis is the tendency to reduce all the root causes of civil war to political needs. There is a multiplicity of causes of most contemporary conflicts, which are intrastate in nature. Some causes are external such as the negative impacts of globalization and external interference which cannot be solved by supplying political needs: democratization which is internal. To believe this would assume that if you have good governance and marketization as promoted by the liberal peace thesis, the civil wars would be resolved and transformed.

Further attempts to define peacebuilding have been made by the former Secretary General for United Nations, Boutros Boutros-Ghali in the *1995 Supplement to An Agenda for Peace*. He stated that the goal of both preventive and post-conflict peacebuilding is 'the creation of structures for institutionalization of peace.' The problem with the conceptualization of peacebuilding by Boutros-Ghali is that he uses the term by connecting it exclusively to the post-conflict support of peace accords and rebuilding of war torn societies (Lederach, 1997:19). Boutros-Ghali tended to view peacebuilding in terms of implementation of the peace agreement. Lederach observes that peacebuilding is understood as a comprehensive concept that encompasses, generates, and sustains the full array of

---

[32]Boutros Boutros-Ghali *An Agenda for Peace, Preventive Diplomacy, Peacemaking and Peacekeeping* (17 June 1992). Available at: http://www.unrol.org/files/A_47_277.PDF. Accessed on 2 May 2010.

processes, approaches and stages needed to transform conflict toward more sustainable, peaceful relationships.

Lederach further notes that the term peacebuilding involves a wide range of activities and functions that both precede and follow formal peace accords. While one would agree with Lederach that peacebuilding is a comprehensive concept that encompasses all the stages of the conflict cycle, he seems to locate some of the stages of peacebuilding within the framework of peace accords. Yet experience has shown that peacebuilding can be implemented without any peace accords. For example peacebuilding can be undertaken even in situations where one party has achieved military victory over the other party, such as was the case of the Rwandan Patriotic Front in Rwanda. The Rwandan Government is currently implementing peacebuilding programmes that largely rely on the Gacaca court system, a traditional conflict resolution and reconciliation mechanism (Reyntjens et al, 2001:128).

Ramsbotham et al (2005:215) have observed that during the last ten years, literature on post-conflict peacebuilding has increased leading a number of scholars within the conflict resolution field to revise their thinking about the complex dynamics and processes of post-conflict peacebuilding. Accordingly, the new thinking includes the idea that sustainable peacemaking processes should not be based on manipulation of peace agreements made by elites but on the empowerment of communities torn apart by war to build peace from below. These scholars observe that the shift in thinking has been in three major areas. First, there has been recognition that embedded cultures and economies of violence provide more formidable barriers to constructive intervention in post-conflict peacebuilding than originally assumed.

Second, that in the specification of the post-conflict peacebuilding and of the idea that formal agreements need to be underpinned by understandings, structures and long-term development frameworks that erode cultures of violence and sustain peace processes on the ground. Thirdly, that there is a need to recognize the significance of local actors and of the non-governmental sector, and the links with local knowledge and wisdom. Ramsbotham et al (2005) note that their shift in thinking about peacebuilding was largely influenced by Adam Curle, who as a result of his experience of the ethnic conflicts in former Yugoslavia concluded that:

Since conflict resolution by the outside bodies and individuals has so far proved ineffective (in the chaotic conditions of contemporary ethnic conflict-particularly, but not exclusively, in Somalia, Eastern Europe and the former USSR), it is essential to consider the peacemaking potential within the conflicting communities themselves (Ramsbotham et al, 2005:218).

The conceptualization of peacebuilding by Ramsbotham et al. emphasizing the empowerment and participation of communities torn apart by conflict is relevant and convincing for achieving sustainable peace. The conventional liberal peace thinking of quick fixes by imposition of external interventions and solutions normally complicates and protracts the conflicts. Moreover, outside interventions most times lack a clear understanding of local context and end up being part of the problem rather than a solution such as was the case of the US intervention in Somalia in the 1990s. These analysts argue that in the new approach of peacebuilding from below, the role of external actors should be to empower local people of goodwill in conflict-affected communities to rebuild democratic institutions, and the starting point for this is to help in the development of the local peacemakers' inner resources of wisdom, courage and compassionate non-violence (Ramsbotham et al, 2005:218) The problem with Ramsbotham et al is that they generalize the local agency and do not specifically pinpoint the particular people of 'good will'.

In most cases the people of good will are women and children who are always victims of violent conflicts. It looks apparent that in the short and medium term, empowerment of these two categories may not change the power dynamics on the ground. Even then, some of the so called the 'bad guys' such as the armed opposition could have been driven to the 'violent path' as a result of the prevailing conditions at the time. It may be prudent to engage rather than isolate them in the post-conflict period with the intention of reforming and transforming them into peace-makers. This mistake was made in Iraq where the former national army was disbanded and later had to be brought back when the situation worsened.

Paris (2004:13) traces the origins of the concept of peacebuilding from the end of the Cold War in the late 1980s and early 1990s. The end of the Cold War and the triumph of democratization and marketization enabled the United Nations, which had been bogged down by the super power rivalries, to take on more roles beyond traditional peacekeeping operations which were limited to cease-fire monitoring and could only be performed by military personnel. Paris observes that UN operations after 1988 focused on post-conflict peacebuilding which allowed division of labor between the UN and other international agencies to assist in rebuilding post-conflict war-torn societies. Such agencies include; NATO, EU, OAS with the World Bank and IMF taking major roles in economic reconstruction of war torn societies.

According to Paris, the distinguishing features of peacebuilding with the multiplicity of peacebuilding agencies in the absence of a centralized peacebuilding authority at the time was that they all pursued the same general strategy: promoting stable and lasting peace in war shattered states through democratization and marketization. Paris notes that the general formula for peacebuilding includes promotion of civil and political rights including free speech, free press as well as freedom of association, movement; preparing and administering democratic elections; drafting national constitutions; training or retraining police and justice officials to understand how liberal democracies work; promoting independent civil society; promoting transformation of formerly warring groups into viable political parties; promoting free market economies; stimulating growth of the private sector and reducing the states' involvement in the economy.

Another important change after the end of the Cold War was that international agencies tended to promote liberalization as a remedy for civil conflicts perceived as the triumph of liberal market democracy as the prevailing standard of enlightened governance across much of the world (Paris, 2004:19). Consequently, in every UN mission in the conflict torn societies, planning elections would always begin immediately including market reforms which in most cases resulted in violence and democratic reversals. Paris points out that the agents of peacebuilding are the United Nations and its specialized agencies especially the UNDP, Organization for Security and Cooperation in Europe, EU, NATO, OAS, Bretton Woods Institutions, National Development Agencies such as USAID, and Nongovernmental Organizations.

Paris agrees with Larry Diamond, who in 1995 offered a paean to liberal democracy as a panacea for so many of the world's problems (Paris, 2004:35).According to Paris, the bulk of recent research on the international dimension of the liberal peace thesis especially on the relationship between liberalism and interstate conflicts has generated a consensus that market democracies rarely go to war against each other. Another finding is that market democracies are generally less prone to intrastate disturbances. Based on these findings, Paris concludes that political and economic liberalization would appear to be a sensible and promising strategy for consolidating domestic peace in states emerging from civil wars.

The liberal peace thesis as advanced by Paris and the United Nations and most of the neo-liberal theorists, has come under criticism by scholars and analysts including Richmond who see it as merely an extension of neoliberal ideas-another form of neo-colonialism (Richmond, 2007:287). First, it assumes that market democracy is a panacea for all the problems in war-torn societies and so if democracy was to become a world religion, there would be perpetual peace. Yet where this formula has been tried in societies that are just emerging from war, it has caused more harm than good. East Timor, Afghanistan and Iraq are good examples where liberal peace peacebuilding has not delivered sustainable peace and security. The prescriptions by the IMF and World Bank on market and democratic reforms as conditionalities for financial assistance to most countries experiencing civil wars especially in Africa have always led to state failure and anarchy. So one wonders how the cause for the sickness can at the same time be its cure.

Other critics see the liberal peace thesis as another form of neo-colonialism top-down imposition that could provide a pretext for foreign intervention in the internal affairs of other countries (Herring, 2008:47). The example of the US intervention in Iraq and the mess it has created is a case in point. More so, the liberal peace thesis focuses on the post-conflict peacebuilding and leaves out other phases such as conflict management and crisis prevention which are crucial in preventing the conflicts from becoming violent and destructive. In other words, the form of peacebuilding advanced by the liberal peace thesis for which Paris is an advocate is likely to disempower the local actors and could in the long-run create resistance and a fresh cycle of violence.

Richmond (2007), one of the critics of the liberal peace thesis, points out that peacebuilding is supposed to both create and promote a vibrant civil society. He argues that peacebuilding receives much of its support and legitimacy in war-torn societies from civil society and local actors, in a sense that the notion of civil society acts as a validation of peacebuilding strategies and objectives. He notes that the key feature of the dominant liberal peace approach to peacebuilding represents a neoliberal marketization of peace, rather than engagement with the agents and subjects of this peace. Richmond (2007:288) further notes that this is a particularly Western and enlightenment driven discourse of peace, which is far from culturally and socially sensitive, and has little chance of establishing a locally self-sustaining peace.

Richmond is particularly critical of the liberal peace thesis for ignoring the welfare dimension in peacebuilding despite the experience of liberal states that stability is easily undermined for individuals by direct economic difficulties (this was the case in Iraq and East Timor), welfare support is institutionally absent in most conflict zones, often supplied by NGOs with meagre resources. He points out that 'peacebuilding welfare policies would, if supported through outside means in the short term, support the creation of stable polities. The argument here is that individuals in these war-torn societies, knowing that peacebuilding entails welfare, might be more predisposed towards the development of a long-term peace process. However, this would require the engagement of an international institution capable of communicating directly with locals about their everyday needs, free of neoliberal prescriptions (Richmond, 2007:291). Richmond observes that while the liberal peace does not discount the need for such institutions, its gradual insertion of neoliberal strategies into peacebuilding for ideological reasons or following the US and Western national interests have undermined the crucial link between welfare and politics in a way which undermines the liberal peace project.

Pugh et al (2007:1) have pointed out that in contrast to the traditionally limited activities of peacekeeping and peacemaking, peacebuilding involves a raft of intrusive practices intended to ensure long-term stability after, and even during conflict. They also observe that international assistance for transition has been elevated to new levels of administration, while often largely disregarding local bodies of knowledge and struggles against universalizing presumptions of a particular liberal-capitalist economic order. These scholars further note that the political economy of post-conflict peace and state-building in a liberal peace framework has involved a simulacrum of empowerment where peacebuilders transfer responsibility to societies without transferring power. Most crucially, populations have been subjected to calculated techniques of discipline under liberal agendas requiring individual self-reliance; a loss of public goods and uninsured 'surplus' population may not be an overt goal, but it is a function of accumulation by dispossession and predatory forms of capitalism associated with it (Pugh et al, 2007:391).

Pugh et al make proposals for peace agendas that should facilitate a paradigmatic shift in negotiation of political economies of peace. These proposals include among others; that peace processes and peacebuilding practices need political roots in local societies, and that political communities should have freedom to set their economic priorities including protection of economic activities from negative effects of global integration. It is noted that a new geometry of power should be assembled with its roots in local community structures which enables a constant feedback of local needs to decision-making. They further observe that gender relations should be renegotiated to examine ways of eliminating the post-conflict backlash against women as well as an ethic of economic regulation which should aim at reconstituting global economic regimes away from silent complicity in 'conflict trade' and freedom for capital towards moral responsibility and discrimination in favour of the uninsured poor and that the 'subaltern geographies of political economy-informal economies. Finally, these analysts advise that borderlands and transnational networks such as diasporas need to be de-securitized and their potential role in peacebuilding realized.

Commenting about the post-war backlash against women, Pankhurst (2007:31) points out how the post-conflict environment is not one where life normalizes for women. Instead, she observes that the upheaval of war in which women have been transformed and livelihood systems disrupted, in which women have assumed certain roles for the first time or come into contact with new ideas, has its own impact on interpersonal relationships and social expectations. She also notes that there is evidence from gendered analyses of post-war situations in Yugoslavia, sub-Saharan Africa, Latin America and Asia which shows that women not only face continuation of some of the aggression they endured during the war, but also new forms of violence.

The observation about the plight of women during war, peace processes and post-conflict peacebuilding by Pankhurst is critical and should inform policy makers and peacebuilders to engender the role of women and their needs if there is going to be sustainable peace in post-conflict societies. The marginalization of women in the peacebuilding processes in Northern Uganda was evident right from the initial stages of the failed peace negotiations. The government peace team did not have women representatives while the rebel LRA had only one woman on their team. With pressure from the civil society organizations and the international community, government was compelled to appoint some women on the peace team.

By and large, one cannot simply dismiss the relevance of the liberal peace thesis in totality. Underpinning most civil wars especially in Africa and Uganda in particular, is the whole issue of political exclusion as opposed to political inclusion and ethnic nationalism, which are governance questions. Most importantly, one finds it convincing that democracies rarely go to war with one another and this seems to have become an established truth (Muravchik, 1996:574). It is also true that internal grievances in democracies rarely degenerate into civil wars because of the availability of several channels to articulate and address grievances such as political parties and civil society. Consequently, one can safely argue that in spite of some limitations, the spread of liberal democracies is likely to increase the zones of peace and stability within and among war torn societies.

It is also true that lack of democracy and the struggle for democratic governance including conducting free and fair elections is always among the root causes of conflicts in most war-torn societies in Africa. Political exclusion in the case of Northern Uganda has commonly been articulated by the various rebel groups including the LRA in spite of its laughable democratic credentials, being a protégé of the Government of Sudan. What this means is that even if former child soldiers were well reintegrated by relying on cultural and indigenous resources, without addressing the root causes of conflict where democratic deficit is at the core, the possibility of re-occurrence of a fresh conflict remains high.

The Neglected Psychosocial Dimensions of Disarmament, Demobilization, Reintegration and Rehabilitation in the Context of Peacebuilding

To survive war is to personally and collectively deal with its aftermath-trauma to the body, psyche and soul, the devastation of communities and the effects on quality of life. The challenge for communities is to come to terms with what has happened and develop a renewed sense of present and future possibilities, and be able to heal as a collective. Yet, these are 'soft effects' because they are about people rather than institutions and their importance easily overlooked. Thinking about communities is seldom a priority of the international funding agencies and policy makers, whose efforts during the post-war period are typically directed towards reconstructing the physical, political, educational.... infrastructures (MacKay, 2004).

This section examines the relevance of psychosocial support in the DDRR of child soldiers as a neglected dimension of peacebuilding. The section explores the magnitude of psychosocial support problems of children involved in armed conflicts, an element most often neglected in academic circles and by the official United Nations led DDRR and other post-conflict liberal peacebuilding programming (MacKay et al, 2004:33). The central thesis for this book is that the provision of psychosocial support in the RR of former child soldiers may play a crucial role in their transition to civilian life. And as earlier noted, the book contends that provision of psychosocial support based on traditional and indigenous resources may be more relevant for successful RR of child soldiers into civilian life and peacebuilding. Provision of psychosocial support based on indigenous and traditional resources in the RR of child soldiers is specifically discussed in Chapter Six.

The realization that violent conflicts affect all aspects of child development-mental, emotional, physical and spiritual has prompted scholars to conclude that successful RR of former child soldiers requires provision of psychosocial support (Machel, 2001:80; Wessells, 2006:39). This position is supported by Article 39 of the Convention on the Rights of the Child which requires State Parties to take all appropriate measures to promote children's psychological recovery and social reintegration.

Article 39 states that:

> State Parties shall take all appropriate measures to promote the physical and psychosocial recovery and social re-integration of a child victim of: any form of neglect, exploitation, or abuse; torture or any other form of cruel, inhuman or degrading treatment or punishment; or armed conflict. Such recovery and re-integration shall take place in an environment which fosters the health, self-respect and dignity of the child (Cohn et al, 2003:131).

Before discussing the magnitude of psychosocial problems that children affected by civil war face and the need to prioritize it in the RR programming of peacebuilding, it is important to define what psychosocial support is all about. According to Wessells (2006:190), psychosocial support or assistance is less about healing individual wounds or mental illness than enabling former child soldiers to integrate socially, to participate in the rhythms of civilian life, to be functional as defined in the local context, and to redefine themselves as civilians. Psychosocial has also been defined as '…the dynamic relationship between psychological and social experience, where the effects of each are continually influencing the other. Psycho refers to emotions, behaviour, thoughts, beliefs, attitudes, perceptions and understanding of an individual. Social refers to a person's external relationships and the influence of the environment on his/her well-being (family, school, peers and local community) (UNICEF et al, 1997).

Machel (2001:80) on the other hand observes that the term 'psychosocial' underlines the dynamic relationship between psychological and social effects, each of which continually influences the other. Psychological effects are those that affect emotion, behaviour, thoughts, memory, learning ability, perceptions and understanding. Social effects refer to relationships altered by death, separation, estrangement and other losses; family and community breakdown; damage to social facilities and services. They also extend to the economic dimension, for the war leaves many families destitute, destroying their capacity to support themselves and maintain a standing in society.

Prendergast et al (2001:334) and Summerfield (1998:29) have revealed that at least 10 million children worldwide have been psychologically traumatized by war. Consequently, Summerfield (1998) observes that addressing the psychological trauma of children caused by war should be a cornerstone of their rehabilitation because time does not heal trauma. According to Prendergast et al (2003) war related trauma experienced by children is divided into two categories: acute and chronic. The acute category is defined as a child's exposure to single abnormal incident in which a child/parent relationship remains intact and the child, with the parents' support, is able to adjust his/her perceptions and return to a normal, safe environment. The chronic trauma or Post-traumatic stress disorder (PTSD) occurs over a long period of time and includes a multitude of symptoms that impede a child's ability to develop emotionally. A combination of circumstances such as separation from parents, combat participation and exposure to violence with unmet food and material needs result in personality and emotional alteration in many children.

According to Singer (2006:194), a survey of former child soldiers in Africa found that 50% had severe nightmares on a regular basis, 25% suffered some form of mutism, and 28% experienced some form of paranoia. Because of children's vulnerabilities, the experience of child soldiering often results in post-traumatic stress disorder (PTSD). According to Singer (2006:194) trauma is an external event that is so intense that it overwhelms the person's capacity to cope or master it. In psychological terms, 'traumatic stressors' are those events that are outside the range of human experience and must be of sufficient intensity to invoke symptoms of distress in most people. Singer observes that because of children's vulnerabilities or lack of coping mechanisms, the experience of child soldiering often results in post-traumatic stress disorder (PTSD). PTSD can result in both physical and mental symptoms such as weight loss, depression, learning difficulties and changes in memory, severe headaches and stomach pains (Bracken, 1998:39).

Singer further notes that there is a worry that the effects of child soldiering may be magnified in children in the long term or that children are likely to suffer from what is known as the 'exhaustion model. The exhaustion model is where even those who develop coping mechanisms to deal with trauma in the short term eventually run out of energy needed for copying with stress in the long term. He however notes that given the newness of the child soldier doctrine, it is premature and without scientific justification to conclude that child soldiers are forever 'damaged goods' or simply beyond rehabilitation. Consequently the need to support rehabilitation for child soldiers becomes imperative.

Singer's observation on PTSD among child soldiers holds true in respect to Northern Uganda. A study conducted by UNICEF which sampled 741 males aged 14 to 30 years in Northern Uganda found out that only three never experienced any traumatic events listed (UNICEF, 2006:10). The study also found that five percent of formerly abducted youths reported being haunted by evil spirits (*cen*) (UNICEF, 2006:10). The problem with Singer's observation is that he prescribes the Western model of physical and mental health treatment for rehabilitation of children which has been found to be lacking and sometimes detrimental in other contexts such as Africa (Kostelny, 2006:10).

Furthermore, a study conducted by Liu Institute of Global Issues et al, (2005:39), found widespread psychosocial trauma in Northern

Uganda. Consequently, the study points out that communities in Northern Uganda have adopted traditional ceremonies and cleansing rituals usually performed by cultural leaders to treat trauma among the former child soldiers as part of the RR processes. This was confirmed by Avola, the Coordinator of Ker Kwaro Acholi, the apex Acholi cultural institution during the fieldwork. Avola pointed out that most communities have been complaining of being haunted by spirits of dead people in places where the rebels committed mass murders. Consequently, Ker Kwaro Acholi has been organizing community wide cleansing rituals and burying the dead to rid the region of evil spirits. These traditional ceremonies and rituals that involve 'stepping on the egg' and the slaughter of a goat are believed to cleanse a person, household or community from bad spirits (Interview with Avola).

Arafat et al (2006:111) who studied the impact of the Israel-Palestinian conflict on Palestinian children found most of them who had been exposed to fighting were traumatized. Arafat et al (2006) observe that in order for children to develop normally, and be psychologically healthy certain basic needs must be met. He points out that children who undergo traumatic experiences of war usually develop special needs such as understanding, emotional resolution, and security, a sense of belonging and self worth. These scholars point out that war can damage children's cognitive and affective processes and could implant emotional and physiological scars leading to distrustful and hostile behaviour and can prevent a child from developing into a productive and social adult.

Through their research, these scholars found out that Palestinian children are under significant psychological strain as a result of violence. The situation of children was being aggravated by a widespread feeling that neither their parents nor teachers can fully care for or protect them which makes them less carefree children. Accordingly, teachers and parents have observed widespread trauma-related behaviour ranging from nightmares and bedwetting to increased aggressiveness and hyperactivity as well as reduced capacity to pay attention.

According to Kostelny (2006:26) armed conflicts expose children to a mixture of discrete risks, such as poverty and lack of access to health care. Consequently, she notes that these risks can have adverse emotional, social, spiritual and physical effects on children. She notes for example that in most cases humanitarian intervention focuses its attention on ameliorating the impact of physical risks such as illness, lack of shelter and danger of an attack. Yet most physical risks also have impact at the social, emotional and spiritual levels. Kostelny further notes that because war zones present multiple risks to children, their situation cannot be understood in terms of a single event such as displacement from home, stepping on a landmine or loss of parents. Based on the risk accumulation model, Kostelny observes that as risks accumulate the likelihood of damage to children increases exponentially. The accumulation of three or more risks can produce ten times, as much damage as a single risk factor (Kostelny, 2006:26).

The impact of war on psychosocial well-being of children is also captured by Summerfield (2004:24) who noted that a study on Sudanese teenagers caught in fighting in south Sudan and displaced to Juba from rural areas regarded as ancestral places showed the resultant loss of social identity and memory. No one could write a history of his or her clan and many did not know the names of their grandparents or the village their clan came from. Not one could name any traditional social ceremonies (Summerfield, 2004). The impact of war on the affected population is further articulated by Herman (1997). Herman (1997:20), commenting on the psychological effect of World War 1 on people in Western Europe, observes that:

> One of the many casualties of the war's devastation was the illusion of manly honour and glory in battle. Under conditions of remitting exposure to the horrors of trench warfare, men began to break down in shocking numbers. Confined and rendered helpless, subjected to constant threat of annihilation, and forced to witness the mutilation and death of their comrades without any hope of reprieve, many soldiers began to act like hysterical women. They screamed and wept uncontrollably. They froze and could not walk ....'

Based on the above analysis it is evident that psychosocial needs of war affected populations especially the former child soldiers who faced shocking traumatic experiences during the war is critical for their RR and general recovery of war-torn societies. It is unfortunate, as MacKay (2004) has noted that most post-conflict peacebuilding interventions overlook paying serious attention to psychosocial support especially psychosocial support based on traditional and indigenous resources. The relevance and limitations of indigenous and cultural approaches are extensively discussed in Chapter Six.

Conclusion

This chapter has examined the concepts of disarmament, demobilization, reintegration and rehabilitation of child soldiers that are commonly used by policy makers, donors and international organizations in regard to post-conflict peacebuilding. As most scholars and analysts point out, most DDRR programming in war-torn societies have been designed using a top-down approach and in most cases without serious considerations for the local context in the affected areas. Most specifically, the DDRR programmes marginalized ex-child soldiers, especially the young women former combatants who have specific challenges and needs and therefore require special attention. The consequences of poorly planned, poorly resourced and managed DDRR programmes which are increased insecurity and criminality in the early phases of post-conflict were discussed.

Peacebuilding was discussed and conceptualized with respect to reintegration and rehabilitation of former child soldiers and rebuilding of war torn societies. It is evident that lack of an agreed definition of peacebuilding could negatively lead to poor DDRR of former child soldiers and reconstruction of war-torn societies. It was also noted that some scholars conceptualize peacebuilding that promotes the neoliberal ideas of the West: marketization and democratization at the expense of providing welfare support to communities emerging from civil war and often fails to establish conditions of sustainable peace. Because of its top-down approach without respect for local cultures and resources, conventional neo-liberal peacebuilding often leads to resumption of hostilities as was the case in Iraq and East Timor. The chapter also examined the psychosocial support of child soldiers which is the neglected dimension of peacebuilding.

By and large, it should be mentioned that for DDRR of former child soldiers to be effective, there is a need for proper planning by policy makers, commitment of adequate resources and commitment by the international community and respective governments to invest in long-term RR of former child soldiers. There is also a need for DDRR programming to galvanize support of all the stakeholders (international and local) and empower the local constituency and local resources, which creates local support and local ownership that ensures sustainability in the longer-term.

Part II

Child Soldiers in the Context of Uganda

CHAPTER FOUR

●────────────────────────────●

Conflict and Political Instability in Uganda: The Emergence of Child Soldiers

Since 1990, Uganda has transcended an unenviable two decade history of decline and trauma to reconstruction. When it achieved independence in 1962, Uganda was one of the most promising countries in Africa. However, twenty years of political strife, economic mismanagement, and armed conflicts left it devastated, with much of its infrastructure destroyed. Uganda's long string of tragedies is legendary. Ten leaders have ruled the country in the four decades since independence, including Idi Amin's 8-year reign of terror where an estimated 500,000 people died (Shaw et al, 2008: 214).

This chapter discusses the political economy and political history of Uganda in the pre-colonial and post-colonial periods. It also discusses the sources of conflicts in Uganda with particular focus to the violent protracted conflict of the Lord's Resistance Army (LRA) in Northern Uganda. The rationale for this chapter is to attempt to trace the origins of the socio-economic and political challenges that have persistently confronted Uganda's quest for peace, stability and development for most of its 56 years of independence which are also linked to the LRA conflict and the child soldiers' phenomenon, the main focus of this book. It is believed that Uganda's political history and political economy are closely linked to violent civil conflicts that have characterized most of the country's post-independence period (1962 to date), including the on-going violent conflict of the LRA. Consequently, a thorough understanding of the political history and political economy of Uganda and the sources of conflicts in Uganda would provide a deeper understanding of the child soldier phenomenon in Northern Uganda. The LRA conflict has produced, sustained and aggravated the child soldier phenomenon in Northern Uganda in proportions never witnessed before in Uganda. It is this child soldier phenomenon that is the subject of this book.

Political History and Political Economy of Uganda

Uganda became a formal state *de jure* in 1894 after the British Government declared it a British Protectorate. It should be noted however, that Uganda's constituent parts pre-dated the British Protectorate since they were in existence long before that period (1894) (Kanyeihamba 2002:1). Before the British renamed and reconfigured the territory, what is now Uganda was an array of kingdoms-Buganda, Bunyoro, Ankole and Toro, and communities located in Lango, Acholi, Madi, West Nile, Bukedi, Bugisu, Busoga, Teso, Karamoja, Sebei and Kigezi regions. In other words, it was a heterogeneous area, with a variety of customary practices, social and political structures that were forcefully brought under one political rule (Moncrieffe, 2004:10).

It should be noted that the different ethnic groups that were brought together to form the present day Uganda were at different stages of state formation. While most of the southern groups at the time were governed under kingdoms (Buganda, Bunyoro, Ankole, Toro and Busoga Pricipalities) most communities in the north and east of the country were still governed under clan heads and chiefs systems (Moncrieffe, 2004).

Commenting on the dilemma of the African post-colonial state, Francis (2006:38) notes that some of the states were carved out primarily to serve the political, economic and strategic interests of the colonial powers and at independence were granted the 'legal fiction' of sovereign statehood. Consequently, these states, especially the small ones, have demonstrated increasing vulnerability to security, and compounded the challenges of building viable regional mechanisms for dealing with peace and security issues. The point being emphasized here is that because the colonialists forcefully brought together different ethnic groups that were at different levels of development without their consent to become one nation. It is this forced nature of state formation that continues to

140

threaten Uganda's political stability as some ethnic groups think they can be better off if they break away.[33]

The British used the Kingdom of Buganda to conquer all the territories that now constitute Uganda and bring them under one authority: the British Protectorate. In return, the British colonialists rewarded Buganda Kingdom with conquered territories which increased her size, power and influence. Most crucially, Buganda was also rewarded with a special status both in the colonial and post-colonial Uganda for collaborating with the British colonists (Kabwegyere, 1995:70). This favoured position of Buganda has remained a major challenge and threat to Uganda's national unity and stability. For example, as a reward to Buganda's support in the conquest of Bunyoro which had fiercely resisted colonial rule, the British gave to Buganda a large part of Bunyoro Kingdom comprising of several counties such as Buyaga and Bagangizi which were added to Buganda and that is how the problem of the 'lost counties' was born (Kanyeihamba, 2002:2). The problem of 'lost counties' was later to become a trigger of the 1966 constitutional crisis which led to the abolition of kingdoms in Uganda and abrogation of the 1962 independence constitution.

The Dawn of Independence, Constitutional Challenges and Political Alliances as Seeds of Destruction

Uganda became independent on 9 October 1962. Milton Obote became the Prime Minister with executive powers, while Freddie Mutesa, who was also the King of Buganda, became the first President of Uganda. The Uganda People's Congress (UPC) led by Obote and Kabaka Yekka (KY) (King Only), a conservative traditional Movement that was pushing for the allegiance to the King of Buganda made a political alliance which defeated the leader of the Democratic Party (DP) Benedicto Kiwanuka. The Democratic Party was largely a Catholic Party formed to champion the interests of the Catholics who felt marginalized by the monarchy of Buganda. As such, the King was determined to neutralize the Democratic Party (Kabwegyere, 1995:206). Commenting on the UPC/KY alliance President Museveni (2007:34) has observed that this

---

[33]*The Independent* Newspaper (2010).'Mao's Election and Secession of the Nile State,' September 11. Available at: http://www.independent.co.ug/index.php/column/guest-column/68-guest-column/2590-maos-election-and-secession-of-the-nile-state. Accessed on 11/9/2010.

was not a true principled political alliance, but an attempt by both parties to use each other for selfish objectives. Museveni (2007:35) declared that:

> The UPC, which had no base in Buganda, was a protestant-based party while the Democratic Party (DP) was largely a party for Roman Catholics (Baganda). The UPC and KY teamed up to form the first post-independence government through an unprincipled marriage of convenience. This was not a true alliance but an attempt by both groups to use each other.

The terms of the alliance agreement were that Buganda would have authority over other kingdoms as well as representation in the National Assembly (Moncrieffe, 2004:16). Because the alliance between UPC and KY was based on political manipulation, apart from the short term political gains of denying the majority Catholic party-DP electoral victory, it could not stand the test of time. Intrigue and counter intrigues that were inherent in the crafting of the UPC/KY alliance could not allow the alliance to govern the country. By 1966, intrigue and power struggles within the alliance government plunged the country into a constitutional crisis which started off a wave of political instability that successive governments have not been able to resolve.

The 1966 Constitutional Crisis

Political commentators on Ugandan politics describe the period between 1962 and 1966 as the period of drama in the development of the Uganda Constitution (Kanyeihamba 2002:73). Kanyeihamba has described this period as the transitional period in which the independence constitution went on trial and was found to be unworkable. The independence constitution created a hotchpotch form of government that was both federal and unitary. The constitution was vague on federal arrangement. Uganda consisted of five federal states (Buganda, Bunyoro, Ankole, Toro and Busoga). Of these, Buganda under the independence constitution enjoyed more powers and privileges than the other four kingdoms which had semi-federal status. The constitution recognized ten districts in Northern and eastern Uganda as unitary. However, it was not clear whether these districts were unitary in relation to the central government or to the federal states. While the relationship between the central government and Buganda kingdom can be said to clearly federal, the same could not be said about the other kingdom or federal governments since the central government had more powers with regard to their affairs than with Buganda kingdom (Kabwegyere, 1995).

The consequence of the confusion caused by the independence constitution coupled with Buganda's favoured status was political jealousy and the wish by people from outside Buganda to reduce its privileges and special status. On the other hand, the people of Buganda were ready to defend their special status and privileges at all costs. This inclination coupled with the unprincipled KY/UPC political alliance resulted into political upheavals that have been called the 1966 constitutional crisis whose effects continue to challenge Uganda's political stability today (Mutibwa, 2008:85).

Following the UPC/KY alliance in 1962, the UPC party emerged the strongest and more powerful political player that would shape most of the early politics of Uganda. By 1965 the alliance had collapsed and KY, the partner had been dropped from the coalition with some of its members joining UPC (Sembuya, 2009:25). In spite of the fact that UPC, the ruling party, was busy poaching members from KY and DP, it soon found itself in trouble generated from within its ranks. Traditional and conservative elements had penetrated UPC and acquired its active supporters leading to political infighting which led to the emergence of factions within the party with capitalist and socialist leanings.

In 1964, the ruling UPC party was torn between two factions: the Kakonge faction, the party's Secretary General on one hand and Obote in alliance with Grace Ibingira on the other. Ibingira and Obote were ideologically said to be leaning to the right. Kakonge was subsequently ousted from the party as Secretary General in 1964 at a delegate's conference. The alliance between Ibingira and Obote did not last long. Soon the alliance collapsed with Obote claiming to be the progressive wing of the party while Ibingira was now the conservative wing. Ibingira claimed Obote was pro-communism. The political instability that ensued in the ruling UPC soon dragged in the army as the politicians sought to strengthen their positions (Mutibwa, 2008:86). In order to secure himself, Obote reshuffled the army. Idi Amin, who had been a deputy to Brigadier Shaban Opolot, was made Army Chief of Staff and overall Army Commander (Kanyeihamba 2002: 89). This act brought the military to the centre stage of Ugandan politics and since then, they have remained a major player in politics and threat to democracy in Uganda.

The political crisis in UPC coupled with the successful referendum on the return of the two 'lost counties' to Bunyoro in 1964 triggered the political crisis of 1966. Aggrieved that UPC had tricked them in the alliance and the loss of the 'lost counties' escalated the hatred and animosity between Buganda Kingdom and the Obote Government. Consequently, the traditionalists at Mengo, the seat of Buganda Kingdom, began to exploit every possible opportunity to undermine Obote. The Mengo traditionalists made alliances with disgruntled UPC members to remove Obote from power through either military or political means (Makara, 2007:55).

The deepening constitutional stand-off culminated in the abrogation of the Independence constitution on 22 February 1966 by Prime Minister Obote. Obote abolished the post of the President and Vice President and assumed all the powers of government. The *Lukiiko*, Buganda Kingdom's Parliament, tried to resist these moves by calling upon the Central Government to remove itself from Bugandan soil which provided an opportunity to Prime Minister Obote for a final showdown with the King of Buganda who was also Uganda's titular President. On 24 May 1966, the army led by the army commander Idi Amin attacked the King's palace and forced him to flee into exile (Mazrui 2001:19). Mutesa died a poor and heartbroken man three years later in exile in the United Kingdom (Museveni, 1997). The Constituent Assembly later discussed and adopted the government's proposals as amended and passed a new constitution for Uganda in 1967 (Kanyeihamba, 2002).

The Republican Constitution of 1967 was a unitary one. Besides President Obote being Head of State and Commander-in-Chief of the Armed Forces, he also became the head of Government. The constitution had combined the presidential and parliamentary forms of government. The constitution retained a multiparty system of government even though the opposition parties remained very weak, experiencing desertions and lacking organizational capacity. In the subsequent years, UPC continued to undermine the opposition and by 1969, Obote declared Uganda a one-party state. What followed was chaos as UPC's internal contradictions intensified and the party degenerated into factionalism, which culminated in the military coup of 1971 that brought Idi Amin to power. Amin suspended the constitution and established a reign of terror where close to 500,000 people were

144

killed between 1971 and 1979 when his regime was overthrown (Shaw et al, 2008).

The Rise and Fall of Uganda National Liberation Front (UNLF) Government

The overthrow of Amin's dictatorship in 1979 was welcomed by majority of Ugandans with a lot of hope and optimism, and paved way for the UNLF to come to power. However, as it soon turned out, the optimism created by the new political order: the UNLF which was supported by the Tanzanian Government did not usher in the peace, stability and development. Instead the period following Amin's downfall was characterized by political anarchy and bloodletting. The Commonwealth Team of Observers wrote in 1979 that:

> Crops were damaged and livestock killed, houses, factories and public buildings were gutted; schools supplies, textiles, and writing materials were looted, food, furniture and clothes were taken from houses and shops, office records were lost or stolen, tools and equipment were taken from shops and thousands of cars and trucks were taken out of the country to Sudan, Tanzania, Zaire and Kenya' (Kanyeihamba, 2002:176).

Formed during the Moshi Conference in Tanzania in 1979, the UNLF's main objective was to form a political group and present it as a credible anti-Amin Ugandan front other than former president Obote, whom other Ugandans thought, was a liability both inside and outside Uganda (Museveni, 2007:109). By the end of the Moshi Conference, delegates elected Professor Yusuf Lule as chairman of a new, broad-based movement. Consequently, upon the fall of Idi Amin, Lule formed the first UNLF Government in Uganda. It is under the watchful eye of Lule that Uganda degenerated into factionalism and political intrigues that led to his sudden downfall.

Revengeful killings and assaults of anyone imagined to be an enemy, supporter or associate or relative of the enemy became common practices in the period after the collapse of Amin's dictatorship. In West Nile, Amin's home region, the UNLF army turned their guns against civilians causing a massive flight and displacement of people into former Zaire now the DRC. Most of these people remained in DRC as refugees until 1987 when they were returned by the Museveni Government.

145

Political observers note that the UNLF Government lacked strong leadership and a sense of direction and degenerated into several political factions which resulted into its eventual collapse (Kanyeihamba, 2002).

President Lule was subsequently, replaced by Godfrey Binaisa. Commenting about the removal of Lule from power which was furiously resisted by his tribe's mates, Museveni noted that:

> When it became clear that Professor Lule would have to be removed, some quiet, informal discussions took place among us to try to find a successor. We decided that we should support Godfrey Binaisa, a Muganda, since we knew that the reactionaries on all sides would use tribal arguments to divide the people (Museveni, 2007:116).

The appointment of Godfrey Binaisa as President by the UNLF did not improve the political situation either. As observers have noted, Binaisa was more interested in business deals than managing the affairs of the state (Kabwegyere, 1995). It is noted that Binaisa turned the State House into a business centre where businessmen frequently flocked to look for business deals. Corruption, suspicion, intrigue and rumour-mongering became rampant yet the country greatly needed a committed leadership to champion the reconstruction process after the war. The deteriorating security, rampant corruption that characterized Binaisa's government combined with political forces that were working for the return of Milton Obote were responsible for Binaisa's sudden exit from power. The removal of Binaisa from power marked the demise of the UNLF and the ascendance to power of the Military Commission led by Paul Muwanga (Mutibwa, 2008)

The demise of the UNLF also marked the return of old political parties and the second Obote Government to power. Paul Muwanga the Chairman of the Military Commission and a close confident of Milton Obote organized the 1980 elections which most observers note were massively rigged in favour of Obote's Uganda People's Congress (UPC).

At the close of elections, the Chairman of the Military Commission announced the creation of a new law which prohibited 'anyone' whether chairman, secretary, agent of the Electoral Commission, or private citizen 'to announce results'. The Military Commission warned that anyone caught doing so would be committing a crime and would be fined the sum of Ug.Shs.500,000 (US$226) or imprisonment for up to five years (Kanyeihamba, 2002:200).

146

Ali Mazrui commenting about Obote's second government notes that, Under both the administration of Idi Amin (1971-79) and the second administration of Milton Obote (1980-85), Uganda experienced, simultaneously, some of the worst excesses of both tyranny and anarchy (Kanyeihamba, 2002). With most political groups accusing UPC of rigging elections, President Museveni and other political groups decided to launch guerrilla warfare against the Obote government mainly from central Uganda. Obote's government responded by using the most crude methods of fighting the insurgence which resulted into the death of many innocent civilians in Luwero Triangle.

It should be noted that the atrocities in Luwero triangle committed by the military under Obote government greatly influenced the civil war in Northern Uganda which is the focus of this book. After the fall of the second Obote government and the military junta led by General Okello, the victorius National Resistance Army led by Museveni especially the newly reintegrated FEDUM of Dr Andrew Kayira carried out revenge attacks in Acholi which prompted many soldiers who had initially surrendered to resort to a rebellion (ICG Report, 2004:2).

Nature of Domestic Politics in Uganda: An Overview

Since Uganda got its independence in 1962, the army has remained a dominant player in the country's politics. Almost all successive regimes in Uganda have relied on the military to rule and to exclude others from power. Consequently, the army in Uganda invokes sad memories among the citizens who since colonial times have suffered at the hands of the army. The army is associated with gross violation of human rights in Uganda. The army's brutality, wanton killings, rape and robberies of innocent civilians with impunity is fresh in the minds of Ugandans. The highest level of military brutality was witnessed during Amin's reign of terror and in Luwero Triangle where the Obote II government used a 'scorched earth policy' of indiscriminate killings while battling Museveni's rebels of the National Resistance Army (NRA) in the early 1980s. The International Crisis Group (ICG) report (2004:2) reveals that massacres in the Luwero Triangle during Operation Bonanza, perpetrated by Obote's troops mainly Acholi and Langi troops are estimated to have cost at least 300,000 lives, mostly of Baganda people, which continues to cast a shadow over attempts to solve the North-South problems.

147

The bulk of the army in Uganda has historically been dominated by people from Northern Uganda. This was no historical accident. Rather, it was a British colonial design of governing the colonized people. Before the Second World War, Ugandans from both south and north were equally recruited into the British colonial force: the Kings African Rifles (KAR). The British changed this policy after 1945 when majority of veterans of the Second World War from southern Uganda started to agitate for the independence of Uganda from colonial rule. In response to the threat these well trained soldiers from southern Uganda posed a threat to the colonial state resulting into the British colonists decision to recruit soldiers mainly from Northern Uganda (ICG Report, 2004:2). The colonists then developed a theory that would justify military dominance of people from Northern Uganda. The theory was that the people of Northern Uganda were more 'martial' and 'warlike' while southerners from the centre and west and most of the east of the country were 'soft' because they ate a staple diet of *matooke* (green bananas), compared to the Northerners' staple diet of millet which is supposed to be more hardy (Museveni 1997:39). This was not true of southern Uganda. On the contrary, pre-colonial history shows that the more advanced social forms had evolved in southern and western areas of what is now Uganda.

Advanced forms of social organization had evolved in Buganda, Bunyoro, Ankole and Toro which were formidable kingdoms with standing armies. It is thought that the colonial rulers feared the military tradition and advancement in these southern kingdoms and set out to undermine it and the higher forms of social organization (Museveni, 1997:39).

Commenting about the evolution of the army in Uganda which was inherited at independence, Kabwegyere (1995:224) has observed that the purposes, organization and progress of the army in Uganda were all in accordance with the entrenchment and achievement of the objectives of the colonial power. A question that begs an answer is what kind of army did Uganda inherit at independence? The Ugandan army was constructed along colonial designs to serve the colonial interests or those in power. Taller soldiers were considered more qualified than shorter soldiers. Those who were believed to be innately martial were considered best qualified to be fighters.

As Kabwegyera (1995) further notes that the colonial army which later became the Uganda Army was made up of people selected on dubious and superstitious grounds and trained to achieve the dictates of their masters. That is how Idi Amin, known for his brutality, had excelled in the KAR and was promoted to a rank of a captain by 1962 at the dawn of independence, the highest rank to be given to an African (Sembuya, 2009:32). As the ICG report (2004) has observed, the post-colonial governments of Milton Obote and Idi Amin inherited the colonial policies about the military since they suited their political interests and this has created a challenge of building a unified nation-state since independence in 1962. Amin's subsequent promotion in the military by the Obote Government was not based on his excellence as a soldier but because he was considered to be insufficiently intelligent to have interest in taking over political power (ICG Report, 2004).

Personal loyalty of the army to the Head of State from 1964 onwards has become the norm in Uganda. Surprisingly one of the ironies in history is that the more the army personifies the head of state, the more likely he will be overthrown by the army (Kabwegyere 1995:225). Indeed this is illustrated by the overthrow of Obote two times by his army commanders; first by Idi Amin in 1971 and second by General Tito Okello in 1985 yet he thought they had personal loyalty to him.

Under the Idi Amin and Obote 11 regimes (1971-1979 and 1980-1985 respectively, thousands of people were killed by the military. The brutality of the army extended to the economy, stretching from '*Kondoism*' (armed robberies) in late 1960's to military businesses (*mafuta mingi*) in the 1970's to rapist-looters in the early 1980's. In politics, Amin destroyed so much life that his overthrow in 1979 seemed to be the end of a century of misery (Kabwegyere, 1995). When Museveni's National Resistance Army (NRA) under Museveni overthrew the Okello military junta in 1985 which had also overthrown Obote's second dictatorship, it looked like the end of militarism in Uganda. But did it end? This question is discussed in the subsequent section.

The Advent of the National Resistance Movement: A Fundamental Change or Mere Change of Guards?

In our view, the period between January 26th 1986, when the NRM took power in Uganda, and 1995 when the country, promulgated a new constitution, the Movement can be credited with a number of spectacular successes. ... Many of these changes have been welcomed by the entire population and are likely to remain permanent features of governance in Uganda (Kanyeihamba 2002: 238).

To most Ugandans especially the people in Buganda sub-region who had suffered greatly under the Obote 11 Government, the NRM victory meant total removal of the military apparatus that had enabled one section of the Ugandan population that came from one part of the country to impose a military/political hegemony on the rest of the country (Mutibwa, 2008, 222). According to Mutibwa (2008), for the first time, the soldiers serving in the Uganda Army were perceived and really seen as belonging to the population of the country they were protecting. This confirms the optimism that was ushered in by the victorious NRA led by President Museveni among the southern population. What is also true is that the victorious NRA was being perceived differently in Northern Uganda, the base of Obote 11 Government. In fact, the NRA in most of Northern Uganda were being perceived as foreigners or Banyarwanda which is partly responsible for the LRA rebellion that was initially supported massively by the local population (Olupot, 2010).

When the National Resistance Movement (NRM) came to power after waging a five, year guerrilla war (1981-86), it inherited a near collapsed state. The economy was in shambles, the infrastructure such as roads, industries, telephones and the railway was in a state of disrepair (Mugyenyi, 2001:62). People lacked basic goods including soap, sugar and salt. These commodities under the Obote II government were being rationed and one had to be closely linked to a political heavyweight to get a coupon in order to access these essential commodities.

Ironically, in comparison to other African countries, at independence in 1962, Uganda's economy was in excellent form. It was one of the strongest economies in Black Africa (Kanyeihamba 2002: 206). Given the economic mismanagement and the political turmoil that characterized the first Obote government, the economy became the first casualty (Mugyenyi, 2001). Economic mismanagement was one of the reasons given by Amin for overthrowing the Obote I Government. Obote's first government adopted and preached socialism and the move to the left while at the same time cabinet ministers and political elites and security operatives were busy grabbing national assets for themselves. Commenting on the economic mismanagement by the Obote 1 government, Kanyeihamba (2002:207) has observed that, 'This was the kind of move to the left, while I take everything on the right'.

The second Obote government, which succeeded the Military Commission did not help improve the economy in spite of the massive donor support the government received after the 1979 liberation war. In order to win international recognition and the badly needed foreign exchange, the Obote 11 Government accepted all the conditionalities imposed by donor countries and the International Monetary Fund (IMF). A study that was commissioned by Sweden revealed that such money did not benefit the common people who would have to bear the burden of paying it back (Mugyenyi, 2001).

Besides poor economic policies prescribed by the IMF and economic mismanagement, most of the economic support that was received by the Obote II Government was wasted on the internal wars and conflicts. During the Obote II period, roads and streets in the country were in disrepair and full of potholes. There were chronic shortages of clean water, electricity, medicine and trained personnel in all Uganda's institutions including the educational system, which had become corrupt with falling standards (Museveni, 2007). It is this state of affairs that was inherited by the NRM when it came into power in 1986.

As part of the democratization agenda, the NRM introduced a 'Ten Point Programme' as a basis for social, economic and political reconstruction of the country. The programme would also become a vehicle to deliver the NRM's promises to the people; a fundamental change that was intended to set it apart from the past rapacious governments that had ruled Uganda. Njuba (2001:210), commenting about the fundamental change, observed that the NRM/A revolution in Uganda was aimed at carrying all the people or at least a great majority through purposive and positive mobilization programmes. To Njuba, the main thrust of the ideology of NRM/A was aimed at doing good for Uganda which was true nationalism. Njuba, who served as a Minister for Constitutional Affairs, later fell out with President Museveni, who he accused of abandoning the ideals of democracy, and joined the opposition Forum for Democratic Change (FDC).

In order to deliver on its commitments, the NRM built a fairly credible coalition, comprised of representatives from former political parties, Bantu southerners and Baganda supporters. Also, the NRM had built a strong army which in principle was not permitted to abuse or kill any member of the public which boosted its image. Museveni's immediate move helped him to build some legitimacy beyond his heartland area in the south and south-west and, importantly, to raise expectations of broad public participation, government accountability and improved welfare (Moncrieffe, 2004:18). This was done through the introduction of the Resistance Council (RC) system of governance starting from the national level to the village level that allowed people to make decisions that directly affected their lives (Nsibambi, 2001:279).

In line with the democracy, security and unity objectives outlined in the 'Ten Point Programme', the NRM expanded the Resistance Councils (RCs) to the entire country. RCs had previously been established in the areas under the NRA/M guerrilla control based on the principle that decision-making power, authority and policy making responsibilities should also be located at the local levels and that citizens should be able to reach and influence representatives and hold them accountable. The overarching question after almost 24 years in power is has the NRM administration under President Museveni delivered the fundamental change?

During the last two decades that the NRM has been in power, Uganda has managed to maintain an impressive annual economic growth rate of 6.4 per cent, largely because of improvement in the policy environment; restoration of peace and stability in most parts of the country; and rehabilitation of infrastructure and increased capacity utilization (Shaw et al., 2008:214). The picture though is different in Northern Uganda where the LRA rebellion which has been raging since 1987 has made it almost impossible for government to rehabilitate the infrastructure and implement any meaningful development programme (PRDP, 2007). Another factor for economic growth has been due to increased inflow of capital and technology from the private sector involving both foreign and local investors, economic liberalization of the 1990's and donor aid assistance.

Donors pronounced that Uganda was indeed, 'a pioneer of macroeconomic stabilization and structural adjustment in sub-Saharan Africa', while even the most strident of critics acknowledged that the Movement's political system deserved to be credited for improving and sustaining peace and security in most parts of the country, allowing a fairly free press and encouraging citizen's participation through a democratically elected government (Moncrieffe, 2004:18).

The dividends of policy reforms that have largely been financed by international donors through foreign aid is evidenced mainly by the expansion in construction, manufacturing-the case of textiles which have tapped into the AGOA (African Growth and Opportunity Act), sugar and UHT milk; telecommunications, water, education and poverty reduction. At a broader level, fiscal discipline ensured macro-economic stability while liberalization, deregulation and privatization created a relatively 'new nation' (Shaw et al, 2008). There has also been a marked increase in access to safe water from 49% in 1998 to 57% in 2000. HIV prevalence declined from 30% in the late 1980's to 6.5% in 2001. The number of women in parliament rose from 18.6% in 1996 to 26% by 2002 thus bringing more women into positions of decision-making. Perhaps the most striking development under the NRM government is in the area of education. Since 1997 when government introduced Universal Primary Education (UPE), primary school enrolment increased from 920,000 pupils to 7.2 million in 2002 (Shaw et al, 2008:217).

At Makerere University, the country's prestigious university, the total student enrolment has since 1986 increased from the mere 5,000 to over than 25,000 which is more than 450% increase in 15 years (Kwesiga, 2000; Musisi and Muwanga, 2003). What is even most interesting is that the female enrolment at Makerere University more than doubled as a result of affirmative action in favor of women introduced in 1989.

The NRM can also be credited for the enactment of the 1995 Constitution which was hailed by most observers as a very progressive constitution, re-enfranchising the people by holding regular and periodic elections, and decentralization. The constitution devolved power to the lower levels to increase popular participation of citizens especially those formerly marginalized such as women, persons with disabilities, workers and youths, and political accountability provided for under Article 178 of the Ugandan Constitution.

In spite of the impressive achievements, on the social, economic and political scene, Uganda still faces serious challenges that if not addressed could easily reverse such achievements (Shaw et al, 2008). For example, Northern Uganda has been experiencing a violent protracted conflict of the LRA for over two decades (1986-2006) (PRDP, 2007). Even when relative peace returned to the region in 2006 with the resumption of peace negotiations between the government and the rebels, the people still live in fear that the rebels may strike again from their bases in DRC and South Sudan. More so, because of the conflicts in Northern and eastern Uganda, both regions have lost out on the NRM's socio-economic divdends. Northern Uganda specifically has not benefited significantly from the macro-economic achievements that the country has witnessed since 1986 when NRM came to power (Shaw et al, 2008).

Poverty levels in Northern Uganda are still unacceptably high especially so in the rural areas and amongst the children. While the colonial legacy can be blamed for creating economic imbalance between Northern and southern Uganda, the current high levels of poverty are largely attributed to the rebellion of the Lord's Resistance Army which for over two decades now has been fighting the government of President Museveni using terror techniques aimed at civilians (McKay et al, 1999). This conflict has led to gross violation of human rights especially of women and children, and has destroyed infrastructure, paralyzed economic activity, led to social and cultural break down and disrupted economic and human development of the region. The LRA rebellion forced over 1.6 million people into Internally Displaced Peoples Camps (IDPs) which made people dependant on relief aid. Generally speaking Northern Uganda remains the poorest part of the country in spite of its huge economic potential (Uganda Bureau of Statistics, 2003).

The stuck reality of the development gap between Northern and southern Uganda has prompted some scholars to define Uganda in terms of two Ugandas. Shaw et al (2008) have observed that while the two Ugandas' always co-exist in tenuous ways; in the new century, the division has become wider with profound implications for prospects of development and democracy, human rights and human security in both parts of the country. While the description of the two Ugandas' has been dismissed by the ruling elites in Uganda, the fact of the matter is that there are glaring development disparity gaps between Northern and southern Uganda which stretch from the colonial past (Moncrieffe, 2004) which any serious developmental state should try to address.[34] Unless the economic imbalance is urgently addressed, it could continue to be a major fault line for future political instability and conflict in which children are being recruited and used as combatants in violation of their

---

[34] During fieldwork, the issue of two Ugandas was put forward by senior government people who requested anonymity. They agree that the there exists regional economic imbalance that needs to be addressed although they blame this on the LRA rebellion and the colonial design. Interviews with government officials were conducted in Kampala in March 2009.

human rights. The regional economic imbalance in development was also the focus of peace negotiations between the LRA and Government in the failed Juba Peace Process and it constituted agenda number two of the Draft Peace Agreement.[35]

When the NRM captured power in 1986, it quickly banned all the political parties accusing them of being sectarian (tribal and religious based), narrow, and responsible for the past woes that had afflicted the country. It introduced the Movement political system-a no party system arguing that it was the most suitable political system for Uganda; a society without a sizeable middle class necessary for multipartism. The Movement system espoused the principles of individual merit by all political leaders which meant that one had to be elected on his/her suitability rather than party affiliation; broad-basedness and popular participation. Ironically, while the NRM continued to ban political parties, it operated like a political party. On many occasions during elections, the NRM sponsored Movement supporters and campaigned against candidates known to promote the return to a multi-party system (Makara, 2007).

After 20 years of political monopoly, the NRM government faced with increasing internal and external pressure to free political parties grudgingly organized a national referendum that allowed the return of multipartism in 2005. The 2006 general elections that were marred by irregularities and malpractices and contested by the opposition as rigged in favor of the ruling NRM presidential candidate were organized under a multi-party system (Kibandama, 2008:143).

The return to a multiparty system did not automatically solve Uganda's democratic challenges. Instead, some new democratic challenges were created. For example, as part of the constitutional reforms that paved the return of multiparty democracy, government influenced the parliament to change the constitution and remove the two term presidential limit that had been provided for by the 1995 constitution. The removal of term limits has ensured that the incumbent President Museveni who has ruled for 32 years can continue to stand for re-election indefinitely. To most observers, the removal of presidential

---

[35] RLP, HURIPEC, Faculty of Law, Makerere University, Agreement on Comprehensive Solutions Between the Government of Uganda and the Lord's Resistance Army/Movement, Juba, Sudan. Available at:
http://www.beyondjuba.org/peace_agreements.php. Accessed on 3/2/2011.

terms limits poses a major threat to Uganda's future stability (Kategaya, 2006). As Museveni's popularity continues to shrink,, his hold on to power has become very costly to the country. Most worrying is that in both the 2001 and 2006 presidential elections, the outcomes were challenged by the opposition as rigged in favour of president Museveni and the outcome had to be decided by the Supreme Court rulings and not the electorate (Gloppen et al, 2008:78).

In the 2006 elections, all the Supreme Court Judges agreed that the elections were not conducted according to the law and that there was election rigging, election violence and involvement of security forces in the election malpractices. Based on the majority decision of judges of four out of seven, the Supreme Court concluded that the effects of election malpractice could not substantially have affected the electoral outcome (Mwesige et al, 2006). Consequently, the court upheld the election results and declared Museveni the winner. The point being made here is that the country's failure to manage credible elections accepted as free and fair, traps the country into political violence as the politicians who think their victory was stolen from them as was the case of Museveni in 1981 will always resort to violence (*Daily Monitor* September 4, 2009). More so, the continued scenario where the outcomes of presidential elections are always decided by the court is likely to erode the citizen's confidence in electoral processes, which ultimately undermines democracy.

Other fundamental challenges facing Uganda under the current political dispensation of President Museveni include rampant corruption in public service (*Daily Monitor* September 8, 2009) a very strong Executive that has successfully controlled the parliament and judiciary and rendered them incapable providing checks and balances and upholding the principle of separation of powers as envisioned by the framers of the 1995 Ugandan Constitution (Kanyeihamba, 2002). Unprecedented levels of corruption and increasing levels of public administration expenditure have now become a major landmark of the ruling NRM party and this could be a source of political unrest and its attendant consequences.

It is also interesting to note that Uganda under the 'reformist' NRM has not successfully been able to remove the threat of the military to democracy. President Museveni's control of power and the survival of the NRM administration largely depends on the army and his ability to

156

direct it against any threat to his power (Mudoola, 2001:237; Makara, 2007). Like other governments before him, Museveni relies on the army. Yet experience has shown that the army has always turned against the very people who use it as an instrument of repression against the citizens' human rights.

Also, under the NRM, the country has witnessed the rise and the fall of a free press and a vibrant print media and critical civil society generally. While in the early years of NRM in power, the media and civil society generally enjoyed relative freedom to participate in nation building including being critical of government actions upon which the NRM administration was able to attract massive donor support; recent trends show a change of policy (Kjaer et al, 2008:180). Government in 2006 enacted a stringent law to control the NGO sector. These government actions have severely cowed down the vibrancy of the civil society sector, yet a free press and vibrant civil society are the tenets of a democratic society (Walubiri, 2004:86-99).

Some analysts have observed that while there has been tremendous improvement in all spheres of development there are fundamental challenges that face the future stability and progress of Uganda. These challenges include: the economic disparity between the north and the south; the urban and rural; erosion of the principle of separation of powers failure to manage free and fair elections that cannot be questionable and the poor government-opposition relations that exist including high levels of corruption in public service that has become acceptable which raise the question of the country's future stability, sustainable development and sustainability of the peace dividends.

Conflict Analysis in Uganda

This section critically analyzes the sources of conflicts in Uganda generally. The rationale for this section is to establish the link between the LRA conflict in Northern Uganda and Uganda's troubled political history. In this section, I argue that the LRA rebellion which has produced and reproduced the child soldier problematic is closely related to other conflicts in Uganda that have either been resolved or are latent and those that are still on-going in other parts of the country such as the one of the Allied Democratic Alliance (ADF) with bases in the DRC. It is noted here that a thorough understanding of the sources of conflicts in Uganda would contribute to the identification of appropriate interventions for conflict resolution, conflict prevention and peacebuilding.

In order to understand the sources of conflicts in Uganda, it is important to define what is meant by the term 'conflict.' Conflict has been defined variously by several scholars. However, according to Ramsbotham et al (2005:13), conflict is an intrinsic and inevitable aspect of social change. It is an expression of the heterogeneity of interests, values and beliefs that arise as new formations generated by social change come up against inherited constraints. Conflict can also be defined as the interaction of different and opposing aspirations and goals in which disputes are processed but not definitively resolved. Most scholars note that conflict is a necessary part of a healthy democratic debate and dialogue provided it remains within the boundaries of the commonly accepted rules of a democratic game.

Harris and Reilly (1989:32) note that conflict itself is not necessarily a negative process. Rather, they argue that conflict is one of the most powerful positive factors for change in a society. They further observe that conflict tells us that something is wrong; conflict is the generator of change and improvement. To these scholars, without conflict society would suffer stagnation. While, it is true that conflict can lead to social transformation, intra-state conflicts in Africa and Uganda in particular have been very destructive and disruptive to development making it difficult for people to appreciate their positive side. However, since conflict is part and parcel of human life, people need to learn to live together with their differences and incompatible goals, interests and aspirations. The subsequent section analyses the sources of conflict in Uganda.

Uganda is a war-prone country and a large part of its post-independence history has been characterized by political anarchy and bloodletting (Mutibwa, 2008). This is evidenced by the fact that even under President Museveni's leadership (1986 todate) during which period the country witnessed impressive socio-economic and political growth, the country has been experiencing a violent protracted war in Northern Uganda and some parts of western and eastern Uganda. In recent times, the situation has been compounded by President Museveni's declining legitimacy due to his longevity in power. President Museveni has been in power for over 32 years;, increasing poverty levels among the population; high levels of unemployment among the youths; growing economic inequalities among regions especially Northern Uganda and high levels of corruption in public service.

Uganda's political troubles started in 1966, four years after gaining independence when the country was plunged into a constitutional crisis which led to the overthrow of President Mutesa, abolition of the 1962 independence constitution and establishment of a republic (Mutibwa, 2008). The political crisis that followed the 1966 resulted into a military coup that brought Amin to power and all the ills of his regime.

After the Tanzanian supported liberation war overthrew Idi Amin in 1979, the Military Commission under Paul Muwanga returned Obote to power through a rigged election in 1980, which prompted several disgruntled political groups to declare armed struggles against the regime. Prominent among these groups was the National Resistance Movement/Army (NRA/M) led by the current President Yoweri Museveni. Facing eminent defeat by the rebels, the Ugandan army in 1985 overthrew the second Obote Government and established a military junta, which was subsequently overthrown by the NRM/A in 1986 (ICG Report, 2004:2).

In spite of the credit accorded to President Museveni by most observers for restoring peace in most parts of the country since 1986; Uganda has been experiencing violent civil wars in the north, south-west and north-eastern regions. In Northern Uganda, the rebellion of the Lord's Resistance Army (LRA) has been very violent and destructive especially to innocent civilians, mostly children, who are abducted and forcefully recruited into the LRA (World Vision Report, 2005:16). Cattle rustling by the Karamajong in north-eastern Uganda, fuelled and sustained by the availability of illegal guns has caused untold suffering to the people in Karamoja and the neighbouring communities, exacerbating environmental degradation, famine and poverty in the north-eastern part of the country.

The rebellion of the Allied Democratic Forces (ADF), an Islamic fundamentalist group led by Jimil Mukulu and supported by the Government of Sudan with bases in the DRC has alleged links with Al-Qaeda. ADF was militarily suppressed in 2002 but their remnants have re-grouped and have been conducting widescale massacres mostly of civilians including children in DRC (IRIN Special Report, 1999). With the arrest and extradiction of ADF rebel leader Jamil Mukulu by the Tanzanian authorities who haded him over to Uganda most people that the back of the rebellion was broken. Ironically, ADF has continued to execute their deadly missions in Uganda and are still active and vicious in the DRC *(Daily Nation, 2015)*[36] In West Nile, although the former rebels of the National Rescue Front, associated with former military dictator Idi Amin returned home from Sudan after reaching a peace settlement with the government, an aura of anxiety still prevails. These former rebels have been demobilized and others reintegrated into the national army and into civilian life, which is a very delicate process. Available information indicates that the senior officers of this group benefited most from the peace agreement at the expense of rank and file soldiers. More so, these former rebels complain that government never honoured some of the elements of the agreement that brought them out of the bush (Makerere University Refugee Law Project, 2004). Such complaints indicate that durable peace has not yet been achieved since these elements can easily start a fresh rebellion out of frustration.

The prevailing socio-economic conditions in Teso sub-region also continue to pose a security threat to the country. The violent Teso rebellion of 1987-1992 by the Uganda People's Army (UPA) led by Peter Otai left behind a ravaged and dislocated society in Teso prone to more conflicts (Makerere University Refugee Law Project Report et al. 2008). The region has since been experiencing severe poverty and famine as a result of loss of cattle during the rebellion. Cattle keeping used to be the main economic activity for the people of Teso before the rebellion. After the rebellion, government failed to implement a successful post-conflict reconstruction programme for the region as funds meant for cattle restocking were embezzled by the politicians and technocrats (Makerere University Refugee Law Project Report, 2008).

Since 2001, the Government of Uganda has alleged the existence of a new rebel group known as Peoples Redemption Army (PRA) linked to the leading opposition leader of FDC, Rtd. Col. Dr Kiiza Besigye. PRA is reported to be based in the DRC. Although the PRA has never launched any known military attack, former soldiers-Colonels Samson Mande and Kyakabale, believed to be the leaders of the rebel group, declared their intentions to oust President Museveni through armed means. The

---

[36]*Daily Nation* (2015). Fugitive rebel chief Jamil Mukulu extracted to Uganda. Also available on Internet at: https://www.nation.co.ke/news/africa/Fugitive-rebel-Jamil-Mukulu-extradited-Uganda/1066-2783544-4bqechz/index.htmlhttps://www.nation.co.ke/news/africa/Fugitive-rebel-Jamil-Mukulu-extradited-Uganda/1066-2783544-4bqechz/index.html. Accessed on 17/10/2018.

presence of these two army deserters in Rwanda was central to the hostilities between President Paul Kagame of Rwanda and President Museveni of Uganda (ICG Report, 2001). The possibility of the existence of PRA rebels creates a sense of uncertainty and fear among Ugandans who seem to be tired of civil wars. To date, the former opposition leader of FDC Dr. Besigye is still facing several charges, which most observers think are politically motivated (Makara, 2007:70). It is against this background that this book is interested to establish the sources of conflicts in Uganda.

The sources of conflicts in Uganda can be traced to the colonial legacy, bad governance or democratic deficit, imbalance in economic development, natural resources scarcity (land) in some parts of the country with high population density and huge mineral deposits in the country including the recent discovery of commercial quantities of oil and gas reserve (oil in 2006), regional spill over, proliferation of small arms and light weapons. These sources of conflicts are discussed in detail below.

One of the sources of conflicts in Uganda at the core of the LRA conflict in Northern Uganda is economic marginalization and imbalance in development which has created the two Ugandas: the underdeveloped north and developing south (Shaw et al, 2008:214). This point has also been underscored by the PRDP, the official Government of Uganda post- conflict reconstruction and peacebuilding programme for Northern Uganda. The PRDP (2007) indicates that government development agenda has led to reduction in poverty nationally, and that welfare indices indicate that Ugandans who are unable to meet their basic needs declined from 56% in 1992 to 38% in 2003 and further to 31% in 2006. However, the PRDP also observes that welfare indices for Northern Uganda have not improved at the same pace as the rest of the country (PRDP, 2007). Poverty income in Northern Uganda remains high, literacy rates are low and access to basic services still poor. The PRDP attributes the high levels of poverty to the violent conflict, which made it difficult to implement development programmes, destruction of the infrastructure and internal displacement of over 1.6 million people. The regional economic imbalance in development which is at the centre of conflict in Northern Uganda is linked to the colonial legacy. Several scholars attribute the contemporary civil wars going on in most developing countries such as Uganda to the effects of colonialism.

According to Mazrui (2008:36), while the most lethal civil wars in Africa have been fought between blacks, the roots of these wars lie in the white colonial legacy. Mazrui argues that the seeds of the post-colonial wars themselves lie in the sociological and political mess which 'white' colonialism created in Africa. This is true in the case of Uganda where the British divided the country into economic zones, in which the north was considered unsuitable for plantation agriculture. Most of the sugarcane, cotton and coffee plantations and better infrastructure (roads, schools and industries) were introduced in the south. Northern Uganda was used as s reserve for supplying cheap labour to the plantations in the south and later in colonial history, soldiers to the army. The consequence of this economic zoning was that it resulted into imbalance in economic development with the south developing at the expense of the north. One of the underlying causes of the conflict in Northern Uganda is the grievance by people that they have been economically marginalized by the government of President Museveni.

Moncrieffe (2004:15) concurs with Mazrui and observes that during the British colonial rule in 1925, the new Director of Agriculture started to encourage cotton production in Northern Uganda but was summarily advised that the 'policy of government' is at present to refrain from actively stimulating the production of cotton or other economic crops in outlying districts on which it is dependent for supply of labour for carrying out essential services in the central producing districts. This economic zoning of the country perpetuated the neglect of, and underdevelopment in Northern Uganda and this has always fermented regional tensions based on economic imbalance in development. Unfortunately, the post-independence leadership in Uganda has never focused their attention to address the regional economic imbalance. It is no wonder that most observers are currently pointing out the existence of two Ugandas (Shaw et al, 2008:216). It should be noted however, that after nearly six decades of independence, Ugandan leaders should not hide behind the claims of colonialism for underdevelopment. In the case of Northern Uganda, it is apparent that no single post-colonial government has attempted to correct the economic imbalance in regional development. As discussed in Chapter Five, even the so called developmental state in Uganda under President Museveni has failed to prioritize the development of Northern Uganda as a conflict management mechanism. The PRDP which most observers thought was going to be a Mashall Plan for Northern Uganda has been politicized; is under-funded, top-down, short-term in nature and lacks political commitment.[37]

While this economic imbalance that gives an outsider the impression of the existence of two Ugandas has been widened in the last two decades by the 24 year old violent conflict, it is the creation of the British colonial rule which is one of the major grievances for the rebellion of the LRA.

Another source of conflict that is also linked to the colonial legacy is that the British colonialists used divide and rule method of administration which polarised the country and deepened ethnic hatred. Moncrieffe (2004:15) observes that the British ascribed a 'martial tribes' thesis that prioritized the Nilotic and Sudanese (Nubians) tribes of Northern Uganda for military service. Accordingly, these groups were considered satisfactorily fit for the theory that soldiers should be of a different race, geographically distant and even hostile to the main groups. The Acholi were thus recruited into the African Kings Rifles with the mandate to 'take action' against the local groups in the Protectorate who engaged in active opposition to the colonial policies. The British colonialists also encouraged the people in the south to take on education and work in the civil service since they were soft but intelligent and therefore suitable for the tasks (Museveni, 1997:39). Consequently, most Ugandans, including people from Northern Uganda came to believe that only groups from the north had the right to bear arms. The immediate post-independence leaders, particularly Milton Obote and Idi Amin, both from the north, emphasized this myth and exploited it to become the source of the bitterest legacies of colonialism in Uganda (Moncrieffe (2004:15; Henderson, 2008:56).

The divide and rule technique of administration used by colonists produced inferiority and superiority complexes among Ugandans with the people from the north thinking that they are militarily superior while those in the south think that they are more civilized and intelligent. The military myth of people from Northern Uganda was challenged in 1986

---

[37]Interview with Nobert Mao, Chairman Local Council 5 Gulu District. Interview was conducted in Gulu in December, 2009 Mao who is also a presidential candidate for the Democratic Party doubts Museveni's commitment to develop northern Uganda which does not support him politically. In two successive presidential elections (2001& 2006) Museveni got the least votes in northern Uganda compared to his closest political challenger Dr Besigye.

when the National Resistance Army (NRA) led by Yoweri Museveni which was largely dominated by soldiers from southern Uganda defeated Uganda Liberation Army, a national army dominated by Northern Ugandans. One of the grievances advanced by the LRA is disrespect and denigration by people from the south who call them abusive names such a '*koko*' or animals.

Another source of conflict in Uganda is the Buganda question. The British colonialists accorded a special status to Buganda Kingdom because of its collaboration role and the military assistance it rendered to bring the entire Protectorate under British rule (Mutibwa, 2008). The unequal relationship between Buganda and other regions was created by the 1900 Buganda Agreement and subsequently legitimized by the 1962 independence constitution. The 1962 constitution in essence institutionalized ethnic tensions and conflict in Uganda. This problem has become entrenched in Uganda's politics and is a constant source of political tension.

Mamdani (1976:242) has observed that although the independence constitution was called 'federal' only one region, Buganda, was given separate and substantial powers independent of the centre. The Buganda *Lukiiko* controlled public services, local government, and its public debt and had separate powers of taxation and its revenue was supplemented by grants from the state as specified in the constitution. Buganda had its own court system and, subject to the control of the Uganda Inspector-General, its own police force. Buganda selected its twenty one representatives to the National Assembly indirectly, through the *Lukiiko*, rather than by popular vote. The constitution provided that none of these powers could be altered by the Ugandan Parliament without the two-thirds concurring vote of the *Lukiiko*. In effect, the 1962 constitution became very difficult to implement and by 1966 Buganda Kingdom had fallen out with the central government, leading to a bloody conflict and the abolition of ethno-cultural kingdoms (Mamdani, 1976).

Museveni reintroduced the ethno-cultural kingdoms in 1993 hoping that they will be controllable, conform to the constitution and contribute to peace, stability and national development. However, currently President Museveni is facing a standoff with the Buganda Kingdom, which is demanding the full restoration of the special status of 1962. In a recent standoff between Buganda Kingdom and the government in September 2009, over 30 people were reportedly killed while over 100 casualties were hospitalized. Commenting on the September 2009 riots in Kampala, President Museveni observed that:

> We need to strictly enforce the principle of separating cultural institutions from politics through enacting the cultural law (*Daily Monitor* September 15, 2009).

Another source of conflict in Uganda is religion. Religious induced conflicts too are linked to the colonial legacy. The religious conflicts in Uganda date back to the 19th century, when Captain Lugard armed Protestants secretly (Kabwegyere 1995:67). Lugard was assured of the Protestant support, since the Church Missionary Society who were British found themselves in competition with White Fathers who were French and the Moslems who were mainly Arabs. The Lord Lugard state-led alliance with the Protestants won the war, and since then the protestant Christians have always dominated politics in Uganda, especially the topmost position of the president. There is a growing feeling in Uganda that the Catholics who are the majority have been marginalized in politics since there has never been a Catholic president. It is no wonder that President Museveni, throughout his period in power, has been trying to balance religious representation in his cabinet and reserving the slot of Vice President solely for the Catholics. Recently, a Minister of State for Local Government accused the Vice President of Uganda, Professor Bukenya of using the Catholic Religion to come to power.[38] The Muslims have also been fighting against what they perceive as political marginalization. In fact the rebellion of the Allied Democratic Front (ADF) is partly motivated by what they perceive as political marginalization of Moslems and their desire to establish an Islamic state in Uganda (IRIN Special Report, 1999).

Additionally, Uganda faces the problem of the availability of so many illegal small arms and light weapons in the country, which are fueling and sustaining conflicts. The problem of easy availability of small arms and light weapons is compounded by the regional spill over of more guns and refugee movements from the various war zones that surround Uganda, including Somalia, Sudan, Burundi, Rwanda and DRC. Mazrui (2008:39) has pointed out that a combination of modern weapons and

---

[38]*The Monitor* (2010). 'Bukenya Denies Using Religion to Get Power.' Available at: http://allafrica.com/stories/201011170105.html. Accessed on 3/2/2011.

less modern armies has proved to be a menacing and destabilizing one to most of Africa. Collier (2009:103) concurs with Mazrui and notes that cheap and plentiful guns may increase the risk of violence but also points out that the availability of guns may also reduce violence since people will be careful with each other. Experience in Uganda has shown that most political groups easily resort to armed violence whenever there is a political difference due to the easy availability of arms and this has trapped the country in a vicious cycle of political violence.

Furthermore, Uganda faces the problem of resource-driven conflicts. As most analysts point out, natural resource abundance and natural resource scarcity can pose a serious problem for developing countries whose economies are natural resource dependent (Indra de Soysa, 2000; Francis 2008:5) such as Uganda. Uganda faces two forms of natural resource-induced conflicts. The first form of resource-based conflict is due to land scarcity aggravated by poor farming systems, fast increasing population growth in some parts of the country, especially in Kigezi which has forced people to migrate into other areas causing ethnic tensions over land (Kisamba-Mugerwa, 2001:311). The areas most affected by land driven conflicts are Bunyoro, Kasese, central Uganda (Buganda sub-region) Teso, Karamoja and Acholi sub-region in Northern Uganda. In Bunyoro sub-region particularly in Kibale district, the land conflict between the indigenous Banyoro and the immigrant Bakiga has already claimed several lives.

In an attempt to resolve the land conflict in Kibale, President Museveni recently proposed that the immigrants should not participate in the politics of the area for the next 20 years and that top electoral positions in the district should be preserved for the indigenous people - the Banyoro. The letter by President Museveni to this effect caused a lot of confusion and drew condemnation from the general public which viewed the President's advice as divisive, sectarian and fueling ethnic politics in the country. In Northern Uganda, a region still recovering from a violent conflict of the LRA, land has become the major fault-line of conflict (World Bank Report, 2008)[39]. Local politicians, including

---

[39] World Bank Report (2008). 'Analysis of Post Conflict Policy and Land Administration: A Survey of IDP Return and Resettlement Issues and Lessons in Acholi and Lango Regions.' Available at:

Members of Parliament from the region have accused government of planning to grab their land and give it to foreign investors; and further marginalize the communities (*Sunday Monitor*, August 30, 2009). The situation is even worse in Buganda sub-region where the Kingdom of Buganda threatened violence if government went ahead to formulate the National Land Policy and amend the Land Act 1998 and give land to squatters (Tebajjukira, 2009).

The second aspect of natural resource-based conflict in Uganda and perhaps the most threatening aspect of natural resources is the discovery of huge oil deposits. Already, Bunyoro Kingdom where most of the oil deposits have been discovered is demanding 65% of the oil revenue share even when no single drop of oil has been drilled. The situation has been made worse by the rush of the political and military elites to acquire large chunks of land in Bunyoro in anticipation of oil being discovered on their land and get compensation. Civil society organizations in Uganda accuse the government of pursuing a policy of secrecy in the whole process of oil exploration (Oketch, 2009). Consequently most analysts point out that unless the oil governance regime in Uganda is made more transparent and accountable and allows civil society and parliament to provide oversight over the prospective oil boom; oil could turn out to be a curse rather than a blessing. This fear is not far-fetched given the experience of other oil producing countries such as Nigeria, Chad and Angola (Bainomugisha et al, 2006:2).

Moreover, conflicts in Uganda are closely associated to bad governance or democratic deficits. Some scholars note that among the political, economic and cultural factors most consistently implicated in civil wars are those related to a states regime type (Henderson and Singer, 2000), its level of economic development (Collier 1998; Collier and Hoeffler, 1998; Henderson and Singer 2000), and its cultural composition (Auvinen, 1997; Collier, 1998). These analysts further observe that the consolidated democracies are more protected from large-scale domestic conflict due to the availability of legitimate channels for conflict resolution (Muravchik, 1996:573; Harris and Reilly, 1998; Henderson 2008:55). The observations are relevant to Uganda's peace and stability in several respects. First, the nature of the Ugandan state is

---

http://www.oxfam.org.uk/resources/leaving/land
right/downloads/northern_uganda_land_study_acholi_lango.pdf. Accessed on 1/7/2010.

historically that of a conquest and repressive state. The state was created by British colonialist through conquest and it sustained itself through repressive policies. It is this repressive state that was inherited by the post-colonial leaders in Uganda who have not reformed it into a democratic state that is accountable to the citizens.

Noteworthy also is that most post-independence leaders in Uganda have always come into power through conquest and have always been removed by force, which traps the country in violent politics (Kabwegyere, 1995). The point being advanced here is that the repressive nature of the state in Uganda has been the source of several violent and latent conflicts in the country's post-colonial history. One of the reasons for the conflict in Northern Uganda, from the standpoint of the LRA, is what their leaders perceive as President Museveni's dictatorship, which they claim must be resisted in order to establish a democratic government. While this reason is laughable given the LRA record of brutality and human rights abuses, one cannot discount the fact that poor governance is a major source of conflicts in Uganda.

The second dimension of the nature of the state in relation to the LRA conflict is that because the state in Uganda was created through conquest serious contenders for political power have occasionally attempted to capture state power through forceful means as opposed to democratic means. The use of force has almost become an institutionalized way of gaining political power in Uganda. Consequently, almost all political groups that seek political power have often attempted or contemplated the use of armed force. It is against this background that this study proposes the need for democratization involving fundamental reformation of the state in Uganda as part of imperatives for the sustainable conflict resolution in Northern Uganda and durable peace in the entire country.

Another source of conflict in Uganda is linked to the democratic transitional process from the "Movement System" to the present Multiparty System in Uganda. As Dahl (2000) has observed, democratic transitions are always tricky, fragile and conflict-ridden, a situation where Uganda currently finds itself. Most observers note that the transition process is very delicate to the extent that some countries suffer democratic reversals or democratic stagnation. The situation is made worse because the current government in Uganda due to the youth dividend is increasingly facing legitimacy challenges among this group who are the majority and don't want to hear stories of 'we liberated this country from political thugs'.

In the 2001. 2006 and 2016 general elections, presidential election outcomes were decided upon by the Supreme Court ruling. With another general election approaching in 2021 and with declining political popularity of the ruling NRM party and demographic composition dominated by the youth, most observers fear that unless these elections are conducted very well, they could plunge the country into political instability. This is based on the threats by the main opposition party, Forum for Democratic Change (FDC) who argue that they will never go back to the court of law over alleged rigged elections.[40]. The history of poorly conducted elections has always been a source of political instability in Uganda.

Henderson (2005) observes that dissidents in semi-democracies rarely have their demands effectively addressed through government channels available to them and consequently are more apt to mobilize their dissidents and pursue insurgency. This observation reflects the pattern of political conflicts in most of Uganda's nearly 60 years of independence, including the LRA conflict in Northern Uganda. Finally, lack of respect for the constitution and constitutionalism has also been identified as a major source of conflict which traps Uganda in a vicious cycle of conflicts. Since independence, almost all heads of state in Uganda have not respected the sanctity of the national constitution. They instead have treated the constitution as a document to be changed to suit their interests. Commenting on how Obote abrogated the 1962 independence constitution and introduced his tailor made constitutions of 1966 and 1967, Kabwegyere (1995:230) observed as follows: That the head of state could abrogate a constitution and replace it with one of his choice was the severest blow at the working of the state. It showed that the constitution was not a sacred and respected document, and that the power of the president was in a sense limitless. The 1967 Obote constitution is not only colored by the immediacy of the situation at the time but also by Obote's personal interests and ambitions.

When Idi Amin toppled Obote in 1971, he too suspended certain parts of the 1967 constitution. Under a Proclamation, Articles 1, 3, 63 and Chapters 1V and V of the Constitution of 1967 were suspended. The

---

[40]The Monitor (2010). War Talk- NRM Officials Criticise Besigye, Available at: http://allafrica.com/stories/201001290270.html. Accessed on 4/2/2011.

suspension meant that the Ugandan Constitution of 1967 was no longer the supreme law of the land. Its provisions and indeed, those of any other law could be overridden by decrees passed by the military government (Kanyeihamba, 2002:139). Consequently throughout his eight year reign of terror, Amin ruled the country by decrees.

The situation has not been any different under President Museveni's era of 'fundamental change.' When the NRM came to power in 1986, the government quickly embarked on a constitution making process which lasted from 1989 to 1995 when it was promulgated. As Kanyeihamba (2002) has observed, the 1995 Ugandan Constitution was hailed as the most progressive constitution Uganda has ever had. Its strength was based on the consultative nature the constitutional making process undertook, the gender responsiveness, and sensitivity to other marginalized groups such as persons with disability, workers, minority groups and youths. Most critically, the framers of the 1995 constitution were informed by the country's political history and set out to make a constitution that would avoid the 'bad old days.' The preamble of the Constitution states that: We the people of Uganda, recalling our history which has been characterized by political instability … do hereby, in and through this Constituent Assembly solemnly adopt, enact and give to ourselves, our posterity, this Constitution….this 22nd day of September, in the year of 1995.

Barely 10 years down the road, the NRM government presided over a constitutional reform process which overhauled the entire 1995 Constitution. It is more disturbing that the two term presidential limit was removed. This paved way for President Museveni to run for a third term, fourth, fifth etc terms. Most Ugandans have complained that this had deprived them a chance to witness a peaceful transfer of power from one President to another. Professor Kanyeihamba (2002:271), himself a founding member of NRM and former Attorney General and Minister for Constitutional Affairs, has observed that: Since 1996, the National Resistance Movement has unveiled many facets which few Ugandans expected from it. It can be stated that since the promulgation of the 1995 Constitution which was arguably the finest hour of the NRM administration, the leadership has appeared to concentrate more on political games of how to stay in power and exclude others from it longest.

Eriya Kategaya, widely considered as number two to President Museveni in the NRM administration, before his death, was shocked by the constitutional change. He noted that:

In my naïve thinking, I believed that President Museveni will live up to the stature of a statesman and be the first President of Uganda to retire as per the Constitution and thereby set a constitutional precedent. I strongly believe that this should be done for the sake of the future stability of this country. I have spent most of my youth running up and down and even went into exile because of bad politics and I don't wish my children to experience the same problems (2006:121).

The current status of the 1995 Constitution is highly contested. In fact, one of the key democratic reforms that civil society and the political opposition parties have persistently demanded include the re-instating of the two presidential term limits which many think would solve the problem of life presidency in Uganda and the problems associated with it.

Emergence, 'Production' and 'Reproduction' of Child Soldiers in Uganda

Because of the magnitude of the suffering of children in Northern Uganda, where the Lords' Resistance Army (LRA) has forcefully recruited thousands of child soldiers through abduction, most of the academic studies and policy analyses have tended to present the problem as though it is limited to Northern Uganda. It should be noted that the child soldier phenomenon is not new in Uganda's political history and did not start with the LRA conflict. Child soldiering can be traced as far back as 1972 during the first war against Idi Amin's reign of terror through the 1978/79 Uganda National Liberation War which finally ousted Amin. The war that was largely fought by the Tanzanian army and Ugandan exiles, massively recruited young people in an effort to beef up the Ugandan armed forces once the Tanzanian army had withdrawn. Former child soldiers who were part of the liberation struggle and have since become prominent personalities include General Salim Saleh, President Museveni's brother and a celebrated general in the National Resistance Army (NRA) and the late Major General Fred Rwigyema, the first leader of the Rwandan Patriotic Front (RPF/A) who was killed in the early 1990's during the war to liberate his country Rwanda. These soldiers were recruited by President Museveni in their teens to join the

Front for National Salvation Army (FRONASA) which fought alongside the Tanzanian army during the Uganda Liberation war of 1979 (Museveni, 2007).

The above observation is confirmed by President Museveni in his book, *Sowing the Mustard Seed: The Struggle for Freedom and Democracy in Uganda.* According to Museveni:

> In August 1971, we brought some boys into Uganda and positioned them on Mt Elgon without any arms, in the hope of buying some later; but the boys were not sufficiently disciplined and soon gave themselves away. A boy called Wafula went into the market in Bumbo where he was arrested and made to talk about his activities. Amin's soldiers then arrested the rest of the group, including Raiti Omongin, and took them to Makindye Maximum Security Prison in Kampala (Museveni, 1997:55).

President Museveni has also confirmed how and why he recruited his younger brother General Salim Saleh, then a 16 years old teenager, into the liberation struggle when he visited him in exile in Tanzania. As Museveni narrated:

> I was very worried about the safety of my family in Uganda... I decided not to send him back, especially as he was the only brother I had. I thought that one day Amin would kill my family simply because they were my relatives. ..... I argued that now was not the time for him to concentrate on studies. It was better to keep alive and make a contribution to the liberation of the country. ...I encouraged him to join the group I had sent to train in Mozambique. As a 16 year-old, he was of course delighted at the prospect. Young people are easily excited by guns, although they may not always know the political implications (Museveni, 1997:91).

It is not surprising therefore that during the National Resistance Army (NRA) guerrilla war (1981-86) which brought President Museveni to power, child soldiers popularly known as '*Kadogos*' played a critical role in toppling both the Obote 11 government and Gen. Okello's military junta in 1985 and 1986 respectively. The NRA justified its recruitment of child soldiers as the best way for protecting orphans whose parents had been killed by government forces and had nowhere to turn to except the army.[41]

According to Kaihura (2000:14), in February 1981 Yoweri Museveni began a guerrilla war against the government of Milton Obote who had come to power through rigged elections in 1980. This war was based in Luwero Triangle in central Uganda. Consequently, the government army launched a campaign to dislodge the National Resistance Army (NRA), Museveni's rebel group, from its bases in Luwero Triangle, which was densely populated. In the process, the army attacked villages, destroyed homes and indiscriminately killed innocent men, women and children (Human Rights Watch, 1997). Many children, especially orphans and those whose parents could not be traced, remained with the NRA.

Kaihura (2000:15) further observes that since the war in Luwero Triangle had no frontline, it was essential that the children be prepared to defend themselves as inevitably they would be caught up in fighting between the NRA and UNLA (national army). When the NRA/M captured power in 1986, child soldiers were briefly demobilized and enrolled in primary schools. Subsequently, most of them were re-absorbed into the army[42]

The number of children among the NRA has never been clearly known. After the end of the war, The Uganda Group of Human Rights based in London wrote to the Ugandan Government and demanded demobilization of child soldiers who were alleged to constitute 15% (about 3,000) of the total number of the national army (Kaihura, 2000:13). The Uganda Government pointed out that the number of child soldiers at the time were only 300 and not 3,000 as claimed by Non-Governmental Organizations and the international community. According to the government's official information, by the end of 1986, a total of 300 *Kadogos* had been registered for demobilization of whom 40 were girls. They ranged between seven and sixteen years of age. Ten of them were under seven years old; the youngest was four years. The *Kadogos* were registered in Bombo barracks and by June 1987 when the *Kadogos* were moved to their new School in Mbarara barracks, the number had increased to 638 (Kaihura, 2000).

---

[41] Interview with Lt Col. Kulayigye, F., Spokesperson for Ministry of Defence and Uganda Peoples Defence Forces in Kampala in March, 2010.
[42]Interview with Lt Col. Felix Kulayaigye, Spokespers of the Uganda Peoples Defence Forces in 2017.

The difference between the NRA and the Lord's Resistance Army (LRA) is that the NRA did not have a policy or military strategy of recruitment and use of child soldiers and soon after the war, they were sent to school with some of them being re-absorbed into the army after their studies. What is also clear is the admission by government that the reintegration and rehabilitation of former child soldiers had limited success. Comparatively, the LRA adopted a strategy of recruitment of child soldiers by abduction and forced conscription (Green, 2008:9). Also, the LRA made children the principal target for its attack and its survival seems to be based on child abduction and use, not on ideological appeal for liberation of their country as was the case of NRA. In fact, it is remarkable that most of the child soldiers that became part of the NRA were looking for security among the rebels who became their guardians, parents and protection since their parents had been killed by government soldiers, especially in Luwero Triangle (Kaihura, 2000:15).

It is worth noting though that there are other former child soldiers that were recruited by the Museveni's NRA who were enabled to advance their educational and military careers. Today, some of them are in important positions in the army. For example, the current head of pharmacy in the Uganda Peoples Defence Forces is a former *Kadogo*.[43] According to Kuluyagye, many former *Kadogos* who completed university and other studies were absorbed into the army and some are currently serving in very senior positions in the army.

It should also be noted that besides the NRA led by Museveni, several other armed groups that were fighting to overthrow President Obote's second government (1980- 1985) recruited and used child soldiers. One example is Captain Semujju, who is a former *Kadogo* but now has a Bachelor's degree in Education. Semujju was 10 years old when he joined Dr Andrew Kahira's FEDEMU in 1981together with his two brothers and other children. He later joined Museveni's NRA upon reintegration of FEDEMU into the victorious NRA.[44]

In spite of the fact that most of the children voluntarily joined the NRA for protection, especially in the war zone, some of them, especially girls, witnessed traumatizing experiences that they will live with for the rest of their lives. An example of a former child soldier under the NRA is

---

[43] Lt. Col. Kuluyagye, Op Cit.,

[44] Captain Semujju is in charge of Finance and Administration, in the Public Relations Office of UPDF. He was interviewed in Mbuya Military Baracks in March, 2008..

China Kaitesi. Kaitesi speaks about how she cannot forget the systematic rapes she suffered and the violence she was forced to commit under the NRA care; a charge fiercely denied by the Museveni government as hoax (BBC News, 25 May 2004). Kaitesi represents several other ex-child soldiers who suffered under the NRA during Uganda's tragic war history but have no forum to express their horror and trauma. It is noteworthy that the NRM leadership seemed never to have been interested in the RR of former child soldiers into civilian life. Most of the former *Kadogos* who were interviewed point out how they were simply re-absorbed into the army after schooling or dropping out of school even when the army was not their preferred option[45].

The Lord's Resistance Army/ Movement Rebellion: Recruitment and Use of Child Soldiers

It was six in the afternoon. We were in the field. My mother and I went home to prepare the food. I saw some strangers, and my mother said that may be they were rebels so I went out to warn the other girls in the field. On the way I met the rebels, and they made me lead them to the other girls - Iris (Save the Children Report, 1999:21).

This section discusses the background and genesis of the LRA conflict. It also discusses the methods of recruitment and use of child soldiers by the LRA and the consequences of the LRA conflict on child soldiers.

Northern Uganda and the Acholi land in particular has been a scene of a bloody and protracted rebellion since 1986 when the NRM government led by President Museveni came into power. The LRA rebellion led by Joseph Kony has been characterized by wanton and indiscriminate killings, child abductions and rape with impunity. Hundreds of people have been killed and maimed while others until recently were forced into internally displaced peoples camps (IDPs) in their thousands. It is estimated that over 1.6 million people, were made IDPs living in appalling unhygienic conditions for over 10 years. The

---

[45] Interview with a former child soldier who was retired from the army in 2010 with bitter memories. He talked about his abduction and forceful recruitment by the victorious NRA, his suffering in the army as a child soldier and the discrimination since he did not come from the correct ethnic group. He did not want his name disclosed since this can cause him problems with the army leadership as he is still a member of the reserve force. The interview was conducted in February, 2010 in Kampala.

United Nations Children Fund (UNICEF) figures show that over 20,400 children have been abducted since 1990 and forcefully conscripted into the rebel ranks where girls are turned into sex slaves for rebel commanders (World Vision, 2005).

The Human Rights Watch (1997), on the plight of children abducted by the LRA in Northern Uganda revealed how the abducted children are subjected to unimaginably brutal methods to become soldiers and slave labourers by the LRA. In order to keep the child soldiers in the bush, the LRA subjects them to cruel punishments including forcing some to kill their friends and relatives who attempt to escape. The girls are distributed to the rebel commanders who turn them into concubines and effectively kept as sex slaves (Lucima 2002:13). What even makes the rebellion more complex is its regional dimension where Uganda and Sudan have through this conflict been fighting a proxy war (ICG Report, 2004), which makes attempts at conflict resolution and peacebuilding extremely difficult. The conflict is linked to other regional conflicts in the Horn of Africa and the Great Lakes regions and is also known to provide a conduit for gun trafficking to regional countries that are experiencing civil wars. The regional dimension makes LRA rebellion pose a national, regional and international threat to peace and security.

The grievances for the LRA rebellion have never been very clearly articulated. What is well known though is that the LRA has been advocating for Uganda to be ruled according to the Biblical Ten Commandments (Green, 2008:9). Ironically, the rebels have committed gross human rights violations including indiscriminate killings, rape, abductions and forced recruitment of children into their ranks. Kony at times claims to be fighting to restore political pluralism in Uganda and for the economic marginalization of the Acholi people by the current government in Uganda. The conflict made it almost impossible for the government and development agencies to carry out meaningful development and reconstruction programmes in the region. The rebellion has had far-reaching consequences on the people of Northern Uganda and the entire country. These consequences include massive human displacement, abject poverty, insecurity and economic stagnation of the region and continues to stifle the country's democratization process.

The origins of the conflict lie in the complex religious traditions of the Acholi people and the deeply-rooted mistrust between the people of

176

Northern Uganda and other ethnic groups in southern Uganda (Briggs, 2005:113). This mistrust is rooted in the colonial distortions by the British colonial administration which concentrated development in the south and left Northern Uganda to provide cheap labour for the plantations in the south and military servicemen (ICG Africa Report, 2004:2). People from Northern Uganda were encouraged to join the army and consequently dominated the military and politics in the post-independence period.

The guerrilla war which brought President Museveni, a southerner, into power in 1986 marked the end of two decades of political and military domination by Northerners. The worst effect of this change was that people from Northern Uganda lost their traditional military jobs and therefore their source of livelihoods (Amnesty International Report, 1999:39). In 1986 when President Museveni overthrew Gen. Okello, a popular revolt was fomented by the ousted troops who formed the Uganda Peoples Democratic Army/ Movement (UPDA/M). Upon defeat of the UPDA by government forces, their remnants were re-organized by a 'priestess', Alice Lakwena to form the Holy Spirit Movement (HSM). Lakwena's HSM massively recruited civilians mostly poorly armed youths to fight against a professional army which led to many of them being killed in battles (Finnstrom, 2005:102).

Inspired by Lakwena, the soldiers of the Holy Spirit Movement inflicted a number of embarrassing defeats on the National Resistance Army who were at first overwhelmed by the sight of thousands of poorly armed soldiers streaming forward, making no attempt to take cover (Green, 2008:9). By 1987, the Holy Spirit Movement's soldiers made it as far as Jinja, only sixty miles from Kampala. At this point, superior technology on the part of government forces won the day. With countless dead, the military wing of the Holy Spirit Movement appeared to be utterly destroyed (Human Right Watch, 1997:68). After the defeat at Jinja, Lakwena fled to Kenya where she died in a refugee camp in 2007.

The LRA leader, Joseph Kony, a cousin of Lakwena, joined the rebellion of the UPDA in 1987 as a spiritual mobilizer (Human Rights Watch, 1997:69). Kony re-organized the remnants of the HSM to form the LRA. The primary motivation of the LRA is the conviction that their struggle against the government is a divine call sanctioned by God through his "prophet" Kony. This ideology is systematically implanted into the minds of the abducted children.

Sudan has since 1994 been central to the survival of the LRA. Sudan has provided to the LRA a safe haven, arms and training (ICG Report, 1997:7). Sudanese support to the LRA is allegedly in retaliation for the Ugandan government support to the Sudan People's Liberation Movement/Army (SPLM/A) insurgency (Woodward, 2001:180). The SPLA/M has been fighting against the imposition of Sharia Law, misrule and socio-economic and political marginalization by the government of Sudan.

The Lord's Resistance Army's Recruitment and Use of Child Soldiers in Northern Uganda

This section discusses the LRA's recruitment and use of child soldiers in Northern Uganda.

Starting from 1987, Kony waged a bloody war targeting civilians, mostly his Acholi community, whom he accuses of betrayal, alleging that they initially supported the LRA war and later abandoned him. Without support from the local population, the LRA resorted to abduction of children as a method of recruitment and indiscriminate killings of suspected government allies to terrorize the population (Briggs, 2005:116; Olupot, 2010). Behind child abductions is a carefully crafted element of war strategy. Children and specifically girls are meant to provide labour and sexual comfort to the rebel commanders, as well as serving as targets of terror against their families and communities. Accordingly, this is intended to create a sense of hopelessness and hatred for the government. When children are killed, parents mourn their death and condemn the army for the failure to protect them (ICG Africa Report, 2004:6).

Whenever the LRA planned raids into Uganda to abduct children and for supplies from their bases in Sudan, they would divide themselves into small bands. In towns and trading centres, they would loot medicines from health centres. In the rural areas, they would loot food and often kill adults and abduct the children (Human Rights Watch, 1997:13). Abducted children would be tied up and forced to carry looted goods. Children who failed to keep up the pace would be killed outright, including those who tried to escape.

Once in the camps inside Sudan, both boys and girls would be trained on how to use weapons and how to fight. During the battle,

178

children are often sent to the frontlines, while the commanders remain safely in the rear to avoid being killed. The LRA adopted a strategy of spiritualization of violence as a powerful psychological tool against child abductees. Children are told that they can overcome bullets and that the spirits will confuse them if they try to escape (Anderson et al, 2005:13). The LRA strategy to abduct children is well designed to ensure that young people who are easily controllable and easy to indoctrinate form the bulk of its forces. Older people are not preferred because they are hard to control, indoctrinate and may question some of the excesses of the LRA, such as wanton killings and destructive behaviour.

Consequences of the LRA Conflict on Child Soldiers

This section focuses on the consequences of the LRA conflict on child soldiers. Children who survive armed conflict have to deal with the horrors they have witnessed. War undermines the very foundations of children's lives, destroying their homes, splintering their communities and shattering their trust in adults. Children spared the direct experience of violence in armed conflict still suffer deep emotional distress in the face of the death or separation of family members and loss of friends (Machel, 1996:80).

Commenting on the consequences of armed conflicts on former child soldiers, Wessells (2006:126) has observed that war creates long-lasting wounds, both visible and invisible. The most visible ones are the physical wounds. Less visible wounds are the hidden ones of the mind, heart and soul. The LRA conflict in Northern Uganda has not been exceptional. Not only have large numbers of children been killed and injured, but countless others have grown up deprived of their material and emotional needs, including the structures that give meaning to their social life.

The report by Human Rights Watch (1997:36) revealed how rebel commanders used the children as shields. When the battle approaches, the children are sent to the frontlines, while the commanders remain in safety behind and watch as the government army guns down the children. Stories have also been told how the children are ordered by their rebel commanders not to take cover, and they are beaten if they attempt to duck down or crouch behind trees or buildings. Consequently, many children have lost their lives during battles with the government army.

The consequences of war on young women combatants in Northern Uganda are worth noting. McKay et al (1999) reveal how child mothers who were former fighters and the babies they gave birth to during fighting had become very vulnerable upon return from the bush. Faced with the evidence of rape (their children) and the violation of cultural taboos, combined with the responsibility of caring for babies and societal resentment, most young mothers have become stigmatized. McKay's story about the child mothers in Northern Uganda has been corroborated by the report by the Liu Institute for Global Issues (2005:73). The report points out that child mothers who are former fighters, find it difficult to reintegrate fully with their families due to rejection by the parents because of the children they returned with. This was confirmed during the fieldwork. It was established that parents are ready to welcome their daughters back but without their children born to LRA commanders in the bush.[46]Consequently, many of these young mothers have ended on the streets of towns as sex workers (Liu Institute for Global Issues (2005).

Another consequence of the LRA conflict on former child soldiers is poverty. It is worth noting that some of the former child soldiers returned to poverty since almost all of them lost out on schooling, which would have accorded them a secure future livelihood. More so, some of them are returning home as total orphans since their parents were killed by the rebels or died from other natural causes. Consequently, most former child soldiers have returned to no homes and to chronic poverty exacerbated by the years of an unending conflict (Liu Institute for Global Affairs, et al.(2005:36). It is this state of affairs that could make most of them fail to transit fully into normal civilian life and they could be easily driven into criminality or fresh rebellions hence constraining reconstruction and peace-building processes.

Furthermore, former child soldiers in Northern Uganda generally return to a society that has been socially and economically disrupted and dislocated. The war resulted in what has been described as 'the world's biggest neglected humanitarian crisis' (World Vision Report, 2005:30). More than 80% of the population in Acholi sub-region estimated at 1.6

---

[46] Most child mothers who are former child soldiers that were interviewed during the fieldwork revealed that their children have been rejected by their parents who demanded that they first take them to their biological fathers. The interviews were conducted in northern Uganda between January and February 2010.

million were displaced into 'internally displaced peoples' camps. Available information indicates that internally displaced people are the most vulnerable to insecurity, poor quality of life and psychological trauma (Liu Institute for Global Affairs & Ker Kwaro Acholi2005:36).[47] It seems that reintegration of former child soldiers into an already traumatized society could become a serious challenge for children who are themselves traumatized. Consequently, it is crucial that the reintegration processes of former child soldiers should go hand in hand with the economic regeneration and reconstruction of the entire society in Northern Uganda.

Also, former child soldiers in Northern Uganda face resentment by their families and the community. During fieldwork, it was established that there cases where family re-unions have broken down with former child soldiers ending up on streets. This is largely due to the fact that most former child soldiers are not used to the dictates of a normal family life with a father as a head of a family or household. The bush life prepared them to obey the armed rebel commander. Some former child soldiers end up questioning the authority of their parents and guardians who they see as civilians and therefore powerless before them. Such behaviours result in quarrels and fights leading to family break ups (World Vision, 2005:16).

Another consequence of the LRA conflict on former child soldiers is the high prevalence of HIV/AIDS, especially among girls and young women who were used as sex slaves by rebel commanders. Most former child soldiers who were tested were found to be infected by HIV/AIDS (World Vision, 2005; PRDP, 2007; McKay, 1999:62).

Emotional stress and social disorder has also been found to be one of the consequences of the LRA conflict on former child soldiers. Because of indoctrination and brutality that former child soldiers were exposed to by the LRA, some of them became seriously affected. A study conducted by Liu Institute for Global Affairs & Ker Kwaro Acholi (2005) found out that some former child soldiers were emotionally distressed. The testimony by one of the rescued child soldiers confirms this point in the following narrative:

---

[47] During fieldwork most of the associations of former child soldiers pointed out that they have since established that there were members of the community who needed psychosocial support such as counselling. Consequently, these associations are offering counselling services to both their members and the community which has also improved their relations with the communities among whom they are reintegrated.

181

I have nightmares and bad dreams. I dream about the bad things they (LRA) used to do, like killing people by cutting them into pieces with *pangas* (machetes). This normally happens at night then I fail to catch sleep and eventually end up sitting in the night... I think even during the day more, especially when I think about them trying to kill me, so even if I am with friends, I think about what happened to me and to my friends (long silence). Sometimes when I sit alone, I think about the machete they used to kill people with and other bad things the rebels did. That haunts me to an extent that I don't want to see any one next to me when I think about it (Liu Institute for Global Affairs & Ker Kwaro Acholi 2005:15).

Furthermore, it has also been noted that formerly abducted children upon return or escape from the LRA captivity have been forcefully recruited into the national army - Uganda Peoples Defence Force (UPDF). Chris Dolan (2000) pointed out that the trauma of abduction does not end with return; some are kept in the UPDF barracks for weeks of questioning while others are incorporated directly into the army and redeployed to fight the rebels. The point here is that the war robbed these children of their childhood and that even UPDF which is supposed to protect them instead perceived them as additional forces to fight the rebels. This constitutes a violation of children's rights under the Ugandan Constitution under Article 17 which prohibits recruitment of children into the army.

One of the disturbing consequences of the LRA conflict on abducted children is that most of them die in captivity. According to Dolan (2000), if all the accounts of children dying or being killed on forced marches or when seeking to escape are true, then several hundreds must have died during their captivity. Some of them are thought to have been killed in skirmishes with UPDF and SPLA while others were alleged to have been sold into slavery in Sudan by the LRA.

National Legal Mechanisms for Protection of Children's Rights in Armed Conflicts in Uganda

This section examines the existing legal framework for the protection of children in armed conflicts in Uganda.

The 1995 Constitution

The Constitution of Uganda as the supreme law in the land provides for protection of children's rights in armed conflicts. Article 17 of the Constitution provides that it is the duty of every Ugandan citizen "to protect children and vulnerable persons against any form of abuse, harassment or ill-treatment". The Constitution also states that children under the age of 16 years "are entitled to be protected from social or economic exploitation and shall not be employed in or required to perform work that is likely to be hazardous or to interfere with their education or to be harmful to their health or physical, mental, spiritual, moral or social development (Article 34). Further, the Uganda Constitution under Article 51 establishes the Uganda Human Rights Commission (UHRC) whose major function is to promote and protect human rights which include children's rights.

Ironically, while the spirit of the Ugandan Constitution is very explicit on the protection of children's rights in armed conflicts, it has not been matched by the practice. Both the LRA and the government army the Uganda Peoples Defence Forces, stand accused of recruitment and use of child soldiers (Global Report, 2008). Noteworthy also, is that UHRC a body established to protect human rights including children's rights, has never brought up any single issue of human rights abuse in respect to recruitment and use of child soldiers in Northern Uganda in spite of the wide spread international condemnation. An interview with the Director of Education and Training at UHRC revealed that the commission lacks adequate financing and staffing to execute its mandate including legal representation of former child soldiers. It was also learnt that UHRC has left most of the issues of former combatants including child soldiers to the Amnesty Commission.

The Amnesty Act, 2000 as Amended in 2006

Another piece of legislation designed to protect children's rights in armed conflicts in Uganda is the Amnesty Act 2000. The Amnesty Act 2000 provides a blanket amnesty to all Ugandans including child soldiers who have participated in various rebellions against the Government of Uganda since 1986 (Amnesty Commission Report, 2008) when the current government of President Museveni came into power. The Amnesty Act establishes the Amnesty Commission whose major task is to promote the Amnesty law, grant amnesty, demobilize and disarm former combatants and resettle combatants including former child soldiers and reintegrate and resettle them into their respective communities (Allen et al. 2006:37). Under the Amnesty Act, a number of former child soldiers in Northern Uganda were granted amnesty and resettled. As will be extensively discussed in Chapter Five, the Amnesty Commission has not performed to the expectation of its framers due to a number of reasons including lack of adequate financing and lack of professional staff to handle DDRR[48]In fact during fieldwork, it was found that there are many former child soldiers who have never been assisted by the Amnesty Commission. Most of these former child soldiers who were not formally reintegrated by the Amnesty Commission revealed that they live in constant fear of possible arrest and prosecution by the government as rebels since they lack amnesty certificates that were provided to others.

The Children Act 1997

The Children Act 1997 is another legal mechanism for the protection of children's rights in armed conflicts in Uganda. The law provides for the care, protection and maintenance of children. The Act defines a child as a person below the age of 18 years. Section 89 (1) states that, 'where a child is arrested, the police shall under justifiable circumstances caution and release the child.' Section 89 (3) states that, 'As soon as possible after arrest, the child's parents or guardians and secretary for children's affairs of the local government council for the area in which the child resides shall be informed of the arrest by the police. Further, the act provides in section 89 (4) that, 'The police shall ensure that the parent or guardian of the child is present at the time of the police interview with the child except where it is not in the best interest of the child.'

The problem with the Children Act is that it legislates for peacetime rather than war-time conditions and as such has not benefited the former child soldiers in Northern Uganda. The children normally report to the army and not to the police before being taken to the reception centres yet the act provides for the police. The interrogation for information is normally carried out by soldiers of the Child Protection Unit in the barracks without parents, guardians or police. Nevertheless the law is an

---

[48]Interview with the Public Relations Officer of the Amnesty Commission in 2010.

important development in the protection of children's rights and can be utilized by child mothers who have been rejected by their parents together with their children. It can also assist to re-unite former child soldiers who have failed to cope with their parents and ended up on the streets. Noteworthy is that the Children Act can be more useful if it is widely disseminated to communities in Northern Uganda and other parts of the country.

Uganda Peoples' Defence Forces Act 2005

The Uganda Peoples' Defence Forces Act, 2005 is another piece of legislation that provides for the protection of children's rights in armed conflicts. The Act prohibits recruitment and use of children in armed conflicts and sets the minimum age for recruitment into the army at 18 years. Section 52 (2) (c) states that, "no person shall be enrolled into the defence forces unless he or she is at least 18 years of age and has attained such level of education as may be prescribed'. Ironically, the Uganda People's Defence Forces (UPDF) has been widely accused of recruitment and deployment of child soldiers, especially the former child soldiers who escaped or it rescued from the rebels of the Lords' Resistance Army, an accusation that the army vehemently denies. The army accepts that sometimes the army recruits people below 18 years mistakenly since most of the young people in Uganda do not have birth certificates and may appear older than their real age."[49]

In terms of ratification of the international legal instruments, Uganda has made significant progress. For example, Uganda ratified the UN Convention on the Rights of Child on September 16, 1990 and did not enter any reservations. Uganda also ratified the Optional Protocol to the Convention on the Rights of the Child in November 2001. Uganda also ratified The Geneva Conventions and Protocols of August 12, 1949. The Rome Statute of the International Criminal Courts was ratified in June 2002 as well as the International Labour Organization Convention No 182 on the Prohibition and Immediate Action for the Elimination of the Worst Forms of Child Labour. Uganda also ratified The African Charter on the Rights and Welfare of the Child in August 1994. Ironically, while the Government of Uganda has done well in terms of ratification and domestication of international law, its record of recruiting former child

---

[49] Interview with Lt. Col. Felix Kulayigye in Kampala in March, 2011.

soldiers rescued from the rebels of the Lord's Resistance Army and re-deploying them in offensives against the same rebels (Global Report, 2004) makes most observers doubt its commitment to its international obligations.

The International Criminal Court Act 2006

The International Criminal Court Act 2006 which came into force in April 2010 is an important piece of legislation for protection of children's rights in armed conflicts. This legislation paves way for the Uganda War Crimes Court to try people accused of war crimes, genocide and crimes against humanity. This is in line with the Rome Statute of 1998, which establishes the International Criminal Court (ICC) that Uganda ratified in June 2002. While at the moment, the International Criminal Court Act 2006 is largely focused on trying the LRA leader Joseph Kony and his top commanders: Okot Odhiambo and Dominic Ongwen, the legislation is likely to work as a future deterrent against recruitment and use of children in armed conflict in Uganda (Mufumba, 2010).[50] In so doing, this legislation could end the cycle of impunity of violation of children's rights, which has been a characteristic of most armed political groups in Uganda. However, this optimism is possible only if the court remains objective. Already, the ICC has come under criticism for its bias against African leaders. For example, David Hoile (2010) who describes the ICC as Europe's Guantanamo Bay observes that:

> The ICC's double standards and autistic legal blundering in Africa has derailed delicate peace processes, thereby prolonging devastating civil wars. The ICC does not have Africa's welfare at heart, only the furtherance of Western European foreign policy and its bureaucratic imperative to exist, to employ more Europeans and North Americans.[51]

---

[50]*The Independent* Newspaper (2010). 'ICC Bill: Why did Mps trap Museveni and Save Kony?' 31March. Available at:
http://independent.co.ug/index.php/column/insight/67-insight/2702-icc-bill-why-did-mps-trap-museveni-and-save-kony. Accessed on 18/6/2010.

[51]*The Independent* Newspaper (2010). 'International Criminal Court: Africa Beware of 'New' Legal Colonialism,' 14 June. Available at:

By and large, no matter how the ICC is perceived, the indictments of several warlords accused of committing crimes against children's rights including high profile personalities such as President Bashir of Sudan, Charles Taylor of Liberia has sent a clear signal that the international law will follow them and punish them. This is likely to act as a deterrent to recruitment and use of children in armed conflicts in Uganda and at least Africa.

Conclusion

This chapter discussed the political history and political economy of Uganda to try to understand the basis for the political woes that have afflicted the country most of its post-independence period that led to emergence of the child soldier phenomenon. The chapter also discussed the sources of conflicts in Uganda which include regional imbalance in economic development or economic marginalization especially of Northern Uganda which stems from colonial economic distortions and lack of political commitment to address colonial economic distortions by the leaders; the nature of the state and bad governance; natural resources scarcity (mostly of land resources) and the substantial oil and gas reserves recently discovered in the country; regional spill over and proliferation of small arms and light weapons in the Great Lakes Region, among others. The chapter also discussed the emergence of the child soldier phenomenon in Uganda, the LRA recruitment and use of child soldiers, as well as the consequences for involvement of children in the LRA conflict. The chapter further explored the existing national legal mechanisms for the protection of children in armed conflicts in Uganda. Like most war-torn societies, Uganda has an enabling legal regime to protect children in armed conflicts, which unfortunately has not been effective.

Children in Uganda continue to be recruited and used in armed conflicts by several armed groups such as the LRA and the Allied Democratic Forces (ADF) as well as the national army. Overall, the chapter presents a picture of a conflict-prone country. It must be pointed out that violent conflicts are not a permanent condition of society

http://independent.co.ug/index.php/column/opinion/86-opinion/3032-international-criminal-court-africa-beware-of-new-legal-colonialism-. Accessed on 18/6/2010.

because conflicts can be practically resolved and transformed. Deepening democratic governance by promoting rule of law, respect for the constitutionalism, undertaking democratic reforms, curbing corruption, tackling economic inequality and effective implementation of the Peace, Recovery and Development Plan (PRDP) in Northern Uganda are some of the interventions that could lead to sustainable peace and stability in Uganda.

CHAPTER FIVE

•────────────────────────────•

Peacebuilding Interventions in the Reintegration and Rehabilitation of Child Soldiers in Northern Uganda

This chapter analyzes the official peacebuilding interventions that have been implemented by the Government of Uganda and Inter-governmental agencies of the United Nations (UN) in the reintegration and rehabilitation (RR) of former child soldiers in Northern Uganda. The chapter also examines unofficial peacebuilding interventions that have been implemented by International Non-Governmental Organizations (INGOs), national Non-Governmental Organizations (NGOs) and Community Based Organizations (CBOs) in the RR of child soldiers. These interventions are critically analyzed to assess their effectiveness and relevance in the RR of child soldiers in Northern Uganda.

It should be noted from the onset that peacebuilding interventions in Northern Uganda are unique in the sense that they are taking place outside the formal peacebuilding processes that are normally implemented by United Nations that follow standard procedures. Peacebuilding interventions in Northern Uganda are being implemented without a formal United Nations brokered peace agreement between the LRA and the Government of Uganda. Peace negotiations between the LRA and the Government of Uganda that were mediated by the Government of Southern Sudan (GoSS) collapsed in 2007 following the refusal by the leader of the LRA Joseph Kony to sign the Final Peace Agreement (FPA). More so, the situation in Northern Uganda cannot be called a post-conflict peacebuilding, since the LRA remains militarily active in the DRC, Central African Republic and Southern Sudan and is poised to attack Uganda given the opportunity (International Crisis,

2007:4).[52] The official peacebuilding interventions have been initiated and implemented by the Government of Uganda with the support of United Nations agencies such as UNICEF, UNDP and bi-lateral development partners, the World Bank and EU. What is common between the usual official UN led peacebuilding interventions and the on-going official Government of Uganda led interventions in Northern Uganda is the top-down approach in terms of planning, design and implementation with the target communities being passive recipients of peacebuilding programmes.[53] As such, the official peace intervention in Northern Uganda like in most contemporary conflicts has tended to focus on short-term assistance rather than on the root causes and underlying issues of the conflict, which adversely affects the quality of the assistance provided (Berdal, 1996:9). Consequently, as this chapter reveals in the subsequent discussions, most of the official government peacebuilding interventions have not been successful in meeting their stated objectives.

Official Peacebuilding Interventions: The Top-Down Approaches

The Peace, Recovery and Development Plan (PRDP) 2007-2010

The official Government of Uganda peacebuilding intervention is the Peace, Recovery and Development Plan (PRDP) for Northern Uganda (2007-2010). The PRDP was designed to be implemented for a period of three years and depending on the evaluation and outcomes, government would make a decision on the longer term development programme for Northern Uganda. The overall goal of the PRDP is to consolidate peace and security and lay a foundation for recovery and development. Because of lack of funds, political squabbles between government and politicians

---

[52] International Crisis Report (2007). 'Northern Uganda: Seizing the Opportunity for Peace.' *Africa Report* No 124-26 April.
Available at:http://www.crisisgroup.org/en/regions/africa/horn-of-africa/uganda/124-northern-uganda-seizing-the-opportunity-for-peace.aspx. Accessed on 15/5/2010.
[53] Namuyonjo, J. (2004). 'Conflicts, Poverty and Human Development in Northern Uganda.' Paper presented at the WIDER Conference on Making Peace Work in Helsinki, June. Available at: http://62.237.131.23/conference/conference-2004-1/conference%202004-1-papers/Nanyonjo-3105
Accessed on 15/5/2010.

from Northern Uganda and misunderstandings between donors and government have led to delayed full-scale implementation of the PRDP which prompted government to extend its implementation up to June 2012.[54]

The Office of the Prime Minister (OPM) that is charged with the overall monitoring and implementation of the PRDP attributes the slow pace of implementation on the donors' failure to commit their pledged contribution. Accordingly, government is supposed to raise 30% while donors are expected to contribute 70% of the overall budget for the PRDP.[55]

The PRDP investment which is estimated to cost Ug Shs 1,341,899,683,840 (equivalent to USD 606,519,297 at the time) plans to achieve its overall goal through four strategic objectives that are mutually reinforcing (PRDP, 2007). These objectives are:

a) Consolidation of state authority. Under consolidation of state authority, government seeks to ensure cessation of hostilities, provision of security and re-establishment of the rule of law in the region.

b) Rebuilding and empowering communities. Through this objective, government seeks to contribute to community recovery, promote improvement in the conditions of quality of life of displaced persons in camps, completing the return and reintegration of displaced populations, initiating rehabilitation and development activities among other resident communities and ensuring that the vulnerable are protected.

c) Revitalization of the economy. Under this objective, government seeks to re-activate the productive sectors within the region, with particular focus on production and marketing, services and industry. This would require rehabilitation of critical infrastructure in the region and ensuring sound management of the environment and natural resources.

d) Peacebuilding and reconciliation. Under the peacebuilding and reconciliation strategic objective, government seeks to ensure continuous prevalence of peace in Northern Uganda. The PRDP observes that peacebuilding and reconciliation processes require increased access to information by the population, enhancing counselling services, establishment of mechanisms for intra/inter communal and national conflict resolution, strengthening local governance and informal

---

[54]Interview with Flavia Waduwa, Undersecretary Office of the Prime Minister in charge of the implementation of the PRDP. The interview was conducted in Kampala in January 2010.

[55] Ibid.

leadership structures and reinforcing the socio-economic reintegration of ex-combatants.

Beyond the four strategic objectives, PRDP has fourteen priority programmes. These are: Facilitation of the Peace Agreement Initiatives; Police enhancement; Prisons enhancement; Rationalization of auxiliary forces; Judicial services enhancement; Enhancing local government; Emergency assistance; Return and resettlement of IDPs; Community empowerment and recovery; Production and marketing; Public Information, Education and Communication; Sensitization and Counselling, Amnesty; Demobilization and Reintegration.

The OPM is officially mandated to spearhead the implementation of the PRDP and is also the coordination office of all the reconstruction and development programmes being implemented by government, UN agencies and civil society in Northern Uganda. A Minister of State for Reconstruction of Northern Uganda is the focal person in the implementation of the PRDP. A Policy Committee and a PRDP Coordination and Monitoring Unit at national level oversee the implementation of the PRDP activities. The Policy Committee is comprised of representatives from sector ministries, donors, UN agencies and representatives from Non-Governmental Organizations.

As a result of two decades of violent conflict between the Lords' Resistance Army (LRA) and Government of Uganda, Northern Uganda has fallen far behind in terms of socio-economic development compared to the rest of the country (PRDP, 2007). The rebellion resulted into over 1.6 million people being forced into internally displaced persons camps (IDPs) where they stayed for over ten years living in appalling poor standards of living (World Vision International, 2005:25). The Government of Uganda has been under intense pressure from the international community and political opposition to close down the IDP camps and improve the living conditions of the people in Northern Uganda. Since the return of relative peace in 2006, following the start of peace talks between Government and the LRA in Juba South Sudan; people left the camps and returned to their original homes.

The PRDP observes that since 1990s, the Government of Uganda has been implementing a development agenda that has led to a reduction in poverty nationally, with visible improvement in many of the welfare indices. It indicates that the number of Ugandans who are unable to meet their basic needs declined from 56% in 1992 to 38% in 2003 and

192

further to 31% in 2006 with simultaneous improvement in other indices relating to access to health, education, and water and sanitation. However, the welfare indices for Northern Uganda have not improved at the same pace as the rest of the country. Income poverty remains significantly high, literacy rates are low and access to basic services is poor (Shaw et al, 2008:217). Government blames the state of poverty and economic underdevelopment and human suffering that has been experienced by the people of Northern Uganda on the prolonged conflict that has lasted for a period of over 20 years now (PRDP, 2007).

According to the World Bank, the proportion of Ugandans living below poverty line declined from 31.1% in 2006 to 19.7% in 2013. The same report observes that progress in reducing poverty has been much slower in Northern Uganda and Eastern Uganda. The proportion of the total number of poor people who live in the Northern and Eastern regions increased between 2006 and 2013 from 68% to 84% (World Bank Report, 2016).[56]

Table 1: Economic Costs of Armed Conflict in Northern Uganda

No	Cost Item	Percentage (%)	Total cost in millions (US $)
1.	Direct Military Expenditure	27.58	367.2
2.	Loss of Income from crops	15.96	212.5
3.	Reduction in tourism	13.90	185.0
4.	Increased medical costs	10.38	138.2
5.	Loss of output due to ill health	7.47	99.5
6.	Loss of income from sale of livestock	4.80	63.9
7	Loss of livestock (cattle)	2.61	34.3
8.	Loss of life-	2.58	34.3
9.	Costs related to West Nile District	2.42	32.2
10.	Loss of foreign exchange earnings	2.27	30.3
11.	Loss of houses	1.46	19.4
12	Loss of tax revenue	1.42	18.9
13	Loss of donor funds due to conflict	1.01	13.4
14	Loss of crops due to forced move to camps	1.00	13.3
15	Loss of household goods and tools	0.98	13.1
16	Loss of investments due to conflict	0.50	6.6
17	Loss of production/income due to illiteracy	0.50	6.6
18	Cost of externalising debt	0.26	3.5
19	Impact of war- related to Lira district	0.24	3.2
20	Environmental and land degradation costs	0.13	1.7
21	Frozen investments in IDP camps	0.11	1.5
22	Roads and Bridges destroyed	0.10	1.3

[56]The World Bank (2016). Uganda Poverty Assessment 2016: Fact Sheet, September 20. Available on Internet at:
http://www.worldbank.org/en/country/uganda/brief/uganda-poverty-assessment-2016-fact-sheet. Accessed on 22/10/2018.

23	Outmigration	0.03	0.4
24	Cost of government offices destroyed	0.01	0.1
Total		100%	$1,331.3

Source: World Vision International Report, 2005, 2nd Edition.

The design of the PRDP and its eventual launch by President Museveni in October, 2007 was largely influenced by the increased optimism and prospects for the return of peace in Northern Uganda. This optimism was based on the peace negotiations between the Government of Uganda and the LRA mediated by the Government of South Sudan (GoSS); in Juba; and the relocation of the LRA rebels from Northern Uganda to DRC, South Sudan and Central African Republic which left Northern Uganda relatively peaceful.

The PRDP and Reintegration and Rehabilitation of Child Soldiers

The PRDP provides for the RR of former combatants under strategic objective four: Peacebuilding and Reconciliation. Under this objective, the PRPD notes that,

> Government of Uganda has established a clear national policy framework for demobilization and reintegration of non-government forces operating in and outside Uganda. The Amnesty Reintegration Programme (ARP) implemented by the Amnesty Commission is based on the framework of the Amnesty Amendment Act (2006) that was amended in 2006 (PRDP, 2007:100).

The RPDP provides three ways by which ex-combatants, including child soldiers can access the Amnesty Reintegration Programme (ARP). This can be through a political framework such as the peace agreement; through a legal framework such as voluntary reporting and through defence framework where these forces surrender to the government army. The PRDP observes that irrespective of the framework the reporters use to access the ARP, they are eligible for amnesty and programme assistance.

While the PRDP provides for the DRR of ex-combatants both by promising to grant amnesty and resettlement assistance, a number of challenges arise in respect to former child soldiers. First, like most official peacebuilding interventions in war-torn societies, the PRDP follows the liberal peacebuilding approaches of top-down quick fixes, time table

194

bound or short-term based programming that never consider that the local actors have anything to offer in rebuilding their lives. Yet as Richmond (2008:288) has observed, peacebuilding receives much of its support and legitimacy in war-torn situations from civil society and local actors meaning that the notion of a civil society acts as a validation of peacebuilding strategies and objectives. Apart from the PRDP which is the official government/international community supported programme being a top-down intervention; it outrightly marginalizes former child soldiers in the demobilization, reintegration and rehabilitation processes.

The PRDP's demobilization and reintegration programme treats ex-combatants as one homogeneous group; yet they are varied with different problems, needs and aspirations. First, most of the former child soldiers were abducted and forcefully conscripted into the rebellion by the LRA. Second, most former child soldiers were tortured and traumatized as part of the training including forcing some of them to kill their friends and relatives in order to prevent them from escaping from captivity. Third, the abducted children missed schooling and lack life skills to earn a living. Fourth, most of the abducted girls were sexually abused and turned into sex slaves and concubines of rebel commanders. Some of them returned with unwanted children they have to look after for the rest of their lives as single mothers. Most of these young mothers or child mothers as they are commonly called have been rejected by their parents and told to return children to their fathers.[57] This has led to most of the child mothers resorting to prostitution in order to survive (Liu Institute for Global Issues & Ker Kwaro Acholi 2005). Jennings (2008:165) has warned against homogenizing DRR based on the experience in Liberia and Mozambique where both foot soldiers and commanders were treated as an undifferentiated mass with same interests, resources and opportunities. In both cases, officers offended at being treated the same as foot soldiers chose to orient their organizational skills and networks towards criminal rather than licit enterprises. Consequently, for government through the PRDP to have treated former child soldiers in the same way as other ex-combatants

---

[57]Interview with M.J. 25, a child mother with three children. During the fieldwork interviews for this book, most child mothers revealed that many of them were living in towns particularly Gulu town with their children where they do petty jobs such as washing houses and cleaning clothes of other people for a small pay. Most of them were worried about the education for their children. The interview was conducted in February 2010.

makes it difficult to effectively rehabilitate and reintegrate them into society.

The other challenges to effective RR for the former child soldiers and those that are still in captivity of the LRA relate to rampant and wide scale corruption that characterised earlier reconstruction programmes to PRDP. The effectiveness of the PRDP's predecessor Northern Uganda Reconstruction Programme (NURP1) and Northern Uganda Social Action Fund (NUSAF) were severely affected by corruption and mismanagement by government officials, yet no serious measures have been put into place to prevent corruption and mismanagement (Tebaijukira, 2008).[58]

Commenting on how the funds meant for NUSAF, the predecessor to PRDP were embezzled, Prime Minister Nsibambi while appearing before Parliament observed that,

...some cases are in courts of law while others are being handled by the police. But it is of great importance for the members of parliament to get copies of the alleged corruption.[59]

Embezzlement of NUSAF funds took all kinds of forms. In some cases members of the Community Project Management Committee (CPMC) connived with contractors to produce shoddy or incomplete work. In other instances, the supplier would be paid for goods that were never delivered. It was also found that in most cases funds were withdrawn from the bank by CPMC executives and diverted for personal use[60] Based on previous experience, it leaves one wondering how funds under the current PRDP will not be embezzled or mismanaged.

Another challenge facing the PRDP that relates to the RR of former child soldiers is its politicization by politicians both in government and opposition at local and national levels. The politicization of the PRDP in form of politicians trying to claim advantage from the programme confuses the target communities who are emerging from a destructive civil war. In fact, there are reports of some districts which failed to submit district work plans which are a basis for release of funds by the

---

[58] Tebajjukira, M. (2008). Shs 2.5 Billion (US$1,129,964)NUSAF Funds Missing. New Vision 10 July. Available at: http://allafrica.com/stories/200807110006.html. Accessed on 14/5/2010.

[59] Ibid.

[60]Interview with a senior official, Office of the Prime Minister who did not want his name disclosed in 2010.

Office of the Prime Minister, simply because local leaders cannot agree on distribution and location of projects.[61] Politicians struggle to have juicy projects located in their constituencies in order to impress the electorate for political advantage. More so, the Museveni Government that has consistently been losing elections in Northern Uganda is eager to use the PRDP to win political support in a region considered an opposition strong hold.[62]

In such circumstances, political expediency takes precedence over objective reconstruction and peacebuilding interventions. The evidence of the above observation is that the PRDP's geographical area, which initially covered 18 districts has now been expanded to cover 40 districts in the areas that were not directly affected by the conflict. Government has defended the expansion of the PRDP coverage on the grounds that the spill-over effects of the conflict through the IDPs and small arms proliferation in the neighbouring districts need to be addressed.[63] This position has been criticised by leaders from Northern Uganda who have interpreted government's action as aimed at gaining political advantage in the new PRDP districts.[64] The point being made here is that politicization of the PRDP activities is causing confusion among the communities that are slowly rebuilding their lives and this could negatively affect the pace of recovery including RR of former child soldiers.

Additionally, there is a challenge of lack of awareness of the PRDP by most of the beneficiary communities in Northern Uganda. During the field-work in Northern Uganda, it was found out that most of the formerly abducted child soldiers are ignorant about the PRDP and how they can benefit from it. Most of them are not able to differentiate the

[61] This statement was made by the Permanent Secretary Office of the Prime Minister at a workshop organized in partnership between Advocates Coalition for Development, Arua Local Government, Greater North Parliamentary Forum and OPM in Arua, West Nile in January 2010. The workshop was organized to assess the progress and challenges in the implementation of the PRDP.

[62] Interview with Mao Norbert former Local Council V Chairperson, Gulu District, in February, 2010.

[63] Wakikhona, D. is a former Minister of State for Northern Uganda in charge of the PRDP. He was interviewed in December, 2009 in Kampala.

[64] Okot Ogong is a Member of Parliament and Chairman of the Greater North Parliamentary Forum. The forum, whose membership comprises all members of parliament from northern Uganda, was created to monitor the implementation of the PRDP. He was interviewed in January, 2010 in Arua.

PRDP from the usual government programmes such as the much publicized 'Prosperity for All' which was President Museveni's campaign slogan during the 2006 presidential elections now being implemented across the country. The implication for this is that communities including former child soldiers are not able to hold their leaders or government accountable for a programme they do not understand (Makerere University, Refugee Law Project 2008:8).

Furthermore, the PRDP effectiveness in the RR of the former child soldiers faces the challenge of the way it was designed. The design of the PRDP was largely a top-down approach although the officers at the OPM claim the design enlisted participation of the target communities[65]. The overwhelming lack of awareness about the PRDP among the beneficiaries, especially the former child soldiers, during the fieldwork interviews, suggests that they were not adequately consulted during the design stage. Lack of adequate consultations and participation of the target communities and the local civil society, in the planning and design of the PRDP, makes the programme become more like the usual UN official externally driven peacebuilding processes that seek quick fixes and neglect local knowledge and local resources that are necessary for local ownership and future sustainability (Richmond, 2007). It is no wonder that former child soldiers who should be key beneficiaries are not specifically targeted for support by the PRDP. Had they been consulted, it is most likely that their unique needs and challenges would have featured more prominently than is provided for in the PRDP.[66]

Another crucial challenge to the PRDP effectiveness relates to the hostile attitude towards civil society that largely exists at the local government level. Most local leaders interviewed accuse civil society of criticising their programmes yet civil society organizations are also not transparent with their own funding and programming.[67] During the field

---

[65]Interview with Mr Othieno, a Commissioner Office of the Prime Minister in 2010.

[66] During the fieldwork exercise in northern Uganda which took place from December 2009 to March 2010, most people interviewed including former child soldiers did not seem to know what was in the PRDP for them and how they were going to benefit. In fact most people confused the PRDP with President Museveni's election Manifesto programme of 2006 called 'Prosperity for All' which is more of an aspiration than a development programme.

[67] A presentation on the roles and challenges of civil society in the implementation of the PRDP in Arua in January 2010 during a workshop organized by Advocates Coalition for Development and Environment and Office of the Prime Minister

work, it was found out that most district local governments now demand that all NGOs and Community Based Organizations must submit their work plans to the district authorities to assist in easy coordination of their activities (The New Vision, 29 June 2010).[68] While on the face of it one would think that local governments are doing a good thing to streamline coordination of peacebuilding interventions, a deeper analysis shows that it is designed to control and silence critical NGOs and CBOs.[69] Yet without a strong and vibrant civil society, the powerlessness and vulnerability that exist, especially among former child soldiers and women, would make it difficult for them to benefit maximally from the PRDP. Prendergast et al. (2002:329) who advocate for strong local civil society involvement in peacebuilding processes observe that,

> ...the greatest comparative advantage that CSOs possess in peacebuilding is local knowledge and deep contextual understanding of barriers and opportunities to making peace at the local level. This local knowledge translates into a set of roles that CSOs can play to foster the implementation of peace agreements and long-term peacebuilding: as transmission belts between communities and national governments, international NGOs ... and as advocates for local communities in national policy debates.

The other challenge is what the politicians from Northern Uganda call lack of political will to reconstruct and develop Northern Uganda by the Museveni Government. Lack of adequate funding and delayed implementation of the PRDP has been interpreted as lack of political will to develop the region that has been hostile to the current government in Uganda. Commenting on government's commitment to reconstruct Northern Uganda, Nobert Mao, Chairman Gulu district which was the

---

generated a heated discussion with each side pointing out the weaknesses of the other. The meeting observed that civil society should be transparent in their operations. It was also noted that local governments should allow civil society to perform their watch dog role if PRDP was to be implemented successfully.

[68] The New Vision, Tuesday June 29, 2010, Northern Uganda NGOs Face Prob. Government is putting pressure on NGOs in northern Uganda to account for the PRDP money, yet they do not get funding from Government. This action could seriously constrain civil society work in the region.

[69] Interview with the General Secretary, Acholi Religious Leaders Peace Initiative during the fieldwork in Arua, January 2010.

centre of the LRA conflict who is also the presidential candidate for the opposition Democratic Party (DP) observed that:

> There seems to be no will to rebuild the north. This started with the slovenly way in which the Shs 18.6b (US$ 8,406,932 at the time) emergency fund was used. In the 2008/2009 budget, money was allocated towards the PRDP but the money is unseen. Recently, the finance ministry said about Shs 120b (US$ 54,238,269 at the time) will be allocated towards the PRDP. We expect the money will be allocated in response to the need and indicative figures disclosed to local government in time.... Some government officials talk as if the money meant for SACCOS, NAADS and similar national interventions are all part of the PRDP....The confusion over the PRDP is a gross betrayal of the people. It is unacceptable that there is no money for PRDP (Mao, 2009). [70]

Based on the above analysis, it becomes evident that the demobilization, disarmament and reintegration of former child soldiers in Northern Uganda were not given any serious consideration by the official peacebuilding intervention. Yet as Berdal (1996:9) has observed, only with clearer appreciation of the context of such attempts at disarmament, demobilization and reintegration can some features that have made success so 'inherently difficult' be identified and their negative influence on the peace process be mitigated. Nevertheless, the PRDP still stands a chance to strategically plan and target the former child soldiers since it provides for periodic review'.[71] During the field work, the Minister of State for Reconstruction of Northern Uganda, Hon. David Wakikhona acknowledged that during the design of the PRDP government lacked technical expertise on DRR which explains why the component is not well conceptualized. He however pointed out that government is willing to take advice from civil society organizations with expertise in the field of DRR. It is against this background that the need for involvement of

---

[70] Mao, N. (2009). Has the Government Moved a Vote of No Confidence in Itself? *The New Vision* Newspaper of 9 February. Available at:
http://www.friendsforpeaceinafrica.org/norbert-mao/345-has-the-govt-moved-a-vote-of-n. Accessed on 14/5/2010.

[71] F. Waduwa is an Under Secretary in Charge of the implementation of the PRDP in the Office of the Prime Minister. Waduwa was interviewed in March 2010 in Kampala.

civil society in the successful implementation of the PRDP becomes imperative.

Northern Uganda Reconstruction Programme (NURP 1)

The Government of Uganda in 1992 designed and implemented the Northern Uganda Reconstruction Programme (NURP 1). The main objective of NURP1 was to address the social economic problems in Northern Uganda with the exception of the districts of Kotido and Moroto in Karamoja.[72] The programme was essentially an emergency operation aimed at restoring basic economic and social activities in the region. Although the implementation of NURP 1 was estimated to cost USD 600 million, only USD 93.6 million was realized and utilized. NURP 1 did not have any specific projects on the RR of former child soldiers. The main focus for NURP1 was to upgrade the infrastructure of the region in the form of roads, water supplies, health facilities and schools with support of IDA loan (Robinson, 2000).[73] Even if the social and economic projects would have indirectly benefited the former child soldiers, the programme faced serious challenges that made it almost a failure. Some of the key challenges that NURP 1 faced include massive embezzlement of project funds by officials and insecurity in the region.
It is noted that most of the money meant for the communities in Northern Uganda ended up in Kampala, the capital city of Uganda benefiting people who did not deserve it. Secondly, projects implemented under NURP 1 were greatly hampered by the insecurity, since it was too risky to reach certain areas in Northern Uganda where the LRA were very active. The third challenge is that the design of NURP 1 followed a top-down approach which lacked community

---

[72] Ministry of Finance and Economic Development (2003) 'Post-conflict Reconstruction: The Case of Northern Uganda.' Discussion Paper 7 (Draft). Available at: http://www.finance.go.ug/docs/Post-conflict%20Reconstruction.pdf. Accessed on 13/5/2010

[73]Robinson, M. (2000). 'Community Driven Development in Conflict and Post-Conflict Conditions: The Northern Uganda Social Action Fund (NUSAF) Project.' Available at: http://www.google.co.uk/#hl=en&source=hp&q=World+Bank%2C+April+2000%2C+Northern+Uganda+Reconstruction+Project%3A+Performance+Audit+Report%2C+Operations+Evaluation+Department.+Report+No.20664&btnG=Google+Search&aq=f&aqi=&aql=&oq=&gs_rfai=&fp=74aa98f7d3a65fd7. Accessed on 8/5/2010.

participation and ownership. This was largely responsible for its failure. Some of the components of NURP 1 that were considered successful such as the Soroti District Development Programmes, the Community Action Programme (CAP) in West Nile region and the Arua District Development Project were developed and implemented with participation of the target communities (Uganda Debt Network, 2004).[74] Another major weakness of NURP 1 as a peacebuilding intervention is that it pursued the economic dimension of peacebuilding, a liberal thinking which assumes that giving people an economic stake in peace rather than war is sufficient to make war less likely (Herring, 2008:48; Selby, 2008:16). Consequently, NURP1 focused on investing in infrastructure development, health, water etc which would improve economic development and deliver peace in Northern Uganda. Over emphasis on the economic dimension of peacebuilding by NURP1, when the root causes of the LRA conflict are complex and diverse including political inclusion, bad governance, historical grievances and regional dimension of the conflict, was central to its failure.

Northern Uganda Social Action Fund (NUSAF)

NUSAF is another Government of Uganda programme which started in 2003 and ended in March 2009. NUSAF was funded to the tune of US$133.5 million of which US$100 was a loan from the World Bank and US$13.3 million came from the Government of Uganda, while US$ 20.2 million was a contribution from local communities. The programme covered 18 districts spanning the Northern region which included the districts of Pallisa, Nakapiripirit, Kumi, Soroti, Katakwi, Kaberamaido, Kitgum, Lira, Apac, Pader, Moroto, Kotido, Gulu, Yumbe, Nebbi, Adjumani and Arua. The targeted community has a population of about 6.3 million people (Uganda Debt Network, 2004). The design of NUSAF was widely acknowledged as being participatory and consultative involving stakeholders from the central government and local communities (Uganda Debt Network, 2004). Its design was coordinated by the Office of the Prime Minister (OPM), which included senior government officials who were representatives of line ministries. The resultant design document was described by observers as highly

---

[74]Uganda Debt Network (2004). Will NUSAF Deliver Northern Uganda out of Poverty? Policy Review Newsletter Vol. 4, Issue 3.

appropriate to the conflict and post-conflict conditions in Northern Uganda (Interview with NUSAF officials).

NUSAF was designed to fulfil several objectives: to eradicate poverty; to promote sustainable development and to create conditions for higher levels of investment in agriculture and rural development; and to complement efforts of other projects the government was implementing in Northern Uganda. NUSAF was based on the realization that the majority of the rural farmers in Northern Uganda are small scale farmers with the barest means of survival which had been greatly undermined by the protracted violent conflict of the LRA. Consequently, it was envisaged that if NUSAF was going to be the vehicle for poverty eradication in the region, it must enable the extreme poor to become productive and generate incomes to enable them to afford the basic needs of survival including food, shelter and clothes.

NUSAF had five components: a) Community Development Initiative with a range of targeted project options covering education, health, water supply and sanitation, economic infrastructure, agriculture and environment; b) Community Reconciliation/Conflict Management; c) Vulnerable Group Support; d) Institutional Development; and; e) the Northern Uganda Youth Rehabilitation Fund. For the purpose of this book, the focus will be placed on two components of NUSAF which are closely related to the RR of former child soldiers: Youth Opportunities Project and Community Reconciliation and Conflict Management. Particular emphasis will be put on the relevance of *NUSAF's Youth Opportunities Project, Uganda* in the RR of former child soldiers since it was focused on the youth, a category where former child soldiers fall.

Northern Uganda Social Action Fund Youth Opportunities Project

The Youth Opportunities Programme (YOP) of NUSAF had three main objectives: 1) to provide youths with specific vocational skills and tool kits to enable them earn incomes and improve their livelihoods; 2) to contribute towards community reconciliation and conflict management; and 3) to build capacity of NGOs, CBOs, and Vocational Training Institutes (VTIs) to respond to the needs of youths. In order to accomplish the objectives set out for YOP, NUSAF developed a highly decentralized community and district driven system of youth vocational training. Organized small youth groups would identify vocational skills of interest and apply to the NUSAF District Technical Offices (NDTOs) for funding. Youth groups whose proposals were approved would receive cash transfer of up to US$ 10,000 through a community bank. These funds were used to enrol in VTIs, buy training materials, and equip graduates with the tools and start-up costs for practicing the trade after graduation. NDTOs were supposed to supervise and provide technical assistance. YOP began with US$1.6 million grant from the Japanese Social Development Fund in 2003. In March 2005, NUSAF decided to scale up the funding and committed about US$ 6 million (Blattman et al, 2009).[75]

While the YOP programme seems to have been a good idea where former child soldiers could have benefited, it faced a number of challenges. First, the criteria by which youth groups' proposals were selected for appraisal and approval in the districts remains unclear. There have been reports of corruption, mismanagement, and fraud levelled at many NUSAF, district, and community officials (Blattman et al, 2009). Secondly, the impact evaluation of YOP found it unclear how districts were able to successfully target the youths to benefit from the programme. Instead, the evaluation found signs that urban and peri-urban youth, educated youth, and well-connected youth were more likely to receive funds than the rural, uneducated and dislocated youths, a category where most former child soldiers fall. Third, it was established that the demand for the youth programme at the community level has been much greater than the supply of funds and staff. Thousands of proposals were received in Districts offices that could not be funded (Blattman et al, 2009).

Fourth, a large number of individual youth projects suffered from poor planning, mismanagement and accountability (Uganda Debt Network, 2004:3). In these circumstances, it was difficult for youth groups of formerly abducted child soldiers most of whom missed out out on schooling to access funds under NUSAF's YOP for their successful RR in communities as productive citizens.

---

[75]Blattman, C. Fiala, N. & Martinez, S. (2009). 'Impact Evaluation of the Northern Uganda Social Action Fund Youth Opportunities Project,' Uganda. Available at: http://www.iza.org/conference_files/ELMPDC2009/martinez_s4899.pdf. Accessed on 8/5/2010.

Community Reconciliation and Conflict Management

Another NUSAF component that was closely linked to the RR of former child soldiers is the Community Reconciliation and Conflict Management. The main aim of this component was to improve peace and security in the region affected by the LRA conflict. The Community Reconciliation and Conflict Management component was designed as a cross cutting component among the other NUSAF components. It included: traditional justice mechanism; cultural ceremony support; community dialogue and peace training or peace education.

While NUSAF implemented these activities with relative success, information on the ground reveals that most of the communities and groups that received funds from NUSAF misused the funds. There are reports of widespread corruption and lack of awareness among the communities that benefited from NUSAF funding. It is noted that most beneficiaries confused NUSAF money with Government micro-finance funds commonly known as '*Entandikwa*' that was misused as most people who accessed this money across the country thought it was a gift from President Museveni for political support (Debt Network, 2004). Despite the fact that NUSAF was well funded, it did not achieve much for the target communities in Northern Uganda. It is common practice to find several sign posts on the same spot for non-existent projects (Interview with Mao). Commenting on the level of corruption and nepotism that characterised NUSAF projects, Gulu District Chairperson Mao observed that:

> This project has been hijacked by the local elites making people victims, not beneficiaries. We continue to receive complaints that NUSAF and district officials pressurize people to give kickbacks to benefit from NUSAF project (*The Weekly Observer*, 6 March, 2008).

Based on the level of corruption that characterised NUSAF and the fact that former child soldiers were not officially planned for by NUSAF, they were not able to get tangible benefits. Most youth groups, not necessarily former child soldiers did not get funding due to the bureaucratic nature of the system and the overwhelming number of applications that were received by districts. The groups that benefited lacked proper management and oversight from the fund and ended up squandering the resources. A case in point is *Tempwoyo* Youth

205

Community Carpentry and Joinery Project in Paicho sub-county, Kitgum district where the executive members disappeared with Shs.10 million (US$4,520 at the time) (Tebajjukira, 2008).[76] By and large, NUSAF did not benefit the former child soldiers in their RR processes. If NUSAF benefited former child soldiers in their RR process at all, it was in an indirect manner that is difficult to pin point under this book. Worth noting is that NUSAF has been incorporated as one of the components of the PRDP.

Northern Uganda Rehabilitation Programme (NUREP)

Northern Uganda Rehabilitation Programme (NUREP) is funded by the European Union for a period of four years (2006-2010) to the tune of 20 million Euros. It aims at strengthening self reliance and protection of local populations in the region and rehabilitation of social infrastructure and improvement of the capacity of Ugandan stakeholders to respond to conflict and disasters. NUREP, which is in the process of being incorporated into PRDP, is a needs-based, demand-driven initiative that seeks to narrow the economic, social and political disparities between Northern Uganda and the rest of the country.[77]

The overall objective of NUREP is 'Increased potential for the restoration and preservation of peace and the creation of an enabling environment for development in Northern Uganda'. In order to achieve its objectives, NUREP is supporting the following activities: conflict resolution and peacebuilding initiatives; livelihoods of conflict affected people and returnees; service delivery by local governments; strengthening respect for the enforcement of human rights and the rule of law and support of the OPM to coordinate PRDP implementation. NUREP is working in Acholi, Lango, Teso and Karamoja sub-regions and Adjumani district in West Nile region. The programme is based on the premise that there cannot be peace without development and vice versa.

---

[76] Tebajjukira, M. Shs 2.5 Billion ($1,129,964) NUSAF Funds Missing. New Vision 10 July 2008. Available at: http://allafrica.com/stories/200807110006.html Accessed on 6/5/2010.xxxxxx

[77]Interview with Othieno, R., a Commissioner in the Office of the Prime Minister working on the implementation of the PRDP in Kampala in March, 2010.

In the course of 2008, a total of 126 projects were implemented under NUREP spread across Acholi, Teso, Karamoja and Lango sub-regions and Ajumani district in West Nile. NUREP is supporting national and international organizations to implement a number of projects. Some of the organizations that have been funded by NUREP include; Concerned Parents Association, GUSCO, War Child Holland, International Rescue Committee, St Monica Women's Group, Oxfam and AVSI some of which are involved in the RR of former child soldiers. Key projects supported by NUREP that are linked to RR of former child soldiers are:

> the reintegration of ex-combatants and returnees, conflict resolution and peacebuilding, empowering youth through training in vocational training, income generating projects, construction of school classrooms and psychosocial support to ex-combatants.

NUREP has been helpful in the RR of former child soldiers in several ways. It has supported their RR processes through income generating projects, vocational training, and support to primary schools where some of the former child soldiers have enrolled. However, it remains to be seen how NUREP, which is being folded into the mainstream PRDP which is facing funding problems, politicization and lack of clarity on the DDRR of former child soldiers, can still deliver on its objectives.

Karamoja Integrated Disarmament and Development Programme (KIDDP) 2007-2010

Karamoja Integrated Disarmament and Development Programme (KIDDP) has been integrated into the PRDP. The overall goal of KIDDP is to contribute to human security and promote conditions for recovery and development in Karamoja. The proposed interventions of the KIDDP aim to achieve this goal through the implementation of a comprehensive and coordinated disarmament programme that will enhance peace building and development in Karamoja. Weapon collection activities are being undertaken within the context of peace building programmes where efforts to remove weapons from society are linked with initiatives to address the root causes of the conflicts, including development activities that reduce poverty.

KIDDP does not directly focus on the RR of former child soldiers since this is not a problem in Karamoja sub-region, which is the major focus of the programme.[78] However, a gun free Karamoja, an area which has always destabilized Northern Uganda through cattle rustling, is likely to create a peaceful environment for carrying out peacebuilding including the RR of former child soldiers.

The Amnesty Commission

The Amnesty Commission (AC) is a body that was created by the Amnesty Act of 2000 amended in 2006. The AC has two key objectives: to persuade reporters to take advantage of the amnesty and encourage communities to reconcile with those who committed the offences; and to consolidate the progress so far achieved through the implementation of the amnesty and ensure that more insurgents respond to the amnesty and that the community is ready to receive them (Hovil et al, 2005:7).[79] The Act provides a blank amnesty to all Ugandans who have participated in various rebellions against the Government of Uganda since 1986 (Amnesty Commission Report, 2008). Besides granting amnesty, the Amnesty Commission through its Demobilization and Resettlement Team is supposed to demobilize, disarm, reintegrate and resettle former combatants, including child soldiers, into communities. According to the Amnesty Commission, there have been 27 different rebel groups who have taken advantage of the Amnesty Act since it came into force in 2000, including the rebels of the Lord's Resistance Army, the majority of who are formerly abducted child soldiers upon surrender and renunciation of armed violence.[80]

---

[78] Republic of Uganda (2007) 'Karamoja Integrated Disarmament and Development Programme 2007/2008-2009/2010.' Available at:
http://www.ugandaclusters.ug/dwnlds/0204Karamoja/KIDDP.pdf. Accessed on 10/5/2010.

[79] Hovil, L. & Zachary L. Z. (2005). 'Whose Justice? Perceptions of Uganda's Amnesty Act 2000: The Potential for Conflict Resolution and Long-Term Reconciliation.' Refugee Law Project, Faculty of Law Makerere University, Working Paper N0. 15 February.

[80] Interview with Draku, M., Public Relations Officer; The Amnesty Commission at their offices in Kampala in February, 2010.

Accurate numbers of former child soldiers and LRA fighters who have so far benefited from the Amnesty Act are not readily available. However according to Draku, the Public Relations Officer, Amnesty Commission, between 5,000- 7,000 former child soldiers had by 2010 been granted amnesty and reintegrated with their families[81]. Apart from offering immunity from prosecution and community sensitization, the commission provides amnesty certificates and resettlement packages to all returnees including child soldiers who surrender their weapons and renounce violence.[82]

The Amnesty Commission provides a basic personal assistance kit, including cooking utensils, a mattress, clothes, flour, seeds and fuel. A cash equivalent to three months of the salary of a police officer or teacher, around US$150; US$10.50 for medical expenses and US$10 for transportation expenses; and information and counselling on available reintegration options are provided to ex-combatants by the commission.[83] Beyond the resettlement packages to returnees, the commission has conducted sensitization workshops as well as radio outreach programmes to educate the population about the amnesty law and how they can take advantage of it[84]

Since the commission does not have expertise in counselling, it outsources other partners, especially NGOs, to provide counselling to demobilized and reintegrated combatants. The commission prepares the communities to receive their children. Accordingly, the commission sensitizes the families and communities that children are also victims of the conflict and if these children are not well received and catered for by the communities; the conflict is likely to go on endlessly

According to the staff of the Amnesty Commission, the institution faces the challenge of inadequate funding. They pointed out that Government's annual funding of Ug Shs. 1.6 billion (US$ 723,177 at the time) is not enough to enable the commission to carry out its mandate. For example it is noted that by 2005, the commission had a backlog of reporters or ex-combatants who had not received funds for re-insertion whose numbers had climbed to 11,200. However, this was eased when the commission received a grant of $US4.2 million funding from the

---

[81] Draku, M. Ibid.,

[82] Interview with Okello, J., a Senior Resettlement Officer with the Amnesty Commission in Kampala in March, 2010.

[83] Interview with Draku, M. Op.Cit.,

[84] Interview with Draku, Ibid.

World Bank in May 2005 (Mallinder, 2009). At the time of conducting this research for this book the commission was largely dependent on a World Bank grant that was slated to end in June, 2010. The second challenge faced by the Amnesty Commission relates to the fact that ex-combatants including former child soldiers are being reintegrated into poor communities which makes people resent these ex-combatants who are largely accused of committing human rights abuses and yet are being given 'special treatment'.

While the AC has demobilized and reintegrated former combatants including child soldiers, most people interviewed, especially former child soldiers, have heard about it but few have benefited from its services (Interview with former child soldiers). It rarely conducts follow up visits to the children and other former combatants which would increase its visibility. Even then the commission does not have a functioning website for disseminating information about its work. During the fieldwork interviews, the Public Relations Officer promised that they were working on the website. A study conducted by Allen et al (2006:37) found out that only about 25% of the formerly abducted child soldiers who have gone through the reception centres confirmed having received an amnesty card; applied for amnesty or even heard about the Amnesty Commission. In spite of its dismal performance in the RR of former child soldiers, fieldwork findings indicate that child soldiers who have received amnesty certificates feel more secure than those who don't have certificates.[85]

---

[85] The interviews with former child soldiers revealed that children who were formally reintegrated by reception centres with the certificate from the Amnesty Commission have been better received by communities than those who came straight from the bush to their families. This certificate is a proof of innocence to the former child soldiers who were abducted by the LRA and without it some feel unsafe. The interviews were conducted in northern Uganda between January to March 2010.

Child Protection Unit (CPU) of Uganda Peoples Defence Forces (UPDF)

The Child Protection Unit (CPU) of the Uganda Peoples Defence Forces (UPDF) was always the first stop centre for the formerly abducted child soldiers in Northern Uganda. Whenever children escaped from the LRA into the villages local leaders or religious leaders would bring them to the barracks[86]The reception centres also would bring the children first to the barracks so that they are officially released to them.[87] At the barracks, children would be handed over to the CPU personnel who are trained in human rights to handle the children. Most of the children interviewed during the field work said that they initially feared the army was going to kill them since the LRA had warned them that the UPDF are non-Ugandans and eat people.[88] However, the warm welcome in the army barracks where returnees would be given water and soap to bathe and wash, first aid to treat the wounded, biscuits and porridge, created trust among them towards the army. V.O. a former child soldier remarked as follows:

> They (army) told me that since I was now out, God has helped me and will continue helping me in the future....they were telling me not to be worried... I am not the only one with such a problem, and that I did not choose to go to the bush... We should also not worry because there is nothing that will happen to us.

The CPU was created within the army specifically to handle returning former child soldiers who were either rescued by the army or escaped from the LRA. The CPU received the children and made them feel safe by promising them security from the LRA.[89] The CPU was also responsible for questioning the children to obtain security information about the LRA. It is this questioning which scared most former child soldiers since at times child soldiers would be required to lead the army

---

[86]Interview with the staff of the Amnesty Commission in 2010.
[87]Owori, A., is a social worker who worked with Gulu Support the Children Organization (GUSCO) to rehabilitate and reintegrate former child soldiers. Interview with Owori was conducted in northern Uganda in January, 2010.
[88]Interview with V.O, one of the members of WACA in Gulu, northern Uganda in February 2010.
[89] Kakurungu is a spokesperson for Uganda Peoples Defence Forces for Northern Uganda. He was interviewed in Gulu in Febraury, 2010.

into the bush to locate the caches of weapons hidden by the LRA. Most child soldiers who were interviewed during the fieldwork pointed out they were too terrified by the experience to consider going back to the bush with the possibility of being re-abducted by the LRA who would have killed them for escaping and betrayal.[90]

The UPDF through the CPU has been blamed for recruiting formerly abducted child soldiers and redeploying them against the LRA; a charge they deny.[91] However, during the field work, one of the former child soldiers said that after his escape from the LRA, he was persuaded by the army officers to join the UPDF where he served for 10 years. He recently deserted the army after his brother was murdered by an LDU (Local Defence Unit).[92] He pointed out that if he had stayed in the army where he had access to a gun, he would have been prompted to take revenge on the person who killed his brother. After questioning the child soldiers, the CPU would hand them over to any of the reception centres for RR. The duration of stay at the CPU was supposed to be 48 hours, however some children deemed to have vital security information would stay longer than 48 hours.

In spite of the criticism levelled at the CPU, it was the first point of psychosocial support provided to former child soldiers since they were assured of security, given first aid, food and clothing which made them trust adults again. Some of the children observed that while in the barracks they were allowed to watch films together with soldiers which changed their perception about the UPDF which had been depicted as killers and foreigners[93] Secondly, since the CPU was working closely with

---

[90] The use of former child soldiers as guides to locate weapons buried by the LRA has always been resisted by most child rights organizations. A Child Rights Advocacy Officer with Save the Children Uganda observed that it was acts like this that led to disagreement between the army and child rights organizations since it amounted use of children in the armed conflict. This interview was conducted in Kampala in March, 2010.

[91] Interview with Lt. Col. Kulayigye, F., Op Cit.,

[92] This former child soldier escaped from the bush only to be lured to join the government army: UPDF. He served in the UPDF for 10 years but when his brother was killed by a Local Defence Unit personnel, he decided to desert the army fearing that he may use the gun at his disposal to revenge the killing. He looks a very bitter and traumatized person who needs psychosocial support. This interview was conducted in northern Uganda in February 2010.

[93] Focus group discussion with former child soldiers of KICA Ber Youth Group IN 2010.

the Amnesty Commission these children were able to access amnesty certificates which entitled them to reintegration packages.[94]

Uganda Human Rights Commission

The Uganda Human Rights Commission (UHRC) was established by the 1995 Constitution of the Republic of Uganda under Article 51. The decision to establish a permanent body to monitor the human rights situation was informed by Uganda's violent political history characterised by arbitrary arrests, detention without trial, and torture with impunity on the part of security organs of government .

Article 52 (1) of the Ugandan Constitution lays down the functions of the UHRC. Some of the functions that directly relate to the RR of former child soldiers are a) To investigate, at its own initiative or on a complaint made by any person or group of persons against the violation of any human rights; b) To establish a continuing programme of research, education and information to enhance respect of human rights; c) To recommend to Parliament effective measures to promote human rights including provision of compensation to victims of violations of human rights, or their families; d) To create and sustain within society the awareness of the provisions of the Constitution as the fundamental law of the people of Uganda; e) To educate and encourage the public to defend this Constitution at all times against all forms of abuse and violation; f) To formulate, implement and oversee programmes intended to inculcate in the citizens of Uganda awareness of their civic responsibilities and an appreciation of their rights and obligations as free people; and g) To monitor Government's compliance with international treaty and conventions on human rights.

Article 52 (2) requires the UHRC to publish periodic reports and submit annual reports to Parliament on the state of human rights and freedoms in the country. The commission has two regional offices in Northern Uganda. The major pre-occupation of the commission has been the investigation of human rights violations committed by individuals and government security forces.[95] The Commission has also been involved in conducting human rights education in the region

---

[94] This was confirmed by Draku, M. Op Cit.,
[95] Interview with an officer of Uganda Human Rights Commission who did not want his identity revealed. Interview was conducted in Kampala in March 2010.

targeting largely the security forces: UPDF and UPF; school children, health workers and local leaders.

The UHRC has not been directly involved in the RR of former child soldiers in Northern Uganda. The commission seems to have left the major task of RR of former child soldiers to the Amnesty Commission, which is legally mandated to implement DDRR of former combatants who include the formerly abducted child soldiers.

However, of particular interest to RR and this book, the UHRC has consistently conducted human rights education targeting the Uganda Peoples Defence Forces (UPDF) and the Uganda Police Force (UPF). Both UPDF and UPF have been directly involved in the conflict in Northern. The UPDF has been particularly involved in the DRR of child soldiers through CPU. The training of the army, police, local leaders, students and school children in human rights has been done through workshops[96] However radio outreach programmes have also been used to reach a wider audience. In 2006 alone, at the time when many abducted children were escaping or being rescued by the army, a total of 20 workshops were organized (UHRC Report, 2006). Most crucially, the UHRC worked closely with the army, the Amnesty Commission, UN agencies and international organizations to lobby the army to establish the Child Protection Unit within the army to handle the returning child soldiers.

The UHRC also continued to be critical of the child soldiering problem in Uganda. The commission, through its mandatory annual reports to Parliament exposed the army's involvement in the recruitment and use of rescued children and other children in auxiliary forces. The UHRC Annual report of 2006 observed that,

Child soldiering continues to be a serious problem in Uganda. A report by the Uganda Parliamentary Form on Children (UPFC) in Northern Uganda estimates that 5,000 children are serving in the UPDF. This report....rejected by Uganda's Minster of State for Defence Hon. Ruth Nankabirwa.... that the UPDF recruitment policy does not allow the recruitment of those under the age of 18. However, UNICEF also reported that no action was taken by the UPDF to release the 1,128 children identified in the LDUs in the year 2005 (UHRC Report, 2006:100).

---

[96]Interview with the Director of Education and Training, Uganda Human Rights Commission in 2010..

Besides conducting human rights education for UPDF and police, the commission has been pressuring the Government of Uganda to comply to international legal commitments including the Convention on the Rights of the Child and United Nations Security Council Resolutions particularly UN Security Council Resolution 1612. The resolution calls upon all parties concerned to ensure that the protection, rights and well being of children affected by the armed conflict are specifically integrated into all peace processes, peace agreements and post-conflict recovery and reconstruction programming. Following exposure by the UHRC and other agencies of the plight of children, the UPDF took steps to implement UN Security Council Resolution 1612. Compliance by the UPDF has been in the form of monitoring human rights violations through its own Human Rights Desk[97]

The UPDF Human Rights Desk monitors the human rights of soldier-to-soldier and soldier to civilian. The UPDF also established the CPU, which assists in the reintegration of former child soldiers and works to rid the army of any children in the ranks of auxiliary forces[98]. The UPDF has also reportedly stopped re-integrating LRA returnees into its ranks since the beginning of 2006 (UHRC Report, 2006). Most crucially, the UHRC, working with UNICEF, Save the Children and United Nations Office of the High Commissioner for Human Rights, have set up a country-wide Monitoring Task Force for monitoring the use of child soldiers in Uganda.

It is should be noted that the UHRC's work in Northern Uganda faces a number of challenges which range from understaffing and underfunding (Human Rights Watch, 2005:54). Besides, UHRC suffers from great political influence by the government. All the UHRC's commissioners are appointed by the president of Uganda and approved by Parliament and have no right of tenure which leaves them vulnerable. At the same time, the war in Northern Uganda seems to be controversial which makes the staff of the commission tread carefully. As Human Rights Watch has observed, the UHRC has made a number of awards of compensation (not for child soldiers though) against the state where about 90% of such awards have not been paid by government (Human Rights Watch, 2005). The point being made here is that lack of

---

[97]Interview with Director of Education and Training, Uganda Human Rights Commission.
[98]Interview with a staff of Save the Children Uganda in 2009.

compliance and enforcement of the UHRC's reports makes the commission's work, including RR of child soldiers, difficult.

Northern Uganda Commonwealth Youth Centre

Northern Uganda Commonwealth Youth Centre is a Government of Uganda initiative supported by the Commonwealth Youth Programme located in Gulu District. The centre which opened with a start up funding of 500,000 Euros, provides vocational and life skills training in brick laying, welding, arts and crafts, tailoring, agriculture and entrepreneurship development; and peace and conflict management skills. Others are HIV/Aids, gender and environment mainstreaming and basic education. According to Tebare, an officer with the centre, the focus of the centre is on young people between 15-25 years mainly from Gulu district but plans to eventually cover the entire Northern Uganda sub-region. The aim is to enable young people outside the school system, especially those from 15 years onwards, to acquire vocational skills.[99] While the centre is expected to benefit former child soldiers, it does not necessarily look out for them. Instead, the centre seeks to serve all the young people in the region since they were all negatively affected by the conflict.[100]

The project was designed to address the challenges of rebuilding Northern Uganda after two decades of a violent conflict which greatly retarded development of the region. It is premised on the understanding that the conflict has affected the youth in many ways: young people in the region have missed the opportunity of formal education; the poverty levels are very high among the youth and the entire population generally and that many of the youths especially former child soldiers are traumatized by the experience of the war[101].

---

[99] Project Hope: Northern Uganda Youth Development. Available at:
http://www.thecommonwealth.org/Internal/152816/152834/177193/project_hope__northern_uganda_youth_development_ce/ . Accessed on 10/5/2010.

[100]Interview with Tebare, L., staff of northern Uganda Youth Centre in Gulu in February, 2010.
[101]Interview with Tebare, Opcit.

The project targets the following categories of people for training:

a. Youth that have missed out on formal education;
b. Youth that have stopped in primary seven;
c. Youth that have stopped in senior four;
d. Youth that have stopped in senior six;
e. Youth that was not able to complete their university education.

The centre which at the moment is still operating below capacity faces a number of challenges. The challenges include lack of adequate funding from both the Government of Uganda and the development partners; lack of electricity and Internet connectivity and lack of transport. The centre also lacks accommodation for the students who are poor which has forced most of them to stay in the deserted semi-permanent houses left behind by the IDPs[102] Finally, the centre is facing an overwhelming demand from many youths who want to acquire vocational skills.[103] The centre which opened its gates in 2007 hopes and that former child soldiers and other youths, all victims of the conflict, will be able to get life-long skills which will help them rebuild their lives and become agents of peace and not agents of destruction (Interview with Tebera). It is against this background that a course in peace education was included on the curriculum for the centre. The centre also provides counselling services which they have outsourced to Watoto Church due to lack of expertise. In terms of enrolment, the centre in 2008 had 70 students; 148 in 2009 while in 2010 the number increased to 300.

While the centre operates below capacity, it is a ray of hope for many youths in Northern Uganda who missed out on education as a result of the conflict. The challenge for the centre is that it is not well funded and lacks infrastructure to meet the current demand. Most of the former child soldiers interviewed view vocational education as the best avenue of bettering their lives. Consequently, a fully operational Northern Uganda Youth and Development Centre is likely to answer the dreams of many desperate youths including former child soldiers.

---

[102] Ibid.
[103] Ibid.

United Nations Development Programme (UNPD)

The UNDP support for the RR of ex-combatants and IDPs human security and peacebuilding in Northern Uganda is being implemented under the Country Programme Action Plan (2006-2010). The Country Programme Action Plan 2006-2010 for Uganda is a five-year framework defining mutual cooperation between the Government of Uganda and the UNDP. Through the Conflict Prevention, Resolution and Recovery component of the country programme, the UNDP is supporting three major areas that if well implemented would enhance effective RR of former child soldiers and other ex-combatants.

The first one is Human Security, peacebuilding and reconciliation. This component is expected to contribute to human security and promoting the conditions for recovery and development. This activity supports DDRR of former combatants in Northern Uganda. UNDP is also supporting the Government of Uganda to address the proliferation of illicit small arms and land mines contamination as well as the Uganda Human Rights Commission's work. UNPD also supported traditional, religious leaders and civil society organizations in Northern Uganda to implement peacebuilding and reconciliation activities.

Further more, the UNDP has continued to work closely with the Ministry of Gender, Labour and Social Development, UNIFEM, UNHCR and UNFPA, UHRC and OHCHR to respond to widespread sexual and gender based violence in Northern Uganda. It is important to mention that women and girls in the war zones suffer disproportionately compared to their male counterparts and may need consistent long term support long after the end of the war. This is consistent with an argument by Pankhurst (2007) who observes that, even when the war ends women continue to be marginalized and discriminated in post-conflict peacebuilding processes. Consequently, there is a need to ensure that reconstruction programmes focus on addressing peculiar challenges, needs and issues of women and girls. By and large, UNDP's work in the RR of former child soldiers remains at policy level and providing funding to other actors directly involved in RR of former child soldiers.

United Nations Children's Fund (UNICEF)

UNICEF is an agency of the United Nations whose major responsibility is to support programs that aid education and the health of children and mothers in developing countries. In Uganda, UNICEF works through collaboration and creating linkages with government ministries, donors, World Bank and local NGOs with similar objectives to support children in areas affected by conflict (Interview with Nsanzugwanko).[104]
In Northern Uganda, UNICEF does its work through:

- Collaboration with government ministries at policy level like the Office of the Prime Minister, Ministries of Gender, Labour and Social Development, Education and Sports, donors and other international agencies that are mandated to handle former child soldiers.
- UNICEF works with World Bank and other agencies like Save the Children Uganda by coordinating all the child protection agencies and liaising with Uganda's Ministry of Gender, Labour and Social Development, which is responsible for child affairs to ensure that social support is provided to the former child soldiers.
- UNICEF has provided funding to local NGOs and CBOs like GUSCO and Kitgum Concerned Women's Association (KIWA) that have been involved in child reception and RR of former child soldiers.
- UNICEF acted as a focal point for child refugees from other countries that neighbour Northern Uganda such as the DRC, Southern Sudan, Chad, and Central Africa Republic. In this case UNICEF links up with MONUC to ensure that child refugees are repatriated and reunited with their families.
- UNICEF, through the Amnesty Commission, ensures that former child soldiers get amnesty and are reintegrated with their families, offered health care, education, protection, food, water and other social care provisions.
- UNICEF has also provided funding to District Local Governments to coordinate the activities of NGOs and CBOs involved with the RR of former child soldiers.

---

[104] Interview with Nsanzugwanko, V., Head of Children Unit at the UNICEF Offices in Kampala in April 2010.

According to Nsunzungwanko, UNICEF in Uganda has keen interest to ensure that after the RR of former child soldiers, government supports their recovery. UNICEF has been deeply engaged in the RR of child soldiers largely through provision of funding and technical support to organizations directly involved, funding government and coordinating other children's rights focused international organizations to ensure that government fulfils its obligations on protection of children's rights.

Unofficial Interventions by International Organizations and Local Non-Governmental Organizations

If there is one overarching lesson to be drawn from the decidedly mixed record of post-conflict interventions since the early 1990s it is that stability cannot be imposed on war-torn societies from the outside (Berdal, 2009:97).

The return of relative peace in Northern Uganda attracted very many organizations which are involved in different peace intervention activities. Research conducted by ACODE found that there are over 2,000 organizations in Northern Uganda.[105] The challenge with such large scale proliferation of organizations (local and international) which are largely externally funded and driven whose programming largely promotes contemporary liberal peacebuilding approaches could further disempower communities that have been traumatizing by two decades of violent conflict. Aware of such a challenge some analysts (Pugh et al, 2008:390) have observed that peacebuilding practices need political roots in local societies, and political communities should have the freedom to set their economic priorities including protection of economic activities from negative effects of global integration.

This section focuses on the unofficial peacebuilding interventions in respect to RR of former child soldiers in Northern Uganda that have been carried out by international organizations, local NGOs and CBOs. The section begins by examining the interventions of international organizations.

---

[105]Bigirwa, E & Komakech, L., Profiles of NGOs and CBOs Involved in the Implementation of the Peace, Recovery and Development Plan (PRDP) for Northern Uganda.ACODE Policy Research Series (Forthcoming).

International Organizations

World Vision Uganda and Children of War Rehabilitation Centre

World Vision Uganda is part of the World Vision global partnership and therefore functions in partnership with World Vision offices across the world (Interview with Obilu Akol).[106] World Vision is a Christian relief, development and advocacy organization dedicated to working with children, families and communities to overcome poverty and injustice. Its work in Uganda started in 1986 at the time when the rebels of the National Resistance Army (NRA) were fighting the government in Luwero Triangle central Uganda (1981-86) which brought President Museveni to power.[107] World Vision moved to Northern Uganda in 1988 to provide relief to the IDPs at the time the LRA rebellion was starting.

Following an upsurge of abducted children escaping and others rescued by the army, World Vision established *The World Vision Children of War Rehabilitation Centre* in 1995. The centre has two components: the Children Rehabilitation Centre and the Community Sensitization Programme. At the height of insurgence, the centre had a maximum of 520 children staying there. When the centre opened; its aim was to help de-traumatize and enhance the psychosocial status of children and young people returning from LRA captivity. According to Obilu-Akol, the opening of this centre was a pioneering work of World Vision on an international scale since there was no blue print anywhere else to copy from.[108] Whenever children were received, their records would be made and entered in a confidential manner for purposes of helping in the family tracing processes. Parents would be notified and invited on the radio to come and meet their children and talk to them in confidence in temporary huts that were built at the centre.

The centre has the following objectives: to provide accommodation to formerly abducted children away from the conflict; to provide health rehabilitation to war-affected children through provision of medical care, nutritional rehabilitation, provision of safe drinking water and basic

---

[106]Interview with Obilu Akol, B., Manager, World Vision Children of War Rehabilitation Centre in Gulu in January 2010).
[107]World Vision in Uganda. Available at:
http://www.worldvision.org.uk/server.php?show=nav.1652 Accessed on 11/5/2010.
[108]Interview with Obilu-Akol J. B., an officer with World Vision Uganda. The interview was conducted in Gulu in March, 2010.

clothing and bedding; to provide psychosocial support, partly through counselling to help overcome their emotional and psychological negative experiences; to contribute to their psychological and emotional recovery by offering recreational activities; provide vocational training in such locally marketable skills as bicycle repairing, tailoring, carpentry and farming; and to resettle the children after the completion of their term at the centre, a process preceded by family tracing, community preparation and training of community voluntary counsellors for follow up and care[109].

Accordingly, World Vision realized from the onset that it would not be possible to counsel children who were tired, sick and hungry. Consequently, food, clothes and medical care were provided to children as soon as they came in.

According to the staff of World Vision, the treatment of physical wounds of the children was instrumental in winning their trust. Whenever children arrived at the centre they would be given full medical check up at Lacor or Gulu Hospital or at a health clinic. It was noted that some of the children had broken bones or open wounds from gun shots. Others were undernourished, tired, and weary and with no hope at all. It is noted that returing children looked scared, would be quiet and did not look to be free. Consequently, World Vision sought to make them feel free, loved and cared for. Some had diarrhoea and scabies which had to be treated. They were also given health education to care about their hygiene. Most girls who had spent a long time in the bush had sexually transmitted diseases (STDs) (World Vision, 2001)[110].

The centre provided psychosocial support using several means. Art and talking therapy are some of the psychosocial supports that were used. This is where children were encouraged to share their stories through drawings and talking. Interpersonal therapy is another psychosocial support World Vision used. This is a sixteen week therapy for groups of children aged between 14-17 years assisted by a counsellor and is done in schools. After 16 weeks, a general assessment of trauma is conducted facilitated by a facilitator. Here children are helped to come up with their own plans. This is one-to-one counselling where a

---

[109]Interview with Obilu-Akol as staff of *The World Vision Children of War Rehabilitation Centre in 2010.*
[110]World Vision (2001). Peace and Reconciliation for the Children of War: Healing Wounds in Northern Uganda.

counsellor engages the child to talk about his/her experiences. This helps the child to re-establish their sense of self and interests. Another method used is the Post Cards Therapy. This was done by arranging correspondence between one group of former child soldiers in Uganda and a group of students in Boston in USA through exchanging post cards. This was done to help establish friendship and for others to appreciate what problems these children went through. At the moment, twinning is done between schools in Gulu municipality and those in the villages.

World Vision has a future plan of using this approach to start exchange visits between schools in western and central Uganda and those in the north. Prayer therapy was also used at World Vision. At the World Vision Children of War Rehabilitation Centre, children were exposed to the Christian teachings which emphasised love and forgiveness of Jesus Christ. Emphasizing Christian values of forgiveness helped to restore trust, hope and confidence among the former child soldiers who had committed crimes such as killing their friends and relatives in the bush.[111] Other psychosocial supports involved use of traditional music, dance, drama, watching selected videos and drawings.

According to Obilu-Akol, most children that passed through World Vision were brought in by the army. In order to improve the situation of the children in the hands of the military, World Vision worked with other civil society organizations to influence the army to create a special unit to receive child soldiers. Consequently, the Children Protection Unit (CPU) was created which worked closely with reception centres in the RR of former child soldiers. World Vision had a first aid clinic with nurses but would refer serious medical cases to Lacor, Gulu Independent and Gulu hospitals. World Vision also reached an agreement with Kampala International Hospital for specialized treatment.

Since these children had missed schooling, World Vision felt that for them to reintegrate fully in society, they needed some life skills. Consequently, World Vision identified vocational schools to train children who passed through the centre. Agreements were entered with vocational training schools and tuition paid. Courses offered included brick laying, carpentry and joinery, and tailoring among others. These would last up to 6 months. Graduates were awarded certificates and tools

---

[111]Interview with officials at the World Vision Children's War Rehabilitation Centre in Gulu in January 2010.

procured for them. Young children were enrolled for formal education in primary schools[112]

At World Vision, counsellors carried out regular assessments of former child soldier's progress. Once the centre was convinced that children were ready physically and psychologically, a preparatory visit would be made to their families and the communities to prepare them receive their children. As part of re-unification with families, children were given bedding, clothes, foodstuffs, seeds and farming instruments. World Vision worked closely with the Amnesty Commission to enable these children get amnesty certificates. Obilu-Akol, observed that follow up visits are organized to find out how the children are coping. However, most former child soldiers interviewed complain of lack of follow up by reception centres. One former child soldier A.J. who was already an adult of 21 years when interviewed observed that:

> I was abducted in 2003 together with my brothers. The rebels killed my brothers in front of me claiming this would make me a brave soldier. I escaped when we were attacked by the UPDF and came back home. The rebels followed me back home and burnt our house when we were sleeping. I escaped with serious burns on my body. I was referred to World Vision where I spent six months undergoing counselling. When they finally took me back home they promised to come back to assist me since I needed a specialized operation at Mulago Hospital. They have never come back.

In the course of RR of former child soldiers, World Vision has faced a number of challenges. First there is the problem of parents' rejection of their daughters who came back with children fathered by rebel commanders. After being rehabilitated by the centre these young mothers and their children were rejected by their families who say are ready to receive their daughters and not their children. An example of such young mothers is A.R. 29 years with five children. A.R. was abducted in 1994 and spent 14 years in the bush as a wife of a rebel commander. She escaped with four children and has since coming back produced a fifth child. Her family refused to take her in with her children. She is currently living in Gulu town where she is struggling to bring up her children as a single mother.

---

[112]Interview with Obilu-Akol, Ibid.

The second challenge relates to funding the education of children who were enrolled in vocational and primary schools since some have no parents while others have parents who are very poor. Most former child soldiers want to study and they look at World Vision as their parent. World Vision also faced the challenge of reintegrating children whose parents were killed and whose relatives sold off their land. Obilu-Akol observed that:

> Some former child soldiers came back and found that their parents had died and their land had been sold off by relatives and as such these have nowhere to go. We decided to refer such cases to the local leaders and the traditional leaders.

World Vision rehabilitated and reintegrated a total of about 14,034 former child soldiers (World Vision, Report 2001) and because of its Christian orientation it could not support traditional rituals and ceremonies although they were never opposed outright.

Box 1: Overview of Counselling Approaches in Reception Centres
World Vision
- Guilt and shame seen as signs of low self-esteem
- Group counselling; discussion on peace; reconciliation; and forgiveness
- Individual counselling; non-judgemental, allowing emotions to surface
- Christian teaching
- Talking therapy
- Use of music, dance and drama
- Use of games and sports.

GUSCO
- Mental well-being assessed through observation of interaction: withdrawal is seen as sign of trauma
- Length of stay at the centre much debated: no consensus on desirable length, decided on case by case basis
- Time spent at GUSCO is influenced by the child's physical, social and emotional well-being
- Children encouraged to talk to social workers about any problems
- Staff try to create a non-judgemental atmosphere of trust.

CPA
- Take away feelings of guilt, suggesting that time with LRA was in a different life
- Clients are told that even after all that happened, they still have the capacity to have a good life

225

- Girls tend to keep quiet during group sessions
- Counsellors find it difficult to assess the individual's progress in group sessions
- Group counselling is playful/using games
- Child soldiers taught basic behavioural skills because these are adults who have the capacity of children.

Save the Children in Uganda

Save the Children in Uganda is part of the world wide Save the Children. It is an independent children's charity. Save the Children in Uganda started supporting the RR of child soldiers in Northern Uganda in 1994. According to Mucurezi, a Child Rights Advocacy Officer, Save the Children was not directly involved in the RR of former child soldiers. Rather, its involvement was in the form of support to Gulu Support the Children Organization (GUSCO), a community based organization based in Gulu. Save the Children provided technical and financial support to GUSCO. It also supported the staff of GUSCO to get training in counselling. Technical experts were brought into the country from Denmark and other countries to assist GUSCO to receive, treat, rehabilitate and reintegrate former child soldiers at the peak of their return.

The organization also engaged a consultant to conduct an assessment of trauma and how trauma was being addressed. The consultant discovered a number of weaknesses including the fact that clinical aspects of trauma were not being treated. The findings were useful in reviewing the psychosocial support that was being offered to children in Northern Uganda[113]. Save the children raised funds that were used to build the office block of GUSCO and provided approximately 90% of GUSCO's overall budget. Beyond the support to GUSCO, Save the Children in Uganda was involved in lobbying and advocacy for children's rights at policy level. For example, working with other organizations Save the Children lobbied the army to establish the Children Protection Unit (CPU) to professionally handle the returning children.

Mucurezi also noted that Save the Children in Uganda, in partnership with other institutions such as UNICEF, UHRC and UNDP, influenced

---

[113]Interview with Mucurezi, D., a Child Rights Advocacy Officer, Save the Children at their offices in Kampala in March, 2010.

the army to provide first aid treatment to children at its military hospital. Save the Children Uganda also lobbied the army to conduct questioning of rescued children in the presence of a social worker and that such questioning should be done outside the barracks to provide a friendly environment to the children. The work of Save the Children in Uganda was sometimes risky. It was for example noted that some soldiers who developed interest in the young women who were returning from the bush would at times want to retain them in the barracks. Mucurezi for example narrated that:

> There was an incident involving a former high ranking LRA officer who surrendered and was absorbed in the government army called Brigadier Banya. Banya picked a girl among the returnees and took her into the barracks claiming she was his wife. The matter went to the President and finally Save the Children went into the barracks and brought out the girl. [114]

Save the Children Uganda faced a number of challenges in their support for the RR of former child soldiers. First, it was risky since it involved dealing directly with the army's handling of children's rights. Secondly, its support to GUSCO which was directly involved in the RR of former child soldiers caused resentment by communities[115]GUSCO used to give former child soldiers a package of farm implements, seeds and bedding as part of the reintegration process.

At the moment, Save the Children in partnership with UNICEF, GUSCO and World Vision Uganda have developed a standby project for the RR of child soldiers who are still in the bush. The organization has also trained staff in RR who would be used to conduct the RR process should the LRA release children.

Caritas Gulu and RR of War affected Children/Child Soldiers

Caritas Gulu is part of Caritas International, which is a Social Services and Development Department arm of the Catholic Church. Through Caritas, the Church plays a pertinent role in advocating for and

---

[114] Ibid.
[115]Interview with Mucurezi, Opcit.

promotion of social justice and positive change[116]. Caritas Gulu has three main areas of focus: Provision of Social Services; Relief and Rehabilitation and Livelihoods and Development.

According to Rubangakene, Caritas Gulu opened up a reception centre in 2001 and started training communities to prepare them to receive the abducted children who were escaping or were being rescued by the army in large numbers. Caritas also started a Community Psychosocial Based Approach programme to train community leaders. This was done through the Church structures throughout Acholi sub-region. Caritas focused mainly on re-unification issues of children with their families dealing with issues of stigma and resentment of children. The trained community leaders were and are still responsible for follow up on re-unification challenges and report to Caritas. Caritas also provided medical care to sick children by partnering with established hospitals with whom they signed Memoranda of Understanding. These hospitals are Dr. Ambrozori Hospital; St. Joseph Hospital in Kitgum and Locor Hospital in Gulu. Caritas RR process included family tracing; preparation of the children and community for re-unification; re-union; and follow up visits.

Rubangakene noted that some children were brought to Caritas by the army, cultural leaders and religious leaders. Some children walked directly from the bush to the centre. Rubangakene observed that:

> On arrival, the staff would welcome children and assure them of safety from any harm. They would be given soap for bathing and washing, food, tooth paste, a mattress, a blanket and a place to sleep. Caritas deliberately avoided setting rules for the children in order to build trust and confidence.

Caritas provided food to child soldiers and in order to avoid suspicion of poisoning since they were programmed like that in the bush, their staff would also eat with them. As part of RR programming Caritas Gulu realized that systematic follow up visits to the reintegrated children was crucial for effective re-union with families and communities. Through these visits, Caritas is able to assess how the reintegrated former child soldiers are coping. Major RR activities implemented by Caritas include;

---

[116]Rubangakene, is a Manager of Caritas- Gulu and was interviewed in Kampala in April 2010.

provision of education support which involved establishment of Pajule Vocational Training School supported by the Austrian Government; facilitating dialogues at community level to improve community relations between returnees and communities, which had been severed by the conflict; support to agricultural livelihoods where social support groups are supported. These groups dig together as it was in the olden days; supporting community healing practices to handle post-traumatic stress disorder. This is done by supporting traditional ceremonies such as *Mato Oput* and stepping on the egg. Caritas has facilitated the burial of 400 bodies and construction of monuments where mass murders took place. This has helped the perpetrators to ask for forgiveness.

According to the staff of Caritas Gulu, a number of challenges confront effective RR of former child soldiers in Northern Uganda. The first challenge relates to the guilty consciences among former child soldiers since most of them were forced to committed atrocities against the communities among whom they have been reintegrated.[117] The second challenge is that most former child soldiers lack a cultural base since they missed out some stages of development where they would be grounded in the cultural norms. The third challenge is that most of the children think they belong to institutions which are providing them with assistance and not the families and communities. This makes the communities feel that organizations like Caritas Gulu are undermining their traditional roles. The fourth challenge is that special interventions to assist these children are creating divisions and resentment of former child soldiers by the society where over 70% of the population were internally displaced and are equally needy (Finnstrom, 2005:110).

The Caritas staff recommended that the RR interventions should target all the disadvantaged persons in the community rather than singling out former child soldiers. Caritas staff further recommended that child mothers have a unique problem and should be specifically targeted for RR. Caritas staff also noted that there is a need to coordinate and regulate NGO and CBO interventions that are causing divisions and duplication of services. Finally, Caritas staff observed that interventions should be designed in a way that does not create perpetual dependence of former child soldiers and target communities on external assistance. It was noted that at the moment some people have made charity a business

---

[117] Interview with Rubangakene, Op Cit., He said that guilt experienced by these children was a major obstacle to their RR processes since they think that society knows the crimes they committed.

with some belonging to more than one group. Caritas reception centre received, cared for, reintegrated and rehabilitated 3,056 formerly abducted child soldiers[118]

Local NGOs and Community Based Organizations

It should be noted that at the time of conducting field work there were almost over 2,000 local NGOs and CBOs in Northern Uganda implementing peacebuilding initiatives, which have both direct and indirect impact on the RR of former child soldiers (Bigirwa et al. (2009).[119] Key local organizations considered relevant for this book are examined below. It should also be noted that while these organizations are considered local, they are funded by external donors and their programmes are externally influenced. Most crucially, because of external donor dependence, most of these local organizations lack long-term sustainability as the proceding discussion shows.

Gulu District NGO Forum

Gulu District NGO Forum is an umbrella organization for Non-Governmental Organizations, Community Based Organizations and Faith-Based Organizations operating in Gulu District in Northern Uganda. Gulu District NGO Forum is a member of the National NGO Forum, which is the national umbrella organization based in Kampala. Gulu District NGO Forum has been implementing several peacebuilding initiatives including the RR of former child soldiers. These projects and activities are discussed below.

The Justice and Reconciliation project which started in 2004 was implemented in partnership with Liu Institute for Global Issues. Through research and advocacy Gulu District NGO Forum worked to create understanding among the policy makers about the interests, needs, concerns and views of the communities: particularly the youths (including former child soldiers), IDPs, traditional leaders and women that have been affected by the conflict. Through this project the organization was able to give a voice to the affected people to influence

---

[118]Interview with Rubangakene
[119] Bigirwa, E. & Komakech, L., Op Cit.,

policy makers in government and the international community to respond to their needs. Key areas of advocacy that have been articulated under this project include: issues and difficulties of RR of former combatants; understanding the traditional justice practices; documenting the experiences of communities who suffered major atrocities and investigating the moral and judicial complexities of abductees who are both victims and perpetrators.

The research under this project was intended to foster the attainment of justice and reconciliation. The research publications under this project have been widely disseminated through policy dialogues and workshops, radio debates and on the Internet.[120]

Since 2006, the organization has also been implementing *The Youth Leadership Project* which aims at addressing the challenges faced by the youth in Northern Uganda. The project also seeks to build the capacity of young people to constructively engage in policy discussions on rebuilding their society by supporting leadership training and capacity building to strengthen grassroots youth groups. The project has implemented the following activities:

a.   Provision of University Scholarships to disadvantaged war affected youth in Acholi sub-region. Since its inception, the project secured 50 scholarships for students to pursue university education. These scholarships are given to the very needy students who would never have joined the university without such support.

b.   Grants to Youth Groups and other Organizations. The organization realized that several youth groups of either former child soldiers or civilian youths that have been formed in the district were not attracting funding from government or donors. Under this project, these groups have been empowered by provision of grants to implement their activities. About US$24,108 has been sub-granted to 20 youth groups in the districts of Gulu, Amuru, Kitgum and Pader.

c.   Capacity Building of Youth Groups and Other Organizations. This component of the project is aimed at equipping youths with life skills in leadership and governance issues, project planning and management, and rights based approach to development.

---

[120] Interview with Okello, R., Programme Officer, Gulu District NGO Forum conducted in Gulu in February 2010.

Currently, over 40 youth groups have benefited from this training.

Another project that was implemented by Gulu District NGO Forum was *The Acholi Youth Strengthening Strategy Project*. The project goal was to promote the rights of Acholi youth and ensure their participation in decision making in reconstruction processes. The project mobilized youths into groups; trained youth groups including former child soldiers in conflict management, human rights, leadership skills and record keeping. The organization also built office premises for two youth groups in Gulu and Amuru districts. It also established a live radio debate platform on Radio King for the youth to champion their issues including the plight of former child soldiers[121].

Gulu Support the Children Organizations (GUSCO)

GUSCO was an indigenous NGO established in 1994 working to promote the well-being of war affected children in Northern Uganda through provision of psychosocial support, capacity building of communities, education, advocacy and peacebuilding. With support from Save the Children and DANIDA, GUSCO established its first reception centre in 1997. GUSCO ran a programme on RR of former child soldiers since its inception as a reception centre. In the RR of former child soldiers, GUSCO employed two broad strategies: A reception centre-based rehabilitation for the formerly abducted people/children where they are received, provided with the physical needs (food, medical treatment, clothes, a blanket and a mattress) and psychological rehabilitation and community based reintegration which strengthened the capacity of communities to support RR processes.

According to Owor, a social worker at GUSCO, child soldiers would be received from the Child Protection Unit of the army. Medical treatment for those who were sick or with bullet wounds would be provided. GUSCO also provided them food, clothes, a blanket, mattress and eating utensils. They were assured that the LRA will not be able to re-abduct them and harm them again. While at GUSCO, children were given counselling which was mainly based on a Western model of one-on-one counselling, talking therapy, playing games, music dance and

---

[121]Interview with Okello, Ibid.

drama. GUSCO was also open to both models of psychosocial support: Western and traditional rituals and sometimes the approaches would be used in combination[122]. The duration of the stay at the centre depended on the period the child would have spent in captivity.[123] According to Owor, the returnees who had stayed in the bush longer had serious psychosocial problems and had to stay longer at the centre undergoing rehabilitation. In addition to counselling of former child soldiers, GUSCO provided the following support: basic skills in tailoring for girls; basic skills in bicycle repair, carpentry and bricklaying for boys and young men.

According to Okeny, Programme Manager, GUSCO, the re-unification of children with their families and communities was always systematically organized. The first step was family tracing which relied heavily on use of radio announcements and programmes where parents would be invited to meet their children at the centre. This was followed by sensitization of families and communities to create a conducive environment for reintegration. Families would be advised how to relate to and to support children rather than stigmatizing them. Former child soldiers were given some package to take home during the reintegration processes. The staff at GUSCO observed that following the RR of former child soldiers, GUSCO staff has continued to organize follow up visits to their homes and IDPs to assess how they are managing. However, during the fieldwork most of the former child soldiers who were interviewed complained that most reception centres including GUSCO and World Vision no longer visit them.

Concerned Parents Association (CPA)

Concerned Parents Association (CPA) is a child advocacy organisation with activities in Gulu, Amuru, Kitgum, Oyam and Lira. It was established in 1996 by a group of parents after the abduction of 139 students from Aboke Girls Secondary School. CPA has four main programmes:

a.   Livelihood Programme - According to Simon Okello, a programme officer, through the Livelihood Programme, CPA

---

[122] Interview with Owor, A., who worked as a Social Worker with GUSCO,

supports parents and youth groups of former child soldiers to start income generating activities to improve their livelihoods. CPA also provides grinding machines, oxen and ox-ploughs, goats and pigs. Follow up visits are carried out to monitor and provide technical support to youth and community groups.

b. Child protection Programme - This programme involves RR of former child soldiers in social aspects using music, dance drama and training in cultural practices.CPA works closely with Ker Kwaro Acholi, the Acholi cultural institution to organize cultural festivals as well as radio programmes on issues of reconciliation and forgiveness (Interview with Okello).

c. Peacebuilding Programme - Under this programme, CPA uses elders to speak on matters of culture on radio stations. It also organises dialogues on topical issues facing RR and peace in the region. CPA works with government child protection committees and Secretaries for Children's Affairs at the local government levels to advocate for children's rights.

d. Parent Support Programme - CPA supports Parent Support Groups through a community structure using people who have been trained to provide psychosocial support to formerly abducted child soldiers. The organization also provides counselling and follow-up activities to the children who were rehabilitated and reintegrated. CPA has trained parents groups in psychosocial support skills such as trauma handling, basic counselling, and training on non-violence and conflict management. The parents replicate these trainings and carry out follow up and referrals in some cases especially for those former child soldiers with bullet wounds and splints on their bodies[124].

CPA uses both Western and traditional approaches of psychosocial support. Where aggression is a problem with a particular case, CPA counsellors use the Western approach. Traditional mechanisms are applied to enhance healing. Comparatively, Okello observed that they have found traditional psychosocial support in the RR of former child soldiers to be more relevant than the Western approach because people identify with it culturally. He also noted that sometimes there is a conflict between parents and children over which approach to use. He however, pointed out that most children with Christian influence prefer Western approaches. Okello gave an example where a particular child had a strong

---

[124]Interview with Okello, Op cit.

disagreement with the parents over what psychosocial approach should be applied on her. While the child preferred the Western counselling and a Christian prayer, the parents wanted *Mato Oput*. About 7,000 children have benefited from CPA's interventions.

War-Affected Children Association (WACA)

WACA was formed in 2002 and registered as an NGO in 2004. It operates in three Sub-Counties of Awach, Lalogi and Patiko in Gulu district. The main objective of WACA is to provide economic empowerment to the formerly abducted children through training in resource mobilization, project planning and management. [125] The specific objectives of WACA are: to improve the quality of life of former child soldiers by providing resources and opportunities; to provide psychosocial support to children/youth formerly associated with armed groups; helping former child soldiers to achieve their potential through provision of education. Founded by former child soldiers, WACA realized that the external assistance provided to them for their RR was not enough and not sustainable. WACA staff also observed that most of their members who were trained in vocational skills lacked business skills, yet economic empowerment is important for their successful RR.

WACA mobilized its members into groups where they make weekly savings. Groups meet weekly where each member contributes Ug.Shs.1,000($.46 cents at the time) . At the time of conducting the field work, there were three active groups of 30 members each. Since 2007 when the Savings and Credit Scheme started the association has bought three ox-ploughs and 12 oxen which have been distributed in three sub-counties in Gulu. The association has also provided seeds such as groundnuts, maize and beans to the groups.[126] Groups draw a weekly time table to follow for their meetings and write down the minutes which were accessed by the researcher.

According to the group leaders, WACA got funding from the ICC *Trust Fund for Victims* channelled to them through Care International to start a project called HOPE. HOPE project has two components: economic empowerment and vocational training. According to V.O., a member of WACA the association has used this support to train 50 war

---

[125]Interview with O.N. a programme officer of WACA.
[126]Interview with members of WACA.

victims mostly child mothers and young men in tailoring, carpentry, catering and brick making. Some of them are still undergoing training in various vocational schools in Northern Uganda.

WACA is providing psychosocial counselling to former child soldiers in the three sub-counties. According to V.O., counselling focuses on domestic violence; group counselling for women who came back with children; peer counselling and child counselling. The association uses the following methods of psychosocial support: drama which involves the victims dramatizing the effects of the civil war and traditional dances. The traditional dances involve mixing victims and non-victims together in performance. This is expected to give victims a sense of being loved, togetherness and belonging to the society.

WACA is currently offering psychosocial support to 300 former child soldiers and 600 community members. Accordingly, WACA has found out that some people who were not abducted but suffered in different ways during the war are also traumatized and need assistance. Consequently, the association has opened its doors to reach out to a wider community beyond its members. Targeting the community as a whole has helped create harmony between former child soldiers and the community and fostered smooth reintegration[127]

Members of WACA observed during fieldwork that most of them are engaged in economic activities where they are earning some income. One of the members, O.D. 24 years, observed that:

> These days we no longer beg for school fees, food and clothes as we used to do.[128] Since we have money we can even afford to change our diet. I mean we can afford to buy meat or fish on some days.

During the group discussion members also noted that their dressing has changed since they can afford to buy new clothes. They no longer save Ug.Shs.1,000 ($.46 cents at the time) per week as they used to do. Instead, each person saves Ug.Shs.2,000 ($.91 cents at the time) since their incomes have increased[129].

---

[127]Interview with V.O a member of WACA.
[128] Interview with a group member of WACA, an association of former child soldiers conducted in Gulu in February 2010.
[129]Interview with members in a group discussion.

WACA is supporting some of its members in secondary and vocational schools by paying school fees and accommodation. The association plans to establish war documentation centres in Gulu, Teso, Lango and southern Sudan to remind people about the horrors of war so thatthe future generations can avoid war[130]

Ker Kwaro Acholi

Ker Kwaro Acholi is the Acholi Cultural Institution which is the custodian of Acholi cultural values and practices.[131]. Ker Kwaro Acholi has been actively engaged in various peace processes in Northern Uganda. In respect of the RR of former child soldiers, Ker Kwaro has been centrally involved in organizing traditional rituals and cleansing ceremonies such as *Mato Oput* and stepping on the eggs to reintegrate children into society. As an apex Acholi cultural organization, Ker Kwaro Acholi is responsible for spearheading the revival of traditional approaches of conflict resolution and reconciliation in the RR of former child soldiers.

According to Avola, traditional ceremonies are credited for psychologically enhancing children's acceptance by society. Ker Kwaro Acholi has organized traditional ceremonies where traditional leaders and children in a particular community take part. The endorsement of traditional cleansing ceremonies by Ker Kwaro Acholi made it possible for other traditional leaders at the lower level to perform these ceremonies for the returning children. Ker Kwaro has been funding traditional ceremonies performed by cultural leaders across Acholi sub-region.

Ker Kwaro continues to organize traditional ceremonies presided over by the Paramount Chief Ben Acan which helped returnees to know that their leaders care.[132] Ker Kwaro has also organized training for Community Volunteer Care Givers. With funding from NUTI (Northern Uganda Transition Initiative), Ker Kwaro has been organizing ceremonies and rituals to cleanse returning children, for purifying areas that were polluted by mass killings which included reburying the remains of the people who were killed during the war but could not get a decent

[130]Interview with WACA members.
[131] Avola, M., is the Coordinator of Ker Kwaro Acholi, the Acholi apex cultural institution. Avola was interviewed in his office in Gulu in February 2010.
[132]Interview with Avola, Ibid.

burial to transit peacefully to the next world. These rituals and ceremonies entail slaughtering of sheep, goats and chicken as sacrifices to appease the dead. According to Avola the cultural ceremonies commonly performed by Ker Kwaro Acholi are: stepping on the egg and *Mato Oput* ceremonies. These are examined in detail in Chapter Six.

Ker Kwaro Acholi is still a weak institution having been restored in 1993 when the current government in Uganda restored cultural institutions that had been abolished in 1966. Most important to note is that the institution has been severely weakened by the two decades of a violent conflict which makes it difficult for it to respond appropriately to community needs. The traditional leaders who are supposed to be the custodians of culture, the Rwods, were also internally displaced and became poor like everybody else which made them lose respect in society. According to Avola, in an effort to boost the role of traditional leaders; government has provided iron sheets, hydra form machines as well as cement for construction of their houses.

During fieldwork, it was established that reception centres and CBOs were using both the traditional and indigenous resources and the Western psychosocial approaches in the RR of former child soldiers. The Coordinator of Ker Kwaro Acholi the apex cultural institution pointed out that the institution found great value by using both the traditional and indigenous resources and the Western approaches during the RR of former child soldiers. Avola pointed out that on a balancing scale, the traditional and indigenous resources were more culturally relevant and sustainable than the Western approach. He, however, noted that since society in Northern Uganda has significantly changed overtime partly as a result of the conflict, which has undermined the cultural values and Western values, it would be good to blend both the traditional and Western approaches. He for instance observed that the advantage with the Western approaches of psychosocial support is that they have a variety of skills that can be applied while the traditional approaches are limited in options.

Gulu War Affected Children Training Centre

Gulu War Affected Children Training Centre was started in 2005. The main objective of the centre was to assist young women who are former child soldiers acquire life time skills to improve their welfare. According to Laham, the Director, the centre started with only five young mothers who were trained in tailoring. By 2006, the centre had enrolled 60 trainees 12 of who were funded by World Vision Uganda. The rest of the trainees were trained free of charge. With the money from the 12 trainees, the centre was able to buy furniture and uniform for the trainees to 'look smart like other students'. Laham, who is a professional designer, used to work alone in the centre for no pay. In 2008 the South African Ambassador visited the centre. The officials were impressed by the work of the centre and decided to donate 10 sewing machines. They also donated a container for storing the sewing machines. The Ambassador also promised to link the centre with a South African company, Eskom to construct a classroom block.

Consequently, Eskom provided funding which was used to build a training centre which currently accommodates offices and four classrooms. Besides training the war affected girls and young women in tailoring skills; the centre also offers training in catering, hair dressing and languages - French, Swahili and Luo. To date the centre has trained over 250 formerly abducted girls and plans to open up rural outreach branches to reach many girls. The Director of the Centre, Laham was herself a victim of the LRA conflict. Both of her parents were killed by the LRA. She first worked with GUSCO as a trainer and when her contract with GUSCO ended, girls followed her to her home and that is how the centre was born. The centre still lacks reasonable funding to pay the teachers' salaries, which makes it dependent on the founder and a few volunteers[133].

KICA Ber Youth Group (Forgiveness is Good)

KICA Ber Youth Group is one of the vivid examples that demonstrate the relevance of traditional and local resources in the RR of former child soldiers which is the focus of this research. KICA Ber Youth Group was formed by seven formerly abducted child soldiers. The overall objective of the group is to unite all formerly abducted youths to rebuild their lives and develop themselves. The group runs a savings and loan scheme for its registered members. It also assists members who are HIV victims by digging, planting crops and building houses for them. The group

---

[133] Interview with Laham, Director, Gulu War Affected Children Training Centre in 2010.

members are also involved in music dance and drama which is intended to mobilize the members and sensitize communities about the plight of former child soldiers and fight stigma.[134] The group carries out training on sexual and gender based violence to promote peaceful co-existence and harmonious living. The group also conducts mine risk education among the community having received training from a Canadian Organization called CIPA (Canadian, Physicians for Aid and Relief).[135]

During the interview with group members they pointed out that the group received assistance from the Window Trust in the form of sponsorship for six members to pursue secondary school education. Some of the members were trained in tailoring by World Vision Uganda. O.D., one of the founder members of KICA Ber, is married with 3 children, runs a retail shop and a piggery project with 10 pigs. He was abducted when he was in primary seven. Since his return from the bush, he returned to school and completed his Ordinary Level Certificate.

In a focus group discussion with the members of KICA Ber Youth Group who are 61 in number, it was noted that that they have greatly benefited from the group. They explained that the group has been able to protect their members from stigmatization by community members. Members have been able to start businesses with loans provided by the group. Members also observed that belonging to the group earns them respect in society since they are seen as being productive. Through the group, some members have been trained in counselling and are helping other members who are still traumatized to cope. Fifteen members of KICA Ber Youth Group participated in a group discussion. The group had about ten male and five female. The interview took place at the association's offices which gave them confidence to participate freely.

On the downside, the members of the group pointed out that the community sees them as beneficiaries of violence since they have attracted some funding which other community members do not have. The group reported that they are still traumatized by the community who call them demeaning names such as rebels, wives of rebels and returnees. Some young women who are married complain that community members tell their husbands that 'you are married to a rebel' which sometimes leads to marriages breaking down. Also, several abductees

---

[134]Interview with O.G member of KICA Ber.
[135]Interview with O.D a founder member of KICA Ber Youth Group at their offices in Gulu in February 2010.

came back with children and most of these children face resentment from the young mother's parents which affects their mothers psychologically as they cannot discard their children.

During the focus group discussion, it was revealed that former child soldiers who passed through the reception centres face less resentment by their families and communities than those who came directly home. The reason is that the reception centres organized re-unions and traditional ceremonies which become a basis for community acceptance. Most of the group members felt that traditional ceremonies were more effective than Western counselling. Commenting on the problems of the Western counselling that involved one-on-one conversation with a counsellor, 20 years old G.O. observed that:

In the case of Western counselling, counsellors treat you like a child which is humiliating to someone.

A small number of former child soldiers during the interviews felt that Western counselling was more helpful to them while others felt a combination of Western and traditional ceremonies worked well for them.

Can Rwede Peke Group

Can Rwede Peke Group comprise of 25 former child soldiers who are now adults. The group operates a village credit and savings scheme. The group meets every Sunday afternoon to discuss issues that affect them and matters related to their credit and saving scheme. Each member of the group contributes Ug. Shs.200 ($.091 cents) every Sunday as a welfare fund. In addition, each member contributes a minimum of Ug. Shs. 500 ($.23 cents) per meeting which takes place once every week. A maximum of Ug. Shs.2,500 (US$1.12) is payable per week by members who are able. Members are allowed to borrow money at an interest rate of 10% per month[136].

During a facilitated group discussion, the members raised a number of challenges they face. These challenges include: lack of school fees for members who want to undertake vocational training courses in tailoring, bricklaying and carpentry. Child mothers who came back with children from the bush are worried about the future of children's education since they lack money to pay school fees. Some members complained that

---

[136]Interview with members during the group discussion.

many people come to them promising assistance, take their photos and never come back. Some of the child mothers are still bitter about the experience of forced marriages in the bush, which ruined their lives. Some members observed that they still live in fear of being re-abducted and killed by the LRA while others pointed out that they experience bad dreams about killings they witnessed in the bush.

One of the testimonies was given by A.M, 22 years old and a mother of two. Her rebel husband died in the bush. A.M. complained of being haunted by the bush memories especially the killings she witnessed. She pointed out that whenever these memories come back, she develops a feeling that she should hide from other people.

It was also established that most of the child mothers' new marriages' to break down as new husbands claim 'that we are mad people from the bush,' one child mother said. Another child mother complained that some community members insult her children since they were born in the bush. During the focus group discussion most of them pointed out that poverty was their major obstacle for successful RR in society. They appealed to government and donors to assist and capitalize their credit and saving scheme as well as paying school fees for their children.

Comparative Analysis of Official and Unofficial Peacebuilding Interventions this section makes a comparative analysis of the official and unofficial peacebuilding interventions in the RR of former child soldiers in Northern Uganda.

To begin with, both the official and unofficial peacebuilding interventions in Northern Uganda are based on liberal peacebuilding approaches. They are top-bottom in a sense that the interventions have been designed without the participation of the affected communities hence overlooking the local capacities and contribution of the affected people in addressing their problems. Also, both approaches are externally funded and implement projects and programmes that are time-bound. Most NGOs and CBOs are funded by donors for specific period of time after which they would simply live. The government official peacebuilding programme: the PRDP was designed to last for three years (2007-2010) although due to failure to attract donor funding in time, the programme was extended to end in June 2012. More so, 70% of the PRDP funded is expected to come from donors while government will contribute 30%. In both cases, over dependency on externally funding makes it difficult to implement successful projects. Most crucially external funding that overlooks local resources and contribution creates dependence among the target communities and prolongs the period for recovery and self-reliance.

Furthermore, both the official and unofficial approaches are poorly coordinated and this is causing duplication of interventions which makes it difficult to have a lasting impact on the ground. Duplication of intervention by many CBOs and NGOs that currently populate Northern Uganda is likely to cause more harm than good to the communities emerging from a torturous civil war. Already there are reports where a number of former child soldiers belonging to several CBOs in order to maximize on the assistance. This is creating a dependency syndrome.

It is worth noting that the unofficial peacebuilding interventions have been able to reach more people in very remote areas that are list served by the government. To this end, unofficial interventions can be credited to be playing a very crucial role of reaching the communities that would have otherwise not be easily targeted by the official peacebuilding interventions.

By far, both official and unofficial interventions have played a complementary role in the RR of former child soldiers in Northern Uganda. However for both interventions to be effective in building of a durable peace, it is important to improve coordination, transparency and aim at supporting capacity building of local resources to ensure future sustainability.

This chapter examined the various peacebuilding interventions - official and non-official that have been implemented in Northern Uganda in the RR of former child soldiers. In the case of the official government and UN agencies peacebuilding interventions, it was established that most of them are top-down in nature based on liberal peace principles of timelines and quick fixes, and therefore lacking community participation and local ownership. The research findings indicate that the main government peacebuilding intervention - the PRDP lacks proper conceptualization of the DDRR of ex-combatants specifically former child soldiers who are bundled together irrespective of their varied experiences, needs and interests. The PRDP was also found to suffer from inadequate funding, politicization and poor coordination which are affecting its effectiveness. PRDP's predecessor official interventions: NURP1 and NUSAF suffered gross mismanagement and massive embezzlement of funds which made them fail to achieve their set objectives.

The unofficial peacebuilding interventions that were examined are largely being implemented by international organizations, local NGOs and CBOs whose operational objectives espouse liberal peace ideas. Research findings established that these organizations depend on external donors for funding which raises the issue of sustainability and foreign dependence by the beneficiary communities. The recent story about loss of jobs by the youth in Northern Uganda as NGOs leave the region in The New Vision of May 15, 2010 confirms the sustainability issue of peacebuilding interventions in Northern Uganda. In the final analysis it was found that both interventions have some striking similarities and challenges including pursuing a neo-liberal peacebuilding agenda that is top-down, short-term and externally driven. It is worth noting that if the official and unofficial peace interventions are going to build durable peace in Northern Uganda, they must aim at rebuilding local capacities by enlisting local ownership and participation in the design, planning and implementation of peacebuilding programmes. They must also invest in ensuring proper coordination and transparency in the implementation of the reconstruction programmes.

Part III

Psychosocial Resources and Reintegration and Rehabilitation of Ex-Child Soldiers in Northern Uganda

CHAPTER SIX

●━━━━━━━━━━━━━━━━━━━━━━━━━━━━━━━●

Importance of Psychosocial Resources in the Reintegration and Rehabilitation of Child Soldiers: Conceptual and Practical Analysis

Violent civil wars in developing countries in which thousands of children have been victims either as bystanders or active participants as child soldiers have profound negative psychosocial effects on their well-being. A study conducted on refugee children who had sought asylum in Europe, found that 60% of them had been exposed to violence (Kostelny, 2006:1). Kostelny (2006) observes that in Rwanda, after the genocide in 1996, 96% of children interviewed had witnessed violence; 80% had lost a family member while 70% had seen some one killed or injured. In Liberia, many child soldiers were counselled because the psychological impacts of the civil war (Sendabo, 2004:80). UNICEF estimates that in the decade from 1990 to 2000, 10 million children suffered from war trauma (Prendergast et al 2002:335).

During the field work for this book, in Northern Uganda, it was established that most former child soldiers who had witnessed killings and had been forced to kill their friends who attempted to escape from the LRA captivity, continued to experience bad dreams and nightmares of being pursued by the LRA.[137] A study conducted by UNICEF in Northern Uganda in 2006 on the state of youth also found that some

---

[137] During the field work conducted in northern Uganda in January and February 2010, in northern Uganda, I interviewed 25 former child soldiers. It was established that all of them said they experienced traumatic incidents including being forced to kill their friends or relatives, beaten senselessly as part of training, participation in fighting with the government army and walking long distances carrying heavy loads of looted food. These traumatic experiences have not left most of them several years after they were rehabilitated by reception centres and reintegrated with their families and communities.

youths affected by the war had psychosocial problems (UNICEF, 2006:10).

This chapter explores the relevance of psychosocial support in the RR of former child soldiers in war-torn societies especially in Africa and specifically in Northern Uganda. Particular focus of the chapter is however placed on examining the importance of the neglected psychosocial support based on traditional and indigenous resources in the RR of former child soldiers in Northern Uganda. The chapter also discusses the limitations of traditional and indigenous resources/approaches in the RR of child soldiers. This is based on the realization that in spite of the highly prized values placed on them including achieving peace through forgiveness, consensus and restorative justice (Osaghae, 2000:217), they too have serious limitations such as gender insensitivity and biases towards women and girls, and the fact that in most war-torn societies, traditional resources/approaches are greatly undermined by the conflicts and legacies of colonial domination.

Traditional and Indigenous Approaches to Peacebuilding in the RR of Child Soldiers and Peacebuilding

African traditions and philosophical approaches have continued to survive despite attempts at marginalization by colonialism, Christianity, and apartheid. *Ubuntu* is an understanding of African philosophy peculiar to South Africa. It represents the embodiment of the political, cultural, economic, and social dynamics of African society.....Moreover, *Ubuntu* has presented formidable and at times contradictory challenges to European discourses of dominance and understandings of the African reality (Masina, 2000:169).

Several scholars observe that while the traditional and indigenous resources/approaches play a crucial role in the RR of child soldiers and general peacebuilding and reconstruction of war-torn societies, they have been neglected in both academic and policy circles (MacKay, 2004). This section examines the significance of the traditional and indigenous approaches/resources in the RR of child soldiers and peacebuilding.

International initiatives aimed at promoting preventive diplomacy, management, resolution of conflicts, reconstruction of war-torn societies and promotion of development in Africa, have traditionally neglected and marginalized the indigenous resource capacities for peacebuilding

248

and reconstruction (Murithi, 2008:16). This is in spite of the existence of Article 39 of the Convention on the Rights of the Child that guarantees the right of children to psychosocial recovery and social reintegration following armed conflict to which most countries are signatories (Machel, 2001:80). In most UN official peacebuilding psychosocial support aimed at addressing war trauma in children, the emphasis has been placed on use of Western approaches whose adherents of the medical model seek to treat mental illness using approaches such as individual or group counselling. As scholars Bracken (1998:55) and Summerfield (1998:30) observe, the universalization of the Western approaches of psychosocial support at the expense of local cultures can be potentially harmful.

The example of this is Rwanda after the 1994 genocide. It is noted that many NGOs implemented psychosocial programmes driven by the assumption of mass traumatisation, despite little familiarity with local culture and conditions (Prendergast, 2002:335). Ironically, as Prendergast (2002) observes, much of the distress that was diagnosed as trauma was in fact normal coping mechanisms in operation. Consequently, scholars (Wessells, 2006:188; Braken et al, 1998) have observed that while the Western approach of counselling is useful in the RR of former child soldiers, in certain circumstances, it has been overused and misapplied in many emergencies as was the case in Rwanda.

The physical difficulties that people face daily to survive are an integral part of their psychosocial suffering. Lack of housing, schools and jobs embody and symbolize the plight of people emerging from civil wars and these rob them of a sense of hope and well-being. Consequently, it would be inappropriate to offer counselling assistance as a singular intervention to individuals with psychosocial problems. Instead, a more holistic approach based on interrelations between children's physical, cognitive, emotional, socio-cultural and spiritual development would be ideal (Wessells, 2006). Kostelny (2006:22) commenting on the relevance of psychosocial support in the RR of child soldiers and peacebuilding observed that concepts of mental health and mental illness vary across cultures. Western psychology mainly focuses on mental illness and concepts of trauma and post traumatic stress disorder (PTSD). Kostelny concurs with Honwana (1997); Wessells (2006) and Marsella et al (1996) that while the Post Traumatic Stress Disorder (PTSD) concept has been validated and has value in some contexts, a focus on trauma alone can marginalize other effects of war such as mistrust, hopelessness, social exclusion and the current stresses of daily life.

Kostelny (2006) further observes that psychosocial support for children in war zones would be best provided through holistic, culturally grounded, family-based and community-based methods. To Kostelny (2006), in order to construct culturally relevant approaches, it is essential to use and learn from local approaches, placing culture at the centre of psychosocial work. Cultural and indigenous psychosocial resources include traditions, human resources, community processes and tools. Accordingly, since these resources reflect values, beliefs and cultural traditions, they give voice to and honour to local people and thus are more sustainable (Kostelny, 2006:29). Murithi (2008:17) concurs with other scholars on the relevance of use of indigenous and endogenous resources. He observes that indigenous and endogenous peace and conflict resolution approaches are not generally recognized by governments as viable alternatives to promoting peace at the grassroots level after the end of conflict. More so, in the aftermath of conflicts, indigenous and endogenous principles are rarely considered in terms of constitutional and legal frameworks to oversee the transition to democratic governance. Murithi (2008) proposes a hybrid approach that relies on a combination of best practices from official and indigenous values, principles and norms.

Consequently, scholars such as Bracken (2006) and Kostelny (2006) recommend an integrated approach of psychosocial support that combines both the best practices from the Western approach and traditional and indigenous values. Accordingly, this approach should be holistic in nature in the sense that it links emotional and social supports which meet the basic needs of war affected children including food, shelter and physical reconstruction. The holistic approach also addresses the needs of whole communities as well as providing vocational training, literacy classes and linking trainees with the job market.

The discussion above demonstrates that psychosocial approaches are important in the RR of children affected by civil war. More so, psychosocial support approaches vary across cultures and therefore the dominance of Western approaches in the provision of psychosocial support to child soldiers and communities affected by war in other settings could harm them further. The section however, recognizes that there are important aspects of the Western approaches that could be blended with indigenous resources to get a hybrid approach that is context relevant.

Advantages of Psychosocial Support in the RR and Peacebuilding Based on Traditional Approaches in the African Context

Peacemaking and peacebuilding in Africa are still predominantly being taught and practiced through models developed from Eurocentric traditions. The mainstream and dominant literature in peace studies works on the premise that the values, resources and institutions that have been developed by Eurocentric Western tradition, broadly defined as the Judaeo-Christian heritage, have a universality and can be transposed on to other societies. The Judaeo-Christian Western traditions have developed their own notions of peacemaking and reconciliation. The greater part of academic research on peacemaking has a distinctly Western and Eurocentric bias (Murithi, 2008:18). This section examines the relevance of provision of psychosocial support in the RR and peacebuilding based on traditional and indigenous approaches in the African context.

Several scholars have observed that violent protracted conflicts that have been experienced in Africa and other regions in the developing world, divide populations, undermine interpersonal relations and social trust and destroy social norms and values that have always regulated societies and held them together (Summerfield, 1998; Osaghae, 2000; Muruthi, 2008). Yet, recovery and sustainable peacebuilding is only possible if international humanitarian intervention is aimed at rebuilding indigenous resources to ensure local ownership and sustainability (Liu Institute for Global Issues et al. 2005:1). Murithi (2008:17) who defines indigenous resources as that which is inherent to a given society but also that which is innate and instinctive observes that indigenous and endogenous processes have been internalized by years of tradition and consequently the values and practices they propose do not seem alien to the affected communities.

While the aim of this chapter is to examine the role of traditional and indigenous resources in the RR of child soldiers in Northern Uganda, evidence from most of Africa shows that most societies that have been affected by wars have indigenous values, institutions and resources for peacemaking and peacebuilding. As scholars have noted, notwithstanding the differences in socio-political organization and levels of development, the nature of conflicts and the strategies devised to deal with conflict management and reconciliation in traditional African societies present striking similarities (Osaghae, 2000:205). Accordingly, these traditional and indigenous approaches of conflict management and reconciliation developed overtime among most African traditional societies can be relied upon to transition from war to peace including the RR of child soldiers since they also have widespread support among the populations. Commenting on the relevance of African traditional conflict management and reconciliation approaches Osaghae (2000:203) observes that,

Tradition is all too clear in present-day African politics and this, in itself, is sufficient reason to consider traditional sources of conflict management. After all, traditional strategies of conflict management are employed at the subnational level in most countries, especially in those where so-called traditional rulers are still respected. Little (1967:185) discovered from his study of the Mende of Sierra Leone that the authority of the Poro society (as well as the Sande and Humui, other secret societies that serve as cultural arbiters) is still widely used to resolve conflicts.

The Rwandan experience provides a good example in respect to the relevance of the African traditional indigenous resources for conflict management, reconciliation and peacebuilding including DDR of ex-combatants who included child soldiers. Following the 1994 genocide which devastated the country, including the judicial system, the new Rwandan Patriotic Front (RPF) Government that captured power had to reinvigorate the Gacaca traditional justice and reconciliation system. Despite its weaknesses, including some people using it to settle political differences, this community-based conflict resolution and reconciliation system helped to promote peaceful settlement of disputes and to reduce the number of cases submitted to the formal judicial structures (Reyntjens el al, 2001:128).

In South Africa, the African National Congress (ANC) Government established the Truth and Reconciliation Commission in 1995 to assist in the healing and reconciliation process after centuries of a repressive apartheid system of governance (Masina, 2000:177). The Truth and Reconciliation Commission (TRC) relied on the Ubuntu, an African traditional restorative justice and reconciliation system common among most South African societies to conduct its work. Commenting on his own experience as Chairman of the TRC, Archbishop Desmond Tutu observed that he constantly referred to the notion of Ubuntu when guiding and advising witnesses, victims and perpetrators during the Commission hearings (Masina, 2000). The TRC was instrumental in the DRR processes of both the former national army and ex-combatants of the ANC who included young fighters. There are several other examples of traditional approaches across Africa, including Bushingantahe, a justice and reconciliation system in Burundi, the Jir Mediation Forum of the Tiv of Nigeria and the Shir Council of Elders in Somaliland (Zartman, 2000).

In spite of the limitations associated with the African traditional and indigenous approaches, including gender biases towards women and its disruption by civil wars discussed extensively in the subsequent section, they are credited with several advantages, which can be relied upon in the RR of former child soldiers and peacebuilding in general.

The first advantage is that since the indigenous approaches have been in use for generations among most societies affected by conflicts, they are familiar, acceptable and have a local appeal to the communities where they are being applied. In any case, these indigenous approaches appeal to people's local cultures, social norms and values making them acceptable and available in the long-term (Deng, 2000).

The second advantage relates to the fact that traditional and indigenous approaches are inclusive in a sense that they are based on the African concept of collective responsibility and togetherness (Masina, 2000). Besides being inclusive, African traditional approaches promote public participation and always endeavour to seek consensus among the parties at conflict in addressing the root causes of the conflict. Public participation of the affected people enlists community support and ownership of the processes and the outcome. The example of traditional approaches that enlist public participation and have been used in RR of child soldiers is the *Mato Oput* justice and reconciliation system among the Acholi people in Northern Uganda[138]. *Mato Oput* is discussed in detail in the next section.

The third advantage of indigenous approaches is that they are sustainable since they depend on local resources, which is necessary to ensure sustainable peace (McCallin, 1998:70). Unlike international humanitarian assistance which is always top-down, externally driven, time

---

[138]Interview with Bishop Ochora, Vice Chairman, Acholi Religious Leaders Association.

bound and financially constrained in the case of United Nations led post-conflict peacebuilding, indigenous resources are resident among the affected communities. And since regeneration and recovery of war-torn societies including RR of child soldiers takes a long time, reliance on indigenous resources ensures long-term commitment. This does not mean that external assistance is not relevant. As Kostelny (2006) has pointed out, the role of external assistance should be largely to assist in rebuilding and empowerment of local capacities and resources to support psychosocial support and peacebuilding of the war affected societies.

The fourth advantage is that indigenous approaches are cost effective to the extent that they rely on the community's own internal resources rather than the infusion of funds from external sources. This helps to build self confidence and re-humanisation of communities and individuals whose sense of humanity and self-worth would have been wounded and undermined by the war. More so, the reliance on indigenous resources/approaches reduces the possibility of dependence that characterizes most societies emerging from civil wars. The above point has also been advanced by Caritas Gulu in Northern Uganda. According to Rubangadeke a staff of Caritas Gulu, external assistance is creating a dependence syndrome among the communities which could perpetually undermine community resilience. Moreso as the subsequent discussions show, indigenous resources such as families, youth and women's groups have been useful in RR of former child soldiers in Northern Uganda.

The fifth advantage is that indigenous approaches put emphasis on mediation and reconciliation processes as opposed to retributive justice. The emphasis of African traditional approaches on mediation of disputes and going beyond mediation to reconcile conflicting parties and build peaceful relationships is considered more appropriate compared to Western judicial approaches which emphasise retributive justice that does not repair broken relationships. In Northern Uganda, *Mato Oput*, which is an Acholi traditional justice system, has been relied upon to reconcile former child soldiers with communities and families [139].

While the African traditional and indigenous approaches embody a number of advantages, they also have limitations. These limitations are discussed in detail in the concluding section of this chapter.

---

[139]Interview with Rtd. Bishop Ochora, Vice Chairman, Acholi Religious Leaders Peace Initiative.

Psychosocial Support Based on Traditional and Indigenous Resources in the RR of Child Soldiers in Northern Uganda

War affects every aspect of a child's development- physical, emotional, intellectual, social and spiritual. Children who have lived through conflict need psychosocial support (Machel, 2001:80).

This section examines psychosocial support based on the traditional and indigenous resources that have been used in the RR of child soldiers in Northern Uganda. Most of the RR of former child soldiers was implemented by reception centres which included; GUSCO, Concerned Parents Association, World Vision's Children of War Rehabilitation Centre and associations of former child soldiers formed after they were reintegrated with their families and communities. The reception centres were the first places where child soldiers found a place to physically heal by providing medical assistance for the sick, counselling, family tracing and advice on how to cope in society outside the bush life. Annan et al (2006) have pointed out that the crucial role played by reception centres is that they became a place in which to transition between two worlds: that of the bush and that of the village.

It should be noted though that not all former child soldiers came back through reception centres. While the majority of the 25 former child soldiers that were interviewed for this book returned through the reception centres about five of them said that they came directly to their homes after escaping from rebel captivity. Findings from fieldwork reveal that most reception centres provided counselling, medical treatment, clothes, vocational training, family tracing and re-unions with families. The final journey which is the family re-union was in most cases concluded by traditional rituals and ceremonies performed by traditional leaders.

Before examining the traditional and indigenous approaches that have been relied upon in the RR of child soldiers in Northern Uganda, it is important to explore the spirituality of the Acholi people who are the main actors in the LRA conflict. The reason for exploring the spirituality of the Acholi people is because the traditional and indigenous rituals and ceremonies used in the RR of former child soldiers in Northern Uganda are anchored in their spiritual beliefs. Traditionally, the Acholi people believe that good health and happiness are situated in the context of the harmony and the well-being of the clan. The ancestral and religious spirit worlds provide guidance to the Acholi people, maintaining the unity of the clans[140].Consequently, conflicts, misfortune and poor health were historically interpreted to have been sent by the angry spirits, and affected not only the offender or violator of the moral codes but his/her family and clan.

Because, in Acholi culture, one person's offence affects other people, it demands collective responsibility to deal with the problem (Liu Institute for Global Issues 2006: 3). A communal society, the Acholi people have a special value for the clan system. Historically, each member of the social unit was expected to fulfil different yet complementary productive, reproductive and cultural roles. The spiritual and religious world among the Acholi which functioned through spiritual and human representatives enforced people's behaviour. While colonial, modern influences and conflict have greatly impacted on their cultural beliefs, most Acholi people believe in the spiritual world (Latigo, 2008). The Acholi believe in *Jok*, a divine spirit, as well as the presence of other ancestral and foreign spirits. Traditionally, each clan had its Jok or Jogi (plural for *Jok*) which was depended upon for blessings, hunting, good harvest and in times of war. Sacrifices were always made to ask for blessings, favour or prevention of calamity. The elders were taken to be close to *Jok* and were responsible for offering sacrifices in shrines.

According to elders, '*Cen*,' an angry spirit is sent to a person for committing a crime against the dead. Such crimes include murder, stealing and abandoning a close relative to die in a demeaning manner. *Cen* manifests itself for a period of time by attacking the family, sub-clan or the entire clan. In this case, the responsibility for setting things right does not rest on the offending individual alone but the entire family and elders within a clan. The types of rituals for chasing or appeasing *Cen* depend on the affected clan and the act, which led to the attack by *Cen*. However, in most cases, a goat or sheep is slaughtered to chase away the bad spirits (Liu Institute for Global Issues 2006).

During the two decade LRA conflict, many of the shrines for *Jok* and witch doctors were targeted and destroyed by the rebels especially the Holy Spirit Movement led by Prophetess *Lakwena* and by the LRA (Human Rights Watch, 1997:66). The traditional approaches for peace making and peacebuilding among the Acholi people are premised on a set of principles: voluntary nature of the process; truth telling as a basis

---

[140]Bishop Ochora Ibid.

for mediation; acknowledgement of wrong doing; compensation and reconciliation through symbolic acts and ritual appeasement.

Depending on the crime committed, compensation was always made in the form of cows, bulls or goats or a virgin girl where murder had taken place[141]. According to Odama, the Acholi traditional justice was guided by the desire to restore the broken relationship rather than punishment. The system never handed down a death sentence for a person accused of intentional or accidental murder. The Acholi traditional approaches of justice and reconciliation are examined in detail below.

Mato Oput Justice and Reconciliation Approach

Most former child soldiers who were interviewed during the field work confirmed that they were assisted in the RR processes by the traditional rituals that were organized for them by traditional leaders and their families to receive them back home. Some of them reported that their fears and sadness were relieved due to the traditional rituals that were performed during the re-unification with families. Some child soldiers who came straight from the bush to their homes and missed out on these ceremonies blame their continued trauma in form of bad dreams and suffering especially due to lack of secure livelihoods on not taking part in traditional ceremonies. According to Avola, Coordinator of *Ker Kwaro*, Acholi, *Mato Oput* and other cultural rituals have been revived and widely used to support RR of former child soldiers in the entire Acholi sub-region.

The Acholi believe that a person is a sacred being whose blood should not be spilled without a just cause. If a person killed another person from the same or different clan intentionally or by accident, the killing would provoke the anger of the deities and ancestral spirits of the victims.[142] It is believed that the angered spirits of ancestors would

---

[141] Archbishop Odama, J. B. (2008). Reconciliation Process (Mato Oput) Among the Acholi Tribe in Northern Uganda. Available at:
http://www.npf.or.jp/peace_prize_f/21/speech_e.pdf. Accessed on 23/6/2010.
Odama is also the Chairperson of the Acholi Religious Leaders Peace Initiative (ARLPI).

[142] Interview with Bishop Ochora, the retired Anglican Bishop of Kitgum Diocese who is the Vice Chairman of the Acholi Religious Leaders Peace Initiative and a strong advocate of the Acholi traditional justice system. He is himself a victim of the conflict.

permit and even invite evil spirits to invade homesteads and harm the inhabitants. Moreover, the killing creates a supernatural barrier between the clan of the killer and the clan of the killed person. After the murder, the two clans stop eating and drinking from the same bowl. Communication and any healthy interaction also break down. According to Bishop Ochora, the separation and lack of cooperation remains until the killing has been atoned for and a religious rite of reconciliation performed to appease the spirits. During this time, the killer is ostracised and treated as an unclean person. Consequently, the offender is prohibited from entering any homestead other than his/her own for fear that he/she is a companion of the evil spirits which would pollute the soil and the homesteads (Latigo, 2008).

In the case of accidental or deliberate killing, the clan of the offender is required to pay blood money as an indemnity to the clan of the dead person. In the meantime, a council of elders appoints a mediator who normally would be a respectable elder from neither of the feuding clans. The mediator is supposed to be impartial and is expected to coordinate the process of paying the compensation. Underpinning the *Mato Oput* approach is that no killing is paid for by another killing.[143] This is based on the belief that killing another person simply means loss of manpower by society which is not beneficial to either party at conflict. The payment of compensation which was always in the form of cows, bulls or goats was preferable since these would be used to marry another woman who in turn would produce children to replace the dead person.

After the payment of compensation, the elders arrange for the customary rite of reconciliation to take place in order to bring the estranged clans together to resume a normal working relationship. The reconciliation ceremony always takes place inan uncultivated field usually located somewhere between the villages or communal settlements of the two clans, away from any footpath or any path commonly used by women and children. The clan of the offender provides a ram and a bull

---

His wife was killed by a landmine, while his daughter committed suicide after being gang raped by the LRA rebels. The Bishop says he has relied on his Acholi tradition and his Christian faith to forgive the rebels. In interviewed Bishop Ochora many times over a period of three years since i have been working with him on the peace process in northern Uganda since 2006. However in respect for this book I interviewed him in September 2009.

[143] Archbishop Odama, Op Cit.

while the next of kin of the dead person provides a goat. Normally new unused utensils are required for the *Mato Oput* ceremony including large quantities of local brew prepared for the occasion. On the appointed day, the appointed master of ceremony, conciliators and elders from both clans assemble at the chosen site and stand facing westwards in a solemn silence. The master of ceremony leads the two parties in a ritual as follows:

Box 2: Example of *Mato Oput* Ceremony
The Master of ceremonies:
'You our ancestors and the children of the Supreme Deity! I now plead with you and ask you to realize that sin is part of man's life. It was started by those who ever lived before us. This man whose fault brought us here has merely repeated the perennial SIN which man has hitherto failed to discard since time immemorial. He killed his own brother. But since then he has repented of his evil deed. He has paid blood money which may be used to marry a woman who will produce children who, in turn, will keep the name of his killed brother for our posterity. We now beseech you our ancestors to let the two families resume a brotherly relationship...' All the assembled elders join in and chant together by saying: Let a man who will be given money to marry a wife be sharp and pick on a vivacious woman... a virgin woman who will produce many and healthy children to grow up well and take over the empty home.' Another master of ceremonies from the clan of the killed person responds to the solemn invocation in the following terms: We are not the first clan to suffer premature death of this kind. The killer has repented his misdeed. He has paid for it. We now supplicate you our ancestors to bless the blood money given to the family to marry a wife to produce a replacement for our killed brother...' All the assembly elders join the invocation and chart together: Let us accept the blood money and wash our hearts clean, and begin to live and work together as we have been doing in the past... Our enemies who have heard of this reconciliation and are not happy that it will now bring peace and prosperity to our two clans ... Let their ill will be carried away by the sun to the west, and sink with it down, deep and deep down ...' (**Source**: Latigo, 2008).

The master of ceremonies using a calabash mixes the pounded extracts from the bitter roots of the oput tree with an alcoholic drink and asks the killer and the next of kin of the killed person to kneel down and drink the herb simultaneously from the same calabash facing each other with their hands behind their backs. It is at this stage in the ceremony that the members of the two clans join to drink from the same vessel for the first time[144]. The master of ceremonies at this point cuts off the head of the ram brought by the killer's clan and the head of the goat from the killed person's clan. The rams head is then handed over to the next of kin of the dead man while the goat's head is given to the killer's clan. Meanwhile, the bull is speared, killed and butchered. The meat is cooked and eaten together symbolizing fellowship again. At this point elders

---

[144]Odama, Ibid.

from both sides mix freely and the two clans re-establish a healthy and normal relationship (Latigo, 2008:105). The bitter roots of the *Oput* tree symbolize the bitterness of the conflict that end in bloodshed. According to Archbishop Odama, the role of the girl as a compensation for premeditated murder was understood as salvation and readiness for the clan to sacrifice their daughter to affirm commitment to peace and co-existence.

The Ritual of Stepping on the Egg (*nyono tong gweno*)

Another Acholi traditional approach that has been used in the RR of child soldiers is the 'Stepping on the Egg' or *'nyono tong gweno'* in Acholi. The stepping on the egg ritual is a firm belief among the Acholi aimed at preserving the sacredness and stability of their homesteads and society. According to an official from the Concerned Parents Association, *nyono tong gweno* is used to welcome home members who have been away from the homesteads for a long period of time. It is believed that being away from home, people could come into contact with spirits which if not cleansed would adulterate and/or bring misfortune to the entire society. The ritual is therefore performed to restore severed relationships and to demonstrate commitment on the part of the community and the affected person to stay together in a harmonious relationship.

Accordingly, stepping on the egg ceremony or ritual is performed at the family or clan level. However, because of the magnitude of the problem in respect to massive abduction of children by the LRA, the ceremony has been organized on a large scale where several formerly abducted children collectively step on eggs in one ceremony. Available information shows that over 12,000 formerly abducted persons have undergone the stepping on the egg ceremony conducted and supported by *Ker Kwaro Acholi* (Latigo:2008:106). The use of the egg represents innocence. The egg is delicate and mouthless. According to Avola, the egg has no mouth to speak words that sometimes cause conflict. By stepping on this delicate egg that is mouthless and innocent the offender becomes purified and innocent again. The stepping on the egg ceremony became very popular to the extent that at one time, Northern Uganda experienced a shortage of eggs.[145]

---

[145] Mao, N., is Chairman Gulu District Local Government, Op Cit.

Cleansing the Body Ritual (moyo kum)

Moyo Kum or Cleansing of the Body ritual is another traditional approach that has been used in the RR of former child soldiers in Northern Uganda. The ritual is complicated and can often last for several days. It is usually performed by elders who come together to bless the returned persons by washing away their misdeeds, chase away the evil spirits and appeal to the ancestors for their blessing. The ceremony involves the act of spearing the goat and dragging it across a compound to rid the clan of *Cen* (evil spirit) that the returning person comes back with. According to Rubangakene, Caritas has supported several cleansing the body rituals in its area of concentration.

Cleansing of an Area (*moyo piny*)

Moyo piny or cleansing of an area is another ritual that has been used in the RR of former child soldiers. *Moyo Piny* involves sacrifice of goats to appease the ancestors and cleansing the area of evil spirits that are believed to dwell in places where mass massacres took place during the war. Most IDPs have been reluctant to return to their original places or plough fields where mass killings took place. The performance of this ceremony by the traditional leaders has facilitated the return and resettlement of communities to their original places which also paved the way for RR of former child soldiers (Interview with staff of CPA).

Bending the Spear (also known as *Gomo Tong*)

Gomo Tong is a ceremony where the two conflicting or warring parties agree to permanently end their violent conflict by bending spears facing the opposite direction of the perceived enemy signalling the end of use of the spear against the enemy. *Gomo Tong* is regarded as sacred which normally invokes the ancestors and once performed it is supposed to mark the end of bloodshed. There exist san historical account where this ritual was used and it worked successfully to prevent war between the Acholi and their neighbours in West Nile (Latigo, 2008).

Apart from the Acholi, other ethnic groups that have been affected by the war in Northern Uganda have their own traditional and indigenous approaches for RR of persons involved in the conflict including child soldiers. Some of these approaches are recognized by the Draft Juba Peace Agreement, 2007 which was never signed by the LRA leader, Kony, and President Museveni. The Langi people have what is called *Kayo cuk* meaning 'biting of charcoal'. This ritual is performed to reconcile parties formerly in conflict and has been used in the RR of child soldiers in Lango sub-region. In West Nile among the Madi people, *Tonu ci koka* traditional ritual has been performed to reconcile parties at conflict especially ex-combatants who include child soldiers. In Teso, where the LRA also abducted a significant number of children, *'ailuc'* traditional ceremonies have been performed to receive children back.

By and large, the Acholi traditional justice and reconciliation approaches are guided by the principle of restoration of broken relationships and voluntarism. Reconciliation is not possible unless the offender accepts responsibility. The voluntary nature of the offender is driven by the fear of *'Cen'* the evil spirit. Most elders interviewed describe the traditional justice approaches as collective and transparent since they are organized in open courts with specific roles of elders and representatives of royal clans and the feuding clans. Research conducted in Northern Uganda reveals that the Acholi people, including the political elites, have strong belief in their traditional rituals and in the spirit world.[146] The decision for the negotiating teams in Juba to include agenda number three on Accountability and Reconciliation was in response to the pressure from the majority of the Acholi people who insisted that they are ready to forgive rebels based on their traditional culture[147].

Most crucially the conflict in Northern Uganda brought to the fore the fact that there exists a rich body of traditional systems in Africa that reflect the principles of conflict management and conflict resolution where the objective is to reintegrate the perpetrators into their communities and reconcile them with their victims. Noteworthy also is

---

[146] Interview with Hon. Oryem, O.H.; Op Cit., Oryem, an Acholi and a son of the former president of Uganda, General Tito Okello Lutwa confirmed that he worships the spirits of his ancestors and has no business with Christianity. The interview was conducted in December, 2009.

[147] Agreement on Accountability and Reconciliation between Government of Uganda and Lord's Resistance Army/Movement provided for use of traditional customary approaches of conflict resolution to end the conflict in northern Uganda. Available at: http://www.beyondjuba.org/peace_agreements/Agreement_on_Accountability_And_ Reconcilition.pdf. Accessed on 24/5/2010.

that the justice aspect of these traditional approaches is distinct from the adversarial one inherent in Western justice or modern formal judicial system used by the courts in Uganda. While the Western justice system produces a clear winner and a loser, the Acholi traditional system produces only winners: both the victim and the offender become winners through the restored relationship that rehumanizes both parties.

Research findings show that the traditional approaches have helped in fostering family re-unions as the families have been made aware that it is their cultural responsibility to accept the children back and reintegrate them as members of society. Further, traditional rituals have fostered community acceptance that children belong to them and it is their responsibility and role to deal with the problem. In fact, during the field work, the staff of Caritas, a Catholic Church organization revealed that the communities have complained that NGOs are undermining their roles of raising community children as most former child soldiers now think they belong to NGOs and not the community. Besides the traditional approaches of conflict management and reconciliation, other local resources in Northern Uganda have played a crucial role in the RR of child soldiers. These local resources include: religious institutions, education institutions, youth and women groups/associations and families. The contribution of these institutions is examined below.

Role of Religious Institutions in the RR of Child Soldiers

Religious institutions, especially the Catholic Church, the Anglican Church and Pentecostal Churches, have played a crucial role in the RR of former child soldiers through preaching forgiveness and unconditional love of Jesus Christ and provision of humanitarian and development assistance. The preaching is said to have enabled some child soldiers to come to terms with their situation and achieve acceptance by the communities they had terrorised to accept them back. O.G., 19 years pointed out that his Church had helped him overcome his troubled mind, revealing that:

> I was abducted with two brothers who are still in the bush. I was forced to kill my friends, I saw innocent children being killed. When I came back, it was difficult for me to sleep. I would dream i was being pursued by the LRA and would wake up screaming. Through prayers and counselling by fellow church members I no longer get bad dreams. I am now praying that my brothers will one day come back alive.

Watoto Community Church, one of the biggest Pentecostal Churches in Uganda, opened a special branch called Watoto Church Gulu in 2008. Through a partnership arrangement with Laroo School of War Affected Children, Watoto is assisting in the rehabilitation of 460 former child soldiers.[148]

Role of Schools in the RR of Child Soldiers

A crucial local resource for RR and peacebuilding in Northern Uganda is schools (primary, secondary and vocational training) which are educating and offering training to former child soldiers. Most reception centres were quick to realize that most former child soldiers needed to be given opportunities for schooling since schooling is critical in addressing psychosocial problems among young people affected by war (Arafat et al, 2006:120). According to Obilu-Akol, an officer working with World Vision, the organization negotiated six months placement for older returnees and enrolled the young ones in primary schools. While not all former child soldiers have accessed schooling opportunities, most of them that were interviewed during field work who are studying appear to be more optimistic and positive about their future.

O.B., 28 years of age, who is offering a bricklaying course in a vocational school observed that his ambition is to become an accountant. O.B observed that, 'My plan is to continue upgrading until I join a university to do a course of my dream'

Role of Women and Youth Groups

Women's groups and youth groups in Northern Uganda have been instrument in the RR processes of former child soldiers. Women's organizations such as Concerned Parents Association (CPA), Kitgum Concerned Women's Association (KIWA) received, counselled and reintegrated former child soldiers. Beyond reintegration, women's groups

---

[148] Ochen, C., is a Social Worker with Watoto Community Church. According to Ochen, Watoto provides counselling and material support to former child soldiers at Laroo School of War Affected Children. Ochen was interviewed at Watoto Church in Gulu in March, 2010.

have continued to conduct community sensitization programmes to foster community acceptance of former child soldiers.[149]

Role of Associations of former Child Soldiers

During field work, it was established that after reintegration and rehabilitation by reception centres and NGOs former child soldiers formed their own associations through which they could champion their needs and get a belonging. Field work findings reveal that these associations have been crucial in assisting the RR of former child soldiers in their communities. Most of these associations are providing psychosocial support to their members through counselling and credit facilities. KICA Ber Youth Group and War Affected Children Association (WACA) are examples of associations of former child soldiers that offer counselling, credit and savings services and scholarships to their members as part of RR activities.[150] Research findings also show that these associations have shielded former child soldiers from community stigmatization since they provide a belonging. Also, the credit and saving schemes, training in business management provided by these associations have enabled former child soldiers to start income generating businesses which have earned them respect in society.[151]

Role of Families in the RR of Child Soldiers

While the Child Protection Unit of the army was the first stop centre of returning child soldiers, the families have been the final destination for the returning children. Most reception centres would first prepare the families through sensitization to accept their children back and urge them to give children all the support they need to recover from the trauma. Findings from the field-work reveal that most former child soldiers (with the exception of child mothers who have been rejected by parents because of the children they returned with) were helped by the warm

---

[149] Interview with the staff of Concerned Parents Association conducted in Gulu in February, 2009.
[150] Interviews with members of KICA Ber Youth Group which took place at their associations offices in Gulu in February, 2009. This group comprise both male and female former child soldiers who are now adults.
[151] Ibid.

reception from their families to settle down. It was also found that most former child soldiers who have high levels of traumatic symptoms such as uncontrolled crying whenever one asks about their bush experience are child mothers who were rejected by families and now live in towns in very difficult conditions.

Commenting about the centrality of families in the RR of child soldiers, Singer (2006:201) argues that:

> ...successful reintegration is as much about whether the families and communities are prepared for acceptance as about whether the children have been properly rehabilitated. .....in one survey in Africa, 80% of adults did not want their children to mix with children who had once served as child soldiers.

Challenges of Traditional and Indigenous Approaches in RR and Peacebuilding

The use of psychosocial support based on traditional and indigenous resources have played a crucial role in the RR of former child soldiers particularly in Northern Uganda. However, in spite of the relevance of traditional and indigenous resources in the RR of former child soldiers, findings from both field-work and literature by scholars show that they have serious limitations.

During fieldwork, it was found out that most of the traditional approaches were not designed to respond to large scale human rights violations that were committed during the war in Northern Uganda. For example, *Mato Oput* was meant to promote reconciliation and restoration of relationships between clans for an intentional murder or accidental killing of one person by a member of another clan and was always mediated by a neutral person from a different clan. The current *Mato Oput* ceremonies have had to be improvised to conduct rituals for mass killings where bodies have been buried in mass graves. What is also challenging is that reconciliation which underpins *Mato Oput* cannot take place since the perpetrators - LRA leaders are still in the bush and have not yet accepted responsibility nor asked for forgiveness which are some of the principles for the *Mato Oput* justice and reconciliation approach.

266

Moreover, it is this improvisation of the traditional rituals among the Acholi that is being challenged by some fellow Acholis as a sham.[152]

The above point was confirmed by an official of *Ker Kwaro Acholi* who said that modifications have had to be made on cultural rituals and ceremonies to address the magnitude of the problem. The point being made here is that these traditional rituals may not be sufficient to address the psychosocial needs of children because they have been simply repackaged and improvised. Mark Avola agrees that while *Ker Kwaro Acholi* has been instrumental in the RR of former child soldiers, it has some weakness and noted that it is necessary to supplement traditional psychosocial supports with Western approaches since the latter use several techniques.

Box 3: Informants Views about Traditional and Western Psychosocial Approaches

Traditional Approaches

Advantages:
a)   Have a cultural basis;
b)   Known by most people in Northern Uganda;
c)   They are locally available and sustainable;
d)   Widespread community acceptance;
e)   Institutionalized with the reinstatement of *Ker Kwaro Acholi*.

Disadvantages:
a)   Have been weakened by the civil war, Christianity, and legislation;
b)   Gender insensitive towards women and girls;
c)   Perpetuate male domination;
d)   Blood sacrifices invoke bad memories among former child soldiers about LRA human sacrifices;
e)   Lack of national appeal, only limited to Acholi sub-region;
f)   Approaches have been repackaged with their validity being questioned;
g)   Have failed to protect child mothers and their children.

Western Approaches of Psychosocial Support

Advantages:
a)   Talking to someone kind to you;
b)   Getting attention and being listened to;
c)   Teaching in life skills;
d)   Counselling gave us hope of new possibilities;
e)   Taught to be respectful to our parents and old people;
f)   Forgiveness;

---

[152] Bigombe, B., an Acholi and former Minister for Pacification of Northern Uganda who led two failed peace negotiations between Government and LRA dismissed *Mato Oput* as a recent invention among the Acholi. She said that people don't know Mato Oput. Bigombe was interviewed in Kampala in August 2009.

g)   Teaching Christian values- love, repentance and forgiveness,
Disadvantages
a)   We were treated like children;
b)   Sharing secrets to strangers;
c)   Cultural differences.

The second limitation of traditional approaches in the RR of child soldiers in Northern Uganda relates to persistent trauma and stigma among former child soldiers in spite of the fact that most of them underwent traditional rituals and cultural ceremonies performed by *Ker Kwaro Acholi*. Most former child soldiers interviewed for this book confirmed they had been purified by traditional rituals sponsored by the reception centres or *Ker Kwaro Acholi*. However, it was also found that most of them complained of being stigmatized by name calling by members of the community, lack of secure livelihoods, loss of parents, uncertain future and family rejection in the case of child mothers. One former child soldier said that whenever they call him a rebel, he feels like fighting back but when it is by an old person, he simply cries.[153] Also, it was found out that most female former child soldiers' were traumatized by failed new marriages which they blame on community perception of them.

A.A, 28 years, is a mother of three. She was abducted at 14 years and spent seven years in the bush. Her LRA husband was killed during fighting in the bush. She returned with two children and remarried. A.A. said that some people have been advising her husband to leave her since she is a risk who can kill him at any time. This is one of the reasons why most female former child soldiers have had run to towns where they end up in prostitution. This finding is also confirmed by a study by Liu Institute (2005:35) which lists name calling and abuses as major causes of stress and stigmatization among the former child soldiers and a challenge to reintegration. The argument being advanced here is that traditional rituals have not helped former child soldiers to fully overcome trauma; neither have they empowered society to forgive and support their RR processes.

---

[153] Interview with a former child soldier whose name remains confidential but is a member of KICA Ber Youth Group or Forgiveness is Good Youth Group in northern Uganda in February 2010.

268

Thirdly, a study conducted by Allen et al. (2006:18) found that the role of local healing in the RR of former child soldiers has been overstated or misunderstood in many reports in respect to Northern Uganda. The study found out that some formerly abducted children are upset by violence in sacrificial ceremonies, and dislike the ritual ablutions because they remind them of the healing rites that were performed by the LRA rebels in the bush. This point was collaborated by Okello, a Programme Officer with Concerned Parents Association (CPA) during fieldwork. He observed that CPA has handled cases where former child soldiers refused traditional rituals in favour of a Christian prayer or Western counselling when their parents favoured the former. Okello noted that in such situations, CPA settled for a compromise where both approaches were used.

The fourth challenge was raised by Bishop Ochora who observes that because of massive internal displacement by the civil war; most traditional and indigenous resources that would have been useful in the RR of former child soldiers were severely weakened including the role of elders, traditional leaders and the family in society. Because of massive internal displacement, people's livelihoods were greatly undermined; most fathers became poor and desperate with some resorting to excessive drinking of alcohol and could not provide for their families as is traditionally expected of a head of a household (Human Rights Focus Report, 2007:24). Families depended on handouts from the World Food Programme and Government.

More so, most of the traditional leaders who were also internally displaced lost respect and authority due to poverty in the camps where they lived a dependent life like everybody else. With the return from the camps, most of them did not have houses to live in which prompted Government to build houses for them (interview with Avola). Consequently, it has become difficult for traditional leaders and elders to spearhead the RR of child soldiers and peacebuilding when most people look at them as ordinary citizens.

Furthermore, reliance on customs, spirit mediums, witchcraft and secret societies by traditional approaches to justice and reconciliation has greatly been weakened by modern influences such as Christianity and formal education which characterise such practices as backward and satanic (Osaghae, 2001:2009). It is not surprising that some of the former

269

child soldiers in Northern Uganda disregarded traditional rituals in preference to Christian prayer.[154]

Another limitation of most African traditional and indigenous justice and reconciliation resources is that they are slow in delivering justice and reconciliation (Murithi, 2008:28). This is because most African traditional reconciliation and justice systems are predicated on the principles of voluntarism and willingness of the parties to achieve consensus which can make the process indefinite. Yet, in a modern society based on rule of law, justice delayed is considered justice denied. For example in *Mato Oput* in the case of the conflict in Northern Uganda, a perpetrator is encouraged to acknowledge responsibility for wrong doing, following the presentation of evidence by the witness a perpetrator is also encouraged to repent and demonstrate genuine remorse; the perpetrator is encouraged to ask for forgiveness from the victims while the victim is encouraged to show mercy and grant forgiveness to the perpetrator. This painstaking process can take ages to complete and this could constrain peacebuilding.

In the case of the war in Northern Uganda, the chief perpetrator Kony and his commanders have consistently backtracked from several peace processes. This means that reconciliation and accountability may go on endlessly. The over reliance on such a mechanism can be frustrating especially on the part of victims who need justice in order to rebuild their shattered lives.

More so, as scholars Denov (2007) and Pankhurst (2008) have observed most peace processes tend to marginalize women and this is most apparent in indigenous approaches to conflict management across much of Africa. Gender insensitivity towards women and girls should be seen as a continuation of another form of violence even after the official conflict has ended. Noteworthy is the fact that some of the cultural practices demean women or violate their human rights. In the case of *Mato Oput* for example, the process of compensation on top of blood money where a person has been killed, a virgin girl is supposed to be given to the clan which lost a person to produce children to replace the dead person[155].

---

[154]Interview with Owor, A., who worked with GUSCO as a Social Worker. Op Cit.
[155]Interview with Archbishop Ondama, the Chairperson of Acholi Religious leaders Peace Initiative.

Even if the 'modernized' *Mato Oput* rituals have removed the compensation of the virgin girl and other negative elements, it has prompted some sections among the Acholi society to say that the practice is diluted while others are opposed to it.[156] While it is true that there exist progressive values within the African traditional approaches, some elements violate the human rights of women. It would be absurd to rely on a system that seeks to deliver justice, peace and reconciliation to some sections of society while abusing the rights of others at the same time- women and girls' rights. Consequently, Devon (2007) observes that because of the historical exclusion and other injustices towards women and girls, psychosocial cultural practices should be pluralistic and sensitive to gender and the dangers of both Western and local practices that perpetuate and reproduce stereotypes and inequalities.

Another limitation is that while most African traditional conflict management approaches have similarities and broad principles; in most cases they are culture and context specific and not flexible which makes it difficult to apply them in other cultures among people who do not subscribe to that culture (Osaghae, 2000:216). For example while the conflict in Northern Uganda is a national conflict and has affected all Ugandans, though differently, the traditional approaches being used are largely from the Acholi people and may not appeal to other ethnic groups. As Osaghae (2001) has observed, any attempt to apply traditional strategies of one ethnic group to modern conflicts across the board, is likely to arouse suspicions of ethnic domination and hegemony in a multi-ethnic post-colonial state such as Uganda and this could cause new tensions. This is a serious limitation on the part of traditional conflict management approaches that have been used in the RR of child soldiers across Africa. This is true of the conflict in Northern Uganda.

While *Mato Oput* and other traditional rituals are popular in Acholi land other neighbouring groups affected by the LRA conflict opted for their own traditional approaches as provided for in Agenda Item 3: Accountability and Reconciliation of the Draft Juba Peace Agreement[157].

---

[156] Interview with Bigombe, B., Op Cit. Bigombe who led two failed peace negotiations between Government and the LRA dismissed *Mato Oput* as a traditional system that is not known by most Acholi people, being fabricated to suit the moment. Interview was made in December 2009 in Kampala.

[157] Agenda Item 3 on Accountability and Reconciliation of the Draft Juba Peace Agreement of 29th June 2007. Available at:
http://www.resolveuganda.org/peaceagreement. Accessed on 24/6/2010.

In this case, while the conflict is a national issue, no single traditional approach commands a national appeal. This limitation calls for rethinking the appropriateness of traditional approaches from a national perspective.

Critics of the traditional justice system especially the one in Northern Uganda point out that it promotes a culture of impunity. Its emphasis on restorative justice rather than the Western formal judicial system tends to be very soft on the offenders who commit human rights violations. For example, most leaders and elites in Northern Uganda have been advocating for a general amnesty for the LRA rebels arguing that 'they are our children and it is us they killed[158]. In fact most of them blame the International Criminal Court (ICC) for failing the peace process in Northern Uganda after it issued arrest warrants for Kony and his top commanders.[159] In Northern Uganda there are key people who have benefited from the Amnesty Act 2000 and traditional justice such as Brigadier Banya and Onen Kamdulu who were some of the top commanders within the LRA that surrendered. Banya surrendered to the government army and was reintegrated and allowed to stay with a wife who was a formerly abducted child soldier. During the field work it was established that on several occasions Banya had battered his wife violently with impunity and it was feared he may onetime kill her.[160]

Kamdulu, himself a former child soldier who rose through the ranks of the LRA to become a Director of Operations of the LRA, was captured by the government army, forgiven and reintegrated into the army. He was subsequently arrested, together with another former rebel commander Major Thomas Opiyo, with semi-automatic rifles and 146 bullets as they attempted to rob local fish sellers in Apac.[161] It is also noted that before Kamdulu was arrested, he had been involved in a

---

[158]Interview with Bishop Ochora, Opcit.

[159] The New Vision, ICC Failed the Kony Talks, Says Oulanya. Available at: http://www.newvision.co.ug/D/8/13/721001. Accessed on 28/5/2010.

[160] Interview with Captain Kakurungu, a Uganda Peoples Defence Forces Public Relations Officer for Northern Uganda conducted in northern Uganda in January 2010.

[161] Ayugi, C. (2007). Pardoned Former LRA members, who allegedly hid their weapons from authorities, are being blamed for a series of gun crimes across northern Uganda. Institute of War and Peace Reporting, Norwegian Council for Africa, Oslo, Norway, 06 December. Available at: http://www.afrika.no/Detailed/15590.html. Accessed on 27/5/2010.

string of other robberies. One of the victims of LRA brutality, Celementina Akoko commenting on the behaviour of former child soldiers accused of robberies, lamented that:

> … the packages should have made the former rebels grateful. How much do these rebels want from us? Iam unable to fend for myself because of bodily harm they inflicted on me, yet they want me to forgive them. But how many times should I continue forgiving someone who intentionally hurts me.[162]

Kamdulu and his colleague are currently serving their sentences in jail.

The point being made is that the romanticization of traditional justice and reconciliation approaches which are too soft on punishment may institutionalize a culture of impunity and trap a society into a vicious circle of violence (Olupot, 2010).[163] More so, most of these traditional practices are based on oral agreements as opposed to written agreements which makes them dependent on the commitment and goodwill of the offender. There is therefore, a need to document these traditional approaches so that they are understood by everybody and are used the same way rather than in a chaotic manner as they are being used today in Northern Uganda. It may be imperative to complement the traditional justice and reconciliation system with the modern judicial system to handle serious violations such as crimes against humanity to break the culture of impunity and build a civic culture based on the rule of law. Short of that conflicts in Uganda and in most of Africa have become a lucrative enterprise where rebel leaders are lured back with 4WD Pajeros, bungalows and huge sums of money as resettlement packages.

Another challenge of traditional approaches in Northern Uganda is their failure to reintegrate child mothers and their children who have been rejected by parents. A fair traditional system should not fail to realize that both the child mothers and their children are victims of the conflict. One wonders why a valued traditional system based on the principles of restoration and forgiveness cannot accommodate the child mothers and their children.

---

[162] Ibid.,

[163] Olupot, M. (2010) 'Aliker raps Otunnu over LRA War Case,' *The New Vision* Newspaper. Available at: http://www.newvision.co.ug/D/8/12/722921. Accessed on 17/6/2010.

Finally, most observers wonder why in spite of the criticisms levelled against Western psychosocial approaches, they continue to be used in most war-torn societies. The reality is that while most of the former child soldiers interviewed said that they were helped by the traditional rituals, there exist a significant number of them who said they found the Western psychosocial support of counselling and other therapies more fulfilling than the traditional ones. Owor who worked with GUSCO as a Social Worker pointed out that:

GUSCO was open to both the traditional and Western models of psychosocial support in terms of counselling. I found the Western approach more effective especially for those who were born again Christians. The traditional approach was mainly advocated by the parents and guardians of the children.[164]

Nevertheless, the traditional and indigenous approaches should not be simply dismissed since they have helped in the RR of child soldiers not only in Northern Uganda but also in other war-torn societies such as Mozambique, Angola and Sierra Leone (Honwana, 2006). Most crucially, they have helped to rebuild societies shattered by decades of violent civil wars and remain a basis for rebuilding such societies. As Kostelny (2006) observes, it is local communities using their cultural resources and supports that are central to the psychosocial well-being of former child soldiers. Despite the fact that traditional approaches/resources would have been disrupted during the war, the role of outsiders should be to help restore traditions by assisting in community empowerment and building local capacities through facilitation and training including provision of technical assistance. On the other hand, it would be unrealistic to dismiss the values of Western approaches based on the findings of this book. Instead, an integrative approach that blends both approaches by picking good elements from either of the two approaches would be ideal for the RR of former child soldiers.

---

[164]Interview with Owor, A., Op Cit.

Conclusion

This chapter has examined the importance of psychosocial support in the RR of former child soldiers in war-torn societies. The chapter also explored the relevance of psychosocial support based on traditional and indigenous resources in the RR of child soldiers in the African context, which is a neglected element of peacebuilding both in policy and academic circles. The chapter specifically discussed the traditional and indigenous resources that have been relied upon in the RR of child soldiers in Northern Uganda including *Mato Oput*, stepping on the egg and bending spears. The chapter also discussed the advantages and challenges of the traditional and indigenous approaches of conflict management and reconciliation.

In the final analysis, empirical evidence in Northern Uganda shows that neither of the two psychosocial supports - African traditional and indigenous approaches and Western approaches alone can effectively reintegrate and rehabilitate former child soldiers. It is against this background that an integrated approach that blends positive elements from both approaches and is holistic is recommended. However, such an approach should be gender sensitive and should as much as possible seek to maximize local participation and cultures.

CHAPTER SEVEN

●━━━━━━━━━━━━━━━━━━━━━━━━━●

National Legal Framework for Reintegration and Rehabilitation of Child Soldiers in Uganda

This chapter examines the relevant national legal framework for the RR of child soldiers in Uganda, as well as the necessary conditions for RR of former child soldiers. The most elaborate legal instrument in Uganda for the RR of child soldiers is the Amnesty Act 2000, amended in 2006. The Amnesty Act provides for the establishment of the Amnesty Commission (AC), a body whose major responsibility is to handle RR of ex-combatants who include former child soldiers (Afako, 2002). The Amnesty Act was mainly enacted to end the vicious circle of armed conflicts in the country particularly in Northern Uganda where the LRA rebels have wreaked havoc across the region (Makerere University, Refugee Law Project, 2005:6).

Article 2 (1) of the Amnesty Act states that, An amnesty is declared in respect of any Ugandan who has at any time since the 26th day of January, 1986, engaged in or is engaging in war or armed rebellion against the Government of the Republic of Uganda by:

a) Actual participation in combat;
b) Collaborating with the perpetrators of the war or armed rebellion;
c) Committing any other crime in the furtherance of the war or armed rebellion; or
d) Assisting or aiding the conduct or prosecution of the war or armed rebellion.

Article 3 provides grounds upon which an amnesty is granted. Article 3 (1) states that, 'a reporter shall be granted the amnesty declared under section 2 if the reporter:

a)   Reports to the nearest army or police unit, a member of the executive committee of the local government unit, or magistrate or a religious leader within the locality;

b)   Renounces and abandons involvement in the war or armed rebellion;

c)   Surrenders at any such place or to any such authority or person any weapons in his or her possession; and

d)   Is issued with a certificate of amnesty ...'

The Amnesty Act establishes the Amnesty Commission, whose major functions include, implementing programmes of demobilization; reintegration; and resettlement of reporters. The Commission is also charged with coordination of programmes including sensitization of the general public on the amnesty law; to consider and promote appropriate reconciliation mechanisms in the affected areas and promote dialogue and reconciliation.

The Amnesty Act also creates the Demobilization and Resettlement Team (DRT) of the Amnesty Commission whose functions are: decommissioning of arms; demobilization; resettlement and reintegration of reporters who include the child soldiers.

As discussed in Chapter Five, the Amnesty Act, through the Amnesty Commission, has demobilized and reintegrated several ex-combatants including the child soldiers in Northern Uganda. According to Draku, an officer with the Commission, the Amnesty Commission's work has been greatly hampered by lack of adequate funding from the government which makes it dependant on external funding. By far, the Amnesty Act is the foremost legal framework that has been used though with limited success in the RR of child soldiers in Northern Uganda.

Another legal framework that provides for the RR of child soldiers in Northern Uganda is the national Constitution. Article 34 (4) of the Constitution of Uganda provides that children are entitled to be protected from social or economic exploitation and shall not be employed in or required to perform work that is likely to be hazardous or interfere with their education or to be harmful to their health or physical, mental, spiritual, moral or social development. This means that child soldiers and children's rights advocates in Northern Uganda could use Article 34 (4) of the Constitution to demand resources and any other support for their RR and development.

More so, Article 5 of the Constitution of Uganda establishes the Uganda Human Rights Commission (UHRC), a body that is supposed to uphold, protect and promote respect for human rights in Uganda. In respect to the RR in Northern Uganda, the UHRC is mandated among other functions under Article 5 to perform the following functions:

1.   to investigate, at its own initiative or on a complaint made by any person or a group of persons, about the violation of any human right;
2.   to establish a continuing programme of research, education and information to enhance the respect of human rights;
3.   to recommend to Parliament effective measures to promote human rights, including provision of compensation to victims of violation of human rights or their families

It was established that the UHRC has not brought any case against government in respect to the violation of former child soldier's rights or failure to protect them against the LRA. However, the constitution empowers the UHRC to exercise its mandate and assist victims of human rights violation such as former child soldiers whose lives were shattered by the LRA conflict.

The UHRC is also mandated to formulate, implement and oversee programmes intended to create civic awareness among the citizens about their civic rights, duties and obligations and to monitor the government's compliance with United Nations Convention on the Rights of the Child and other human rights treaties. In an interview with staff of the UHRC, the institution has been conducting human rights awareness and sensitization programmes in Northern Uganda. However, the UHRC needs to design specific programmes that address the challenges and needs of former child soldiers in Northern Uganda. For instance, the UHRC needs to address the issues of landless children born in the bush, rejection of child mothers by their families and community stigmatization of former child soldiers which undermines their effective RR.

Another important legal instrument for the RR of former child soldiers is the Children Act 1997. Beyond protection of the rights of the child in peacetime conditions, some sections of the Act can be relied upon to promote RR of former child soldiers in conflict situations. Article 10 of the Children Act mandates local government councils to safeguard children and promote reconciliation between parents and children. Article 10 (1) states that, 'It is the duty of every local government council from the village to the district level: a) to safeguard and promote the welfare of children within its area; and b) to designate one of its members to be the person responsible for the welfare of children; and this person shall be referred to as the Secretary for Children's affairs.

Article 10 (3) enjoins the local government to mediate in any situation where the rights of a child are infringed upon especially with regard to the protection of a child, the child's right to succeed to the property of his or her parents and all the rights accorded to a child in section 5. Critical for RR of former child soldiers who may have become disabled during the conflict is Article 10 (5) which provides that, 'A local government council shall keep a register of disabled children within its area of jurisdiction and give assistance to them whenever possible in order to enable these children to grow up with dignity among other children and to develop their potential.

The Children Act would be a useful instrument for assisting family reintegration in Northern Uganda where there are reported cases of family breakdown after re-union due to disagreements between children and parents which has forced such children to street life (Liu Institute for Global Issues, 2005). The Children Actcan assist in the RR of the disabled children who were maimed during the armed conflict. These face additional trauma in their RR processes as a result of their disability making them seem more of a liability than assetsto their families. Worth noting is that in spite of the existence of the Children Act, most local governments are not directly involved in the RR of former child soldiers, yet they are mandated to protect the rights of children generally.

The final national legal framework relevant in the RR of child soldiers is the International Criminal Court (ICC) Act 2006. The ICC Act that was enacted on 10 March, 2010 seeks to operationalize the Rome Statute; Uganda's War Victims Court in Uganda and to facilitate the implementation of the ICC Trust Funds for Victims in Northern Uganda. The ICC has a multi-faceted reparations scheme that is not widely known. The Rome Statute created a hybrid institution- The Trust Fund for Victims (TFV). One part of the ICC is the court itself, the other part is the Trust Fund for Victims, both established in 2002 (Stuart, 2009).[165] The ICC Act 2006 also paves the way for the trial and

---

[165] Stuart, V.H. (2009). The ICC Trust Fund for Victims: Beyond the Realm of the ICC. Available at:

conviction in Uganda of people accused of war crimes, genocide and crimes against humanity (Mufumba, 2010).[166]

Article 75 of the Rome Statute mandates the court to lay down the principles for reparations for victims, which may include restitution, indemnification and rehabilitation. The court has authority to order that this reparation be paid through the Trust Fund for Victims which was set up by the Assembly of States Parties in September 2002.

Both President Museveni and the ICC Prosecutor, Luis Moreno Ocampo have called for compensation of the LRA war victims in Northern Uganda which is part of their RR (*Daily Monitor*, June 1 2010).[167]

In spite of what seems to be a robust body of national legal mechanisms to protect children's rights in armed conflicts, children continue to be major victims of most conflicts in Uganda. Both the LRA and the government army stand accused of recruitment and use of children in armed conflicts (Global Report, 2008). Consequently, one can safely say that national legal mechanisms for protection of children's rights in armed conflicts have largely remained paper protection mechanisms.

Necessary Conditions for Reintegration and Rehabilitation of Child Soldiers

There are a number of challenges that affect successful and long-term RR of child soldiers in most war-torn societies, particularly in Northern Uganda. The findings of this study reveal that the most significant challenges facing RR of child soldiers in Northern Uganda revolve around education, economic and employment opportunities, family and community acceptance and lack of committed long-term official RR programming. These challenges are discussed in detail below.

---

http://static.rnw.nl/migratie/www.rnw.nl/internationaljustice/specials/commentary/0 90204-ICC-TFV-redirected. Accessed on 2/6/2010.
[166] The Independent Newspaper (2010) ICC Bill: Why did MPs trap Museveni and Save Kony? Available at: http://independent.co.ug/index.php/column/insight/67- insight/2702-icc-bill-why-did-mps-trap-museveni-and-save-kony. Accessed on 2/6/2010.
[167] Daily Monitor (2010). 'LRA Victims should be Compensated - Ocampo,' Tuesday June 1. Available at: http://www.monitor.co.ug/News/National/-688334/929644/- /x0ab2i/-/index.html. Acessed on 2/6/2010.

Based on fieldwork research, most local organizations and agencies dealing with the RR of former child soldiers have tended to focus more on humanitarian and psychosocial needs with less emphasis on education and economic empowerment. For example, while reception centres provided the most secure environments to child soldiers escaping from LRA captivity which included counselling, treatment of diseases, wounds, provision of farming tools and home utensils during the re-unification with families, most former child soldiers complain of lack of follow up support and false promises by the reception centres[168].

Ker Kwaro Acholi, the apex Acholi cultural institution has conducted region wide cultural rituals and ceremonies to promote community reconciliation and acceptance. According to Avola, in spite of these efforts by *Ker Kwaro Acholi*, some former child soldiers continue to be stigmatized as a result of other unmet needs. In order for effective RR of former child soldiers in Northern Uganda there are certain material conditions that need to obtain as discussed below:

Education

Most former child soldiers that were interviewed gave education as a priority for their effective RR into society. In fact for some of them who think they have already missed out on education such as child mothers, provision of education to their children is considered their top priority. A.P., who is a 25 years old with a six year old daughter, employed as a security guard noted that her ambition is to enrol for an adult literacy course and learn how to read and write and be able to educate her daughter. A study by the World Bank revealed that increases in school enrolment of former child soldiers contributes to the safety of the community and reduces the probability of another civil war (Guyot, 2007).

Scholars and analysts (Machel, 2001; Honwana, 2006) observe that education can promote respect for human rights and helps to bind communities by bringing together children, parents, educators and local officials for a shared purpose. Almost all the 25 former child soldiers interviewed for this study regard education as key to their secure future livelihoods. Some of them with school age children are already worried

---

[168]Interview with members of KICA Ber Youth Group.

about their children's educations. One former child soldier at the International Review Conference for the ICC in Kampala observed that, 'My children are of school going age already, so I need help to see them through school (*Daily Monitor,* 2010)[169]. However, as Brett et al (2004:131) have noted, education should be tailored towards the current labour market. Most importantly, education opportunities should be sensitive of the special needs of female former child soldiers to avoid their marginalization.

Economic Empowerment and Employment Opportunities

The second necessary condition for effective RR of child soldiers is the availability of economic support or employment opportunities to enable them to start income generating activities to ensure sustainable livelihoods. Some scholars and analysts (Brett et al, 2004) observe that economic hardships among former child soldiers may drive them back into fresh rebellions and criminality and result in failure to reintegrate fully into society. Wessells (2006:179) points out that if poverty, conflict, and child soldiering linkage is worrying from a child rights perspective, it is of equal concern from a peace perspective. Research findings show that one of the greatest worries of most former child soldiers in Northern Uganda is economic insecurity and widespread unemployment. It was found out that youths that have been supported by NGOs and their own associations such as, *Can Rwede Peke* Group and KICA Ber Youth Group to start their own income generating activities are more positive and optimistic about their future and are working hard to improve their lives.

One former child soldier who is a member of KICA Ber Youth Group observed during a focus group discussion,

These days' people in the villages respect us because we no longer go around begging from them as before. With the loans from our group, we have been able to support ourselves and families.

Members of KICA Ber Youth Group (both male and female) borrow money from the group and return it at a low interest rate. Majority of male members are engaged in brick making and agriculture while females

---

[169] Daily Monitor (2010). War Victims Turn to ICC for Compensation, Thursday June 3. Available at: http://www.monitor.co.ug/News/National/-/688334/931164/931164/-/x0q6ix/-/index.html. Accessed on 3/6/2010.

are engaged in small scale businesses mostly selling farm produce and charcoal.[170]

Other scholars point out that income generating activities for former child soldiers and youths in war-torn societies steer them away from risky occupations including joining criminal gangs (Guyot, 2007:9). While income generating activities for youth affected by the war are crucial to ensure effective RR and peacebuilding in Northern Uganda, these activities are being offered by NGOs, CBOs and youth groups in a manner that is uncoordinated and unsustainable. The official Amnesty Commission that is charged with the RR of ex-combatants including child soldiers has been largely ineffective citing lack of funding and capacity limitations.[171]It should be noted that economic empowerment for former child soldiers should take community-based strategies rather than targeting them alone to avoid community resentment and conflict. However, socio-economic reintegration and rehabilitation programming should be gender sensitive to avoid marginalization of former female combatants.

Participation of Former Child Soldiers in Designing RR Programmes

A crucial condition for successful RR of former child soldiers is their participation in the planning and programming of the initiatives designed to assist thier transition into civilian life. Scholars such as Guyot, (2007:8) observe that programming for the RR of child soldiers should recognize their potential and should not treat them as mere passive recipients of donor support. Participation of former child soldiers in design and implementation of their RR programmes is also supported by Jareg (2005) who notes that participation of former child soldiers in planning and execution of RR programmes helps them neutralize the feelings of helplessness and distrust often associated with their traumatic experiences. It is further observed that participation turns around the ways in which children were trained to behave in military environments where they received orders that were not negotiable. Involvement of former child soldiers in RR planning and programming would not only

---

[170] Interview with members of KICA Ber Youth Group conducted in northern Uganda in February 2010.
[171]Interview with Draku, Op Cit.

ensure ownership and skills transfer in planning and sustainability but also provides psychosocial therapy to them since it restores self-confidence eroded by the conflict. In the case of Northern Uganda, the design of PRDP which is the official peacebuilding programme never enlisted the participation of the target beneficiaries including former child soldiers.

Addressing the Structural Causes of Child Soldiering

Most analysts observe that as long as war persists, children will always be caught up in the fighting either as bystanders or as active combatants since they are so vulnerable to rebel commanders' and government forces' recruitment methods which may be coercive or voluntary (Singer, 2006). Honwana (2006:159) observes that regardless of community healing practices which seem to be effective with the RR of war-affected children, such practices cannot sustain long-lasting results if young people do not have jobs, are not going to school or have no skills to earn a living. If former child soldiers are not given a chance to improve their lives, they will be absorbed into violence, be it urban gangs, illicit business dealings, or rebel militias in new civil wars (Singer, 2006; Wessells, 2006). In Northern Uganda, the conditions that caused the rebellion still exist including economic underdevelopment, widespread poverty and unemployment that were worsened by massive internal displacement of the population in camps, and ethnic hatred due to colonial distortions (PRDP, 2007).

In fact some analysts note that effective RR of former child soldiers is possible only if it is done as part of a wider peacebuilding programme that seeks to comprehensively address the root causes of the conflict (Honwana, 2006). The above analysis is confirmed by fieldwork interviews with some of the former child soldiers who live in fear of possible re-abduction by the rebels since they refused to sign a peace agreement and are still active in Sudan and DRC.

Family and Community Acceptance

Family re-unification and community acceptance have been found to be crucial conditions in the RR of child soldiers (Boothby, 2006:170; Brett, 2004; MacKay, 2006). One of the findings during field work, is that most former child soldiers were well received by their families and communities particularly those who were reintegrated by the reception centres. However, it was also established that some family re-unions have broken down parents complaining that their children don't respect them. This has led to some of these youths ending on the streets especially in Gulu town and Kampala city doing odd jobs to survive. There are also some former child soldiers who complained of rejection and stigmatization by families and the community. They noted that some members of community call them rebels, wife of the rebel, and other bad names. B.A., 19, is an example of family rejection. She was seven years old when the LRA abducted her and spent six years in the bush. She escaped when they were attacked by the government army. B.A., a single mother of two children, returned home but found that her mother had died and the father remarried. The Respondent pointed out that:

My step-mother does not want me at home. She made my life unbearable so I decided to take my children to go to my uncle. My uncle's wife also did not want us there. That is how we ended in this town to look for work.

Research findings also established that there are several cases of parents who refused their daughters back with children born in the bush. These child mothers have ended on streets doing odd jobs for a living. As Wessells (2006:202) observes, although returning child soldiers' need for money is undeniable, it is intertwined with their burning desire to avoid stigma and to achieve a modicum of dignity and respect.

RR Programming Should Target Communities

Another important finding is that most communities in Northern Uganda are unhappy at the material support that NGOs and CBOs are providing to former child soldiers as a special group when everybody else suffered during the war. An interview with staff of Caritas Gulu revealed that communities view the support to former child soldiers as a reward for committing atrocities against their families and communities during the conflict. This attitude is likely to lead to resentment and stigmatization and could render RR initiatives unable to achieve their objectives. The staff of Caritas pointed out that as a result of community complaints Caritas has since re-designed their programming to assist the entire communities in their areas of concentration.

286

Consequently, it is advisable that RR initiatives for former child soldiers in Northern Uganda either by government, NGOs and CBOs should also target entire communities as well as promoting community reconciliation and social healing between communities and former child soldiers.

Harmonization of Psychosocial Support for Former Child Soldiers

During fieldwork, it was established that most former child soldiers received psychosocial support in form of traditional rituals and healing ceremonies as well as Western counselling that involved one-on-one counselling, talking therapy, drama, music and dance. The majority of the former child soldiers who were interviewed said they found the traditional approaches more helpful to them. However, there are some who pointed out that they found Western approaches relevant. There are also reports where children refused traditional rituals and were being forced by their parents to accept them (interview with staff of CPA). Conflicting psychosocial supports to RR of child soldiers can be confusing and harmful to the intended beneficiaries. Consequently, it would be good to harmonize these approaches. Government, UNICEF and traditional institutions need to coordinate a process that would come up with a hybrid model of psychosocial support that embodies good elements from both approaches (Kostelny, 2006).

Empower the Amnesty Commission

The Amnesty Commission is mandated by the Amnesty Act, 2000 to disarm, demobilize, rehabilitate and reintegrate ex-combatants including child soldiers. Research findings show that the commission has implemented its mandate with limited success. There are many former child soldiers who returned to their homes without going through the army's Child Protection Unit and reception centres where they were given amnesty certificates and resettlement packages by the Amnesty Commission. Most of these children live in fear of being arrested by government since they were not officially reintegrated. The staff at the Amnesty Commission admitted that the institution has not been able to execute its full mandate due to underfunding and lack of expertise. Findings reveal that former child soldiers need the services of the Amnesty Commission - amnesty certificates as an assurance for their

287

security and resettlement packages to settle down into civilian life. Consequently, government, the UN agencies and development partners should provide adequate funding to the Amnesty Commission to enable it implement its mandate.

Long-term Support for RR of Child Soldiers

Analysts note that the RR of child soldiers is the most difficult process because of the added psychological and physiological scars they carry (Singer, 2006:193). Consequently, it is advised that RR programming should have a long-term perspective that ensures sustainability even after the conflict has ended. Unfortunately, the PRDP which is the official peacebuilding framework is short-term. Initially, the PRDP was designed to last three years (2007-2010) although it has now been extended to June 2012 which is still a short time to make a lasting impact. Also, most of the NGOs and CBOs involved in RR of former child soldiers are donor dependent, funded on a short-term basis. Successful RR of former child soldiers needs long-term programmatic support of five years and above (Guyot, 2007).

Future Research Agenda

This section examines critical areas that are relevant to this book but were beyond its scope and could constitute a future research agenda.

Impunity and Traditional Approaches of Conflict Management

Ugandans have been subjected to extensive human rights violations under successive regimes including Idi Amin's reign of terror (1971-79) where close to half a million people are estimated to have been killed; the Obote 11 Government and now the LRA rebellion in Northern Uganda (Kanyeihamba, 2002:155). Unfortunately, no systematic efforts have ever been made to prosecute the perpetrators which can be partly blamed on weak governments or weak legal systems (Afako, 2002). When the Government introduced the Amnesty Bill in 2000, which gave partial amnesty to the LRA and other armed groups, the Acholi Religious Leaders submitted a memorandum which they claimed represented the views of the Acholi at home and in the diaspora advocating for general

288

amnesty for the entire LRA leadership. Throughout the LRA conflict both the religious and traditional leaders in Acholi have voiced their support for peace through traditional justice mechanisms.

The question here is whether or not traditional approaches of conflict resolution and peacebuilding are promoting nation building or a culture of impunity which traps the country into a vicious circle of violence. New research could help to establish whether these amnesties advocated for by traditional and opinion leaders are promoting sustainable peace or a culture of impunity.

African Traditional Approaches and Gender Issues

The research findings show that to some extent most of the African traditional approaches of conflict management and reconciliation violate or marginalize the rights of women or girls (Denov, 2007; Murithi, 2008). For example, *Mato Oput*, a justice and reconciliation system among the Acholi in Northern Uganda provides for compensation by a virgin girl to the offended party who is expected to produce children and replace the murdered person of another clan. In the current application of *Mato Oput*, this element has been removed although these adjustments also raise questions of acceptance and validity. Furthermore, the failure of the two peace processes led by Betty Bigombe to deliver a peaceful settlement in Northern Uganda is largely attributed to the Acholi male dominated traditional system that cannot allow a mere woman succeed where men have failed[172]Most scholars have observed that women and children suffer most during war and are also marginalized by peacebuilding processes (Pankhurst, 2008). It would be important to study in detail the relationship between African traditional approaches and women's rights and peacebuilding in respect to Northern Uganda.

Land Question and RR of Child Mothers and their Children

Uganda is an agricultural based economy with the majority of the population dependent on agriculture and the environment for survival (Tumushabe et al. 2004). Effective RR of former child soldiers in Northern Uganda is going to depend on whether or not they access land

---

[172]Interview with Betty Bigombe, former chief peace negotiator between the LRA and Government.

for production. Land in most of Northern Uganda, especially in Acholi land, is owned communally on a clan basis. There are serious cases where former child soldiers who are child mothers have been refused return to their homes simply because they have children who don't belong to their parent's clans and cannot inherit land (Allen et al, 2006:87).Rejection of such children makes them landless and yet access to land for production is crucial in agriculture dependent societies such as Uganda. It would be important to conduct research on the land question in Northern Uganda in respect to the issue of child mothers and their landless children.

Conclusion

This chapter examined the national legal framework relevant for the RR of former child soldiers. The legal framework includes the Amnesty Act, 2000; The Ugandan Constitution; the Children Act 1997; and the ICC Act 2006. The chapter also discussed the necessary material conditions for effective RR of former child soldiers in Northern Uganda. These include availability of economic and employment opportunities, educational opportunities, community and family acceptability among others. The chapter also proposed a future research agenda relevant to this research which could not be covered due to its limited scope. The future research agenda could include but not limited to the question of impunity and traditional approaches to conflict management and reconciliation; the gender issues and the land question in Northern Uganda.

CHAPTER EIGHT

●━━━━━━━━━━━━━━━━━━━━━━━━━━━━●

Conclusions

Proposing a New Framework for Post-Conflict Peace-building in Northern Uganda

Study Overview and Findings

This study has used a conflict resolution frame-work which draws from various disciplines in order to have a deeper understanding of the complicated nature of new wars currently going on in the developing countries and their impact on communities, especially the children who are drawn into these wars as combatants. This book cannot claim to have been exhaustive in addressing the issues that relate to the plight of child soldiers and their RR into civilian life in Northern Uganda. However, the book contributes to the debate and the understanding on how better to end violent conflicts and rebuild war-torn societies through RR of child soldiers based on the use of traditional and indigenous resources: the neglected element of the dominant liberal peace approach to peacebuilding (Richmond, 2007). As Richmond (2007:288) observes, the liberal peace approach to peacebuilding is a Western and Enlightenment-derived discourse of peace, which is far from culturally and socially sensitive, and has little chance of establishing a locally self-sustaining peace. This book established that traditional and indigenous resources in Northern Uganda including traditional rituals and cleansing ceremonies, cultural leaders, families, women and youth groups have played a crucial role in the RR of former child soldiers.

The research for this book was premised on a number of arguments. The first argument is that the effective reintegration and rehabilitation of former child soldiers into civilian and productive life would contribute to conditions of peace and security in Northern Uganda. The second argument is that the neglect and marginalization of former child soldiers

291

in most of the reintegration and rehabilitation processes causes more wars, long wars, increases criminality and hampers any efforts towards building durable peace in war-torn societies (MacKay, 2004; Singer, 2006). The third argument is that the provision of psychosocial support based on traditional and indigenous resources, which is the neglected element of peacebuilding is very crucial in the RR of former child soldiers.

Based on field work and literature review, the following constitute the major research findings in respect to the RR of former child soldiers in Northern Uganda.

This book established that all the 25 former child soldiers selected for this research experienced traumatic experiences during their captivity by the LRA. These traumatic experiences included, witnessing killings; being forced to kill one's friend or relative; being beaten senselessly as part of training, extreme hunger and long walks carrying looted food and medicine which sometimes took them into Sudan, sexual slavery and forced marriages. Children also participated in fighting with the government army where many of their colleagues were killed. All these events have left emotional and physical scars on former child soldiers.

During the fieldwork, some former child soldiers revealed that they dream about killings and being pursued by the LRA who seek to kill them. Other examples of trauma established by this research include uncontrolled crying especially by child mothers who have been rejected by their parents and live in very difficult conditions; complaints about stigmatization by the community who call them abusive names; disagreements between children and parents that lead to breakdown of family re-unions and constant fights among former child soldiers.[173]

The book also established that psychosocial support based on traditional and indigenous resources has been widely used in the RR of child soldiers in Northern Uganda. Ker Kwaro Acholi, the main Acholi cultural institution has worked with traditional leaders to conduct regional wide traditional rituals and cleansing ceremonies such as *Mato Oput* and stepping on the egg to welcome children back and to sensitize communities to accept them. It was also established that some reception centres used Western approaches of psychosocial support in the RR of child soldiers while others combined both approaches. World Vision

---

[173] Interview with a Social Worker with Watoto Community Church conducted at Watoto Church in Gulu in March 2010.

only used Western approaches and Christian prayers and discouraged any use of traditional rituals and ceremonies during reintegration with families.

Most of the 25 former child soldiers that were interviewed during the fieldwork observed that they found traditional rituals and ceremonies which included *Mato Oput*, stepping on the eggs and sprinkling with water more useful and relevant in their RR. Traditional and indigenous resources in Northern Uganda enjoy widespread support and respect rooted in the history and spirituality of the people (Latigo, 2008). However, it was also established that there are some former child soldiers especially those from Christian families who said they were greatly assisted by Western approaches of psychosocial support. It was also found that some former child soldiers resent traditional rituals since they remind them of similar blood rituals performed by the LRA in the bush.

The research further established that while traditional and indigenous approaches of psychosocial support were widely used in the RR of former child soldiers in Northern Uganda, they have been greatly weakened by the two decades of the civil war and the effects of colonialism. For example most people in Northern Uganda particularly Acholi sub-region had forgotten most of the traditional approaches such as *Mato Oput*. Consequently, these traditional approaches have had to be recreated which makes them challenged by other people especially the elites. Secondly, Christianity and Western education which are linked to the British colonial legacy greatly undermined traditional rituals and ceremonies since they regarded them as backward and satanic. Above all, traditional and indigenous resources were found to be gender insensitive towards women and girls since the Acholi culture is male dominated.

In spite of the identified weaknesses, indigenous and traditional resources including traditional rituals and ceremonies, and local institutions such as families, cultural leaders, youth and women's groups were found to have contributed a great deal to the RR of former child soldiers. At the same time, Western psychosocial approaches were found to have been widely used by child reception centres whose contribution is greatly appreciated in the absence of a robust government response. As Kostelny (2006) has noted, there are good elements in both approaches that should be harnessed. Consequently, an integrated and holistic model that blends both approaches is recommended.

Furthermore, most organizations involved in the RR of former child soldiers in Northern Uganda, observed that many members of the community among whom former child soldiers are being reintegrated, are traumatized due to the impact of the war.[174]. Community wide traumatization is said to be linked to widespread poverty and many years of IDP life that was dehumanizing and traumatic experiences. This is likely to make it difficult to successfully reintegrate and rehabilitate former child soldiers. Interviews conducted among 25 former child soldiers revealed that even if these people were given psychosocial support by reception centres which were supplemented by traditional rituals by the cultural institutions, most of them remain traumatized. Former child soldiers continue to be traumatized by members of communities who call them bad names. Fear of re-abduction by the LRA, economic insecurity and fear that their children (in the case of young mothers) will suffer the same fate of missed education opportunities are further examples of traumatization.

The young mothers who have been rejected by their families with their children and live in poor conditions in towns seem to be the most traumatized group. During the interviews, some of them were continuously sobbing. It was also established that associations of former child soldiers are very helpful to their members. These associations provide psychosocial support to members through counselling and encouragement in addition to offering savings and credit facilities. Most of the members interviewed said that their groups are a source of protection and security from society that sometimes does not understand their problems.[175]

Additionally, the field work and literature review show evidence that children and women suffer most during civil wars going on in developing countries (Machel, 2001; Singer, 2006; Honwana, 2006,). Children are systematically targeted for recruitment by armed groups and government forces. In Uganda, the LRA has greatly violated the children's rights which prompted the ICC to indict top LRA commanders. Research findings also show that in spite of the existence of a robust international legal mechanism to protect the rights of children in armed conflicts, they have remained ineffective due to international politics, double standards

---

[174]Interview with Caritas staff, Op Cit.
[175] Interview with members of Can Rwende Peke Group in conducted in northern Uganda in February, 2010.

294

and the different conceptualization of a child; childhood and child soldier across cultures.

The fieldwork revealed that educational opportunities, especially vocational training, are crucial for effective RR of former child soldiers. Most former child soldiers who were interviewed individually and collectively through focus group discussions look at education as the most immediate investment that they need to secure a bright future.[176] Worth noting is that most of the leaders of former child soldiers' associations that were visited during fieldwork, are those people who were able to pursue studies after returning from the bush.

Income generating activities were also found to be crucial in the RR of former child soldiers. Most of the former child soldiers observed that their involvement in income generating activities has earned them respect among the communities since they are seen as being productive to society. More so, land ownership was found to be critical to successful RR. Culturally among the Acholi, land is owned communally by clans. Since the children who returned with young mothers do not belong to their mothers' clans, they cannot be allowed to inherit other clans' land. That is why young mothers have resorted to prostitution in towns. The land question is making RR of young mothers and their children difficult.

From the research findings, it is also evident that the assistance being provided to former child soldiers by some NGOs and CBOs is causing resentment by the communities which could hamper the RR processes. Two reasons are given why communities resent preferential treatment of former child soldiers. First, communities still blame former child soldiers for committing atrocities against them during the war since the LRA forced children to kill relatives or people in their communities in order to alienate them. Second, as staff of Caritas observed, the communities are equally poor and needy like former child soldiers.[177] Consequently, it is important that any development assistance to former child soldiers should take a community wide approach to avoid creating more conflicts and stigmatization of child soldiers.

It was also established that lack of follow up on former child soldiers by reception centres is hampering effective RR in Northern Uganda. Most former child soldiers interviewed complained of empty 'promises' by reception centres. During the RR processes, reception centres seem to

---

[176] Ibid.
[177] Interview with Rubangateke, Op Cit.

have raised a lot of expectations among former child soldiers. Interviews with some of the reception centres indicate that they too lack adequate funding to implement follow up activities.[178] Since former child soldiers established strong bonds and trust with reception centres, follow up visits to assess how they are coping and further support are crucial for their successful transition into civilian life.

Research findings further revealed that many organizations have mushroomed in Northern Uganda involved in peacebuilding activities including RR of former child soldiers. The numerous organizations coupled with weak coordination of peacebuilding activities by government is likely to cause more harm than good including institutionalizing dependence of communities and former child soldiers, and duplication of services.[179] Consequently, there is a need for government to take stock of all the organizations operating in the region with a view to streamlining their activities to ensure proper coordination, harmonization, effectiveness and accountability. Government also needs to review the PRDP and design specific projects targeting former child soldiers. Such projects should be designed in such a manner that benefits the communities to avoid resentment.

Based on the finding of widespread traumatization of communities in Northern Uganda (Liu Institute for Global Issues 2006), it is important that government and the international community come up with an affirmative action for the region. Affirmative action should emphasize the integrated psychosocial support model that blends both the Western and indigenous approaches of psychosocial support. Such a model should be holistic in nature in the sense that it addresses broad issues of poverty, education, employment opportunities, reconciliation and good governance that are at the core of the conflict in Northern Uganda. As Honwana (2006:159) observes, effective RR of former child soldiers cannot be possible without comprehensively addressing the root causes of child soldiering, which means addressing the root causes of the conflict in which these former child soldiers are trapped.

---

[178]Interview with the staff of CPA in Gulu in February 2009.
[179] Research conducted by Advocates Coalition for Development and Environment, Op Cit. The research paper that is still undergoing publication which was requested by the Office of the Prime Minister also found out that because of the existence of many organizations, it is making monitoring and coordination of their activities difficult. (The Policy Research paper is forthcoming).

Available information shows that the Government of Uganda has not treated the issue of RR of former child soldiers seriously. Yet as scholars have noted, failure to invest substantive financial and political resources in the RR of child soldiers could result in some of them resorting to criminal activities, as the case of Kamdulu who is currently in prison testifies, and the possibility of being re-recruited into fresh rebellions. Since the PRDP provides for continuous review, government should commit adequate funding for the DDRR of former child soldiers and also equip the Amnesty Commission to implement its mandate.

In the final analysis, based on the findings of this research one can safely conclude that most of the arguments stated in the research were valid. For example, the research established that effective RR of former child soldiers is into civilian life greatly contributes to successful peacebuilding in war-ton societies (MacKay, 2004) such as Northern Uganda. It was established that marginalization or the neglect of former child soldiers in most of the RR processes causes more wars, long wars, increases criminality and hummpers any efforts towards building durable peace in post-conflict societies as was the case in Sierra Leone and Mozambique (Honwana, 2006). The case of Kamudulu a former child soldier who is now a jail sentence for organizing a series of robberies in Northern Uganda is a good example of poor RR process in Northern Uganda. Furthermore, it was established that the provision of psychosocial support based on traditional and indigenous resources, is very crucial in the RR of former child soldiers evidenced by the situation in Northern Uganda where they have been widely used. However, contrary to the research argument on the relevance of traditional and indigenous resources in the RR of former child soldiers, the research findings established that they also have limitations including being gender insensitive, promotion of impunity and the fact that they have been greatly been undermined by the war and the colonial legacy.

Overall, this study reveals that traditional and indigenous resources are still popular and have been widely used in Northern Uganda in the reintegration and rehabilitation of former child soldiers. The majority of former child soldiers who were interviewed observed that they found traditional and indigenous resources more helpful than the Western models of psychosocial support. However, it was also established that there is a significant section of former child soldiers who found Western models more relevant in their reintegration and rehabilitation processes. Based on these findings, the study recommends an integrative and holistic model of psychosocial support that blends good elements from both traditional and indigenous resources and Western approaches with greater emphasis on the former.

Bibliography

Books, Book Chapters and Journal Articles

Amone-P'Olak, K. (2007). 'Coping with Life in Rebel Captivity and the Challenge of Reintegrating Formerly Abducted Boys in Northern Uganda',*Journal of Refugee Studies* Vol. 20, No.4. Oxford: Oxford University Press.

Arafat, C & Musleh, T. (2006). 'Education and Hope: A Psychosocial Assessment of Palestinian Children', in, Boothby, N., Strang, A. & Wessells, M. (eds.) *A World Turned Upside Down: Social Ecological Approaches of Children in War Zones*, Bloomfield: Kumarian Press, Inc.

Ball, N. (1996). 'The Challenge of Rebuilding War-Torn Societies', in, Crocker, A. C., Hampson, O. F. & Aall, P. *Managing Global Chaos: Sources and Responses to International Conflict.* Washington, D.C.: United States Institute of Peace Press.

Bangura, K. A. (2008). 'The Politics of the Struggle to Resolve the Conflict in Uganda: Westerners Pushing Their Legal Approach Versus Ugandans Insisting on their Mato Oput'. *The Journal of Pan African Studies,* vol.2, no.5, July, p. 142-178.

Behrend, H. (2001). 'Is Alice Lakwena a Witch? The Holy Spirit Movement and its Fight Against Evil in the North', in, Hansen, H.B. & Twaddle, M. (eds.) *Changing Uganda*, Kampala: Fountain Publishers.

Berdal, M. (2009) *Building Peace After War*, London: Routledge.

Berdal, R. M. (1996). *Disarmament and Demobilization after Civil Wars*, Oxford: Oxford University Press.

Boothby, N. (2006). 'When Former Child Soldiers Grow Up', in, Boothby, N., Strang, A. & Wessells, M. (Eds.) *A World Turned Upside Down: Social Ecological Approaches of Children in War Zones*, Bloomfield: Kumarian Press, Inc.

Boothby, N. (2006). 'The Keys to Reintegration and Reconciliation', in, Boothby, N. & Strang, A. & Wessells, M. (2006).*A World Turned Upside Down: Social Ecological Approaches to Children in War Zones.* Bloomfield: Kumarian Press, Inc.

Boothby, N., Strang, A. & Wessells, M. (2006).*A World Turned Upside Down: Social Ecological Approaches to Children in War Zones,* Bloomfield:Kumarian Press, Inc.

Bracken, J.P. & Petty, C. (1998). (eds.) *Rethinking the Trauma of War*, London: Free Association Books Ltd.

Bracken, J. P. (1998). 'Hidden Agendas: Deconstructing Post Traumatic Stress Disorder', in, Bracken, J.P. & Petty, C. (eds.) *Rethinking the Trauma of War*,London: Free Association Books.

Brett, R. & Specht, I. (2004).*Young Soldiers: Why They Choose to Fight*, London: Lynne Rienner.

299

Briggs, J. (2005). *Innocence Lost: When Child Soldiers go to War*. Cambridge: Basic Books.

Call, T. Charles (2008). *Ending Wars, Building States, in, Call, T. C & Wyeth, V (eds.) Building States to Build Peace. London: Lynne Rienner.*

Chesterman, S.(2001). (ed.)*Civilians in War*.London:Lynne Rienner.

Cockell, G. J. (2000). *Conceptualizing Peacebuilding: Human Security and Sustainable Peace*, in, Pugh, M. (ed.) Regeneration of War-Torn Societies. London: Macmillan Press Ltd.

Cohn, I. & Goodwin-Gil, G.S. (1994).*Child Soldiers: The Role of Children in Armed Conflicts*, New York: Oxford University Press.

Cohn, I. & Goodwin-Gill, S.G. (2006).*Child Soldiers: The Role of Children in Armed Conflicts*. Oxford: Clarendon Press.

Collier, P. & Sambanis, N. (2005). (eds.) *Understanding Civil War: Evidence and Analysis*. Volume 1, Washington DC: The World Bank.

Collier, P. (2009). *Wars, Guns & Votes: Democracy in Dangerous Places*, London: The Bodley Head.

Collins, A. (2007). (ed.) *Contemporary Security Studies*, New York: Oxford University Press.

Cousens, M. E.; Kumar, C. & Wersmester, K. (2001). *Peacebuilding As Politics: Cultivating Peace in Fragile Societies*, London: Lynne Rienner.

De Soysa, I. (2000). 'The Resource Curse: Are Civil Wars Driven by Rapacity or Paucity?' in, Berdal, M. & Malone, D.M. *Greed and Grievance: Economic Agendas of Civil Wars*. London: Lynne Rienner.

Deng, M.F. (2000). 'Reaching Out: A Dinka Principle of Conflict Management', in, Zartman, W.I. *Traditional Curses for Modern Conflicts: African Conflict 'Medicine'* London: Lynne Rienner.

Dudenhoeffer, Anne-Lynn (2016) 'Understanding the Recruitment of Child Soldiers in Africa,' Africa Centre for the Constructive Resolution of Disputes. Also available on Internet at: https://www.accord.org.za/conflict-trends/understanding-recruitment-child-soldiers-africa/. Accessed on 10/10/2018.

Dzinesa, G. (2007). 'Post Conflict Disarmament, Demobilization, and Reintegration of Former Combatants in South Africa', *International Studies Perspectives*, Oxford: Blackwell Publishing, pp. 73-89.

Farah, A.Y. (2001). 'Roots of Reconciliation in Somalia', in, Reychler, L. & Paffenholz, T. (eds.) *Peace-Building: A Field Guide*, London: Lynne Rienner.

Fay, B. (1996). *Contemporary Philosophy of Social Science: A Multicultural Approach*. Oxford: Blackwell.

Finnstrom, S. (2005). "For God & My Life' War & Cosmology in Northern Uganda', in, Richards, P. (ed.) *No Peace, No War: An Anthropology of Contemporary Armed Conflicts*, Oxford: Ohio University Press.

Flick, U. (2009).*An Introduction to Qualitative Research*, (4th Edition) London: Sage Publications Ltd.

300

Fithen, C. & Richards, P. (2005). 'Making War, Crafting Peace: Militia Solidarities & Demobilization in Sierra Leone', in, Richards, P. (ed.) *No Peace, No War: An Anthropology of Contemporary Armed Conflicts,* Oxford: Ohio University Press.

Francis, J. D. (2006). *Uniting Africa: Building Regional Peace and Security Systems,* Aldershot: Ashgate.

Francis, J. D. (2007). 'Paper Protection' Mechanism: Child Soldiers and the International Protection of Children in Africa's Conflict Zones', in, *Journal of Modern Studies,* 45, 2, pp.207-231. London: Cambridge University Press.

Francis, J. D. (ed.) (2008). *Peace and Conflict in Africa.* London: Zed Books.

Galtung, J. (1996). *Peace By Peaceful Means: Peace and Conflict, Development and Civilization.* London: Sage Publishers Ltd.

Galtung, J. (2000). 'Conflict, War and Peace: A Bird's Eye View; in, Galtung, J., Jacobsen, G.C. & Brand-Jacobsen, F. K. (eds.) *Searching for Peace: The Road to Transcend* (2nd Edition) London: Pluto Press.

Gloppen, S., Kasimbazi, E. & Kibandama, A (2008). 'Elections in Court: The Judiciary and Uganda's 2006', in, *Electoral Democracy in Uganda: Understanding the Institutional Processes and Outcomes of the 2006 Multiparty Elections,* Kampala: Fountain Publishers.

Green, M. (2008). *The Wizard of the Nile: The Hunt for Africa's Most Wanted: A Bloody Conflict, a Messianic Madman, an Army of Child Soldiers.* London: Portobello Books Ltd.

Hampson, O. and Aall, P. (2001).*Managing Global Chaos: Sources of and Responses to International Conflict.* Washington, D.C.: United States Institute of Peace Press.

Hansen, B.H. & Twaddle, M (2001).*Changing Uganda,* Kampala:Fountain Publishers.

Harris, P. and Reilly, B. (eds.) (1998).*Democracy and Deep-Rooted Conflict: Options for Negotiations.* Stockholm: Institute for Democratic Electoral Assistance (IDEA).

Harvey, R. (2001) *Children and Armed Conflict: A Guide to International Humanitarian and Human Rights Law,* A Publication of the International Bureau for Children's Rights (IBCR) and Human Rights Centre of the University of Essex, September.

Haward, P. (2009). *Looking Back: Tragedies of Ugandan Women and Children 1970-2000,* Kampala: Fountain Publishers.

Henderson, E.A. (2008). 'When States Implode: Africa's Civil Wars 1959-92' in, Nhema, A. and Zeleza, P.T. (eds.) *The Roots of African Conflicts: The Causes and Costs, Zimbabwe, Lethetho, Kenya, Sudan, Uganda, The Horn of Africa,* Pretoria: UNISA Press.

Herring, E. (2008). 'Neoliberalism Versus Peacebuilding in Iraq', in, Pugh, M. Copper, N. Turner, M. *Whose Peace? Critical Perspectives on the Political Economy of Peacebuilding,* London: Palgrave Macmillan.

301

Honwana, A. (2006). *Child Soldiers in Africa,* Pennsylvania: University of Pennsylvania Press.

Hovil, L. and Zachary Lomo, Z. (2005). *Whose Justice? Perceptions of Uganda's Amnesty Act 2000: The Potential for Conflict Resolution and Long-Term Reconciliation,* Kampala: Refugee Law Project, Faculty of Law Makerere University, Working Paper No. 15 February.

Human Rights Watch (2003).*Stolen Children: Abduction and Recruitment in Northern Uganda,* March, Vol.15, no. 7 (A).

Human Rights Focus (Gulu) (2007). *Fostering the Transition in Acholiland: From War to Peace, from Camps to Home,* Kampala: Human Rights Focus (Gulu), September.

Human Rights Watch (1997).*The Scars of Death: Children Abducted by the Lord's Resistance Army in Uganda.* New York: Human Rights Watch.

Human Rights Watch (2005).*Uprooted and Forgotten: Impunity and Human Rights Abuses in Northern Uganda.* New York: Human Rights Watch September, Vol. 17, no. 12(A).

Human Rights Watch (2015). We Can Die Too: Recruitment and Use of Child Soldiers in South Sudan. New York: Human Rights Watch December 14. Also available at: https://www.hrw.org/report/2015/12/14/we-can-die-too/recruitment-and-use-child-soldiers-south-sudan. Accessed on 11/10/2018.

Human Rights Watch, 2016. ICC First Lord's Resistance Army Trail Begins: Thousands of Victims Participating in the Case. Also available at: https://www.hrw.org/news/2016/12/05/icc-first-lords-resistance-army-trial-begins. Accessed on 14/10/2018.

Hutchful, E. (2000). 'Understanding the African Security Crisis', in, Fatau Musa, A. & Fayemi, J.K., *Mercenaries: An African Security Dilemma.* London: Pluto Press.

International Alert (2008).*Building a Peace Economy in Northern Uganda: Investing in Peace.* September, Issue No 1.

International Criminal Court (2005).*Rome Statute of the International Criminal Court,* International Criminal Court.

International Peace Academy (IPA) Report (2002). *The Infrastructure of Peace in Africa: Assessing the Peacebuilding Capacity of African Institutions.* New York: International Peace Academy.

Jareg, E. & Petty, C. (1998). 'Conflict, Poverty and Family Separation: the Problem of Institutional Care', in Bracken, J.P. & Petty, C. (eds.) *Rethinking the Trauma of War.* London: Free Association Books.

Jeong, H. (2000). *Peace and Conflict Studies: An Introduction.* Burlington: Ashgate Publishing Ltd.

Kabia, J.M & Sola-Martin, A. (2007). (eds.) *UNAMSIL Peacekeeping and Peace Support Operations in Sierra Leone,* Africa Peace Research Series No. 1,

Bradford: Africa Centre, Department of Peace Studies, University of Bradford.

Kabwegyere, B.T. (1995). *The Politics of State Formation and Destruction in Uganda.* Kampala. Fountain Publishers Ltd.

Kaihura, K. (2000). Uganda: *The Integration of Child Soldiers into the School System.* France: Published by the Association for the Development of Education in Africa (ADEA).

Kaldor, M. (2006).*New & Old Wars: Organized Violence in a Global Era* (2nd Edition) Cambridge: Polity Press.

Kanyeihamba, G.W (2006). *Kanyeihamba's Commentaries on Law, Politics and Governance,* Kampala: Renaissance Media Ltd.

Kanyeihamba, G.W. (2002).*Constitutional and Political History of Uganda: From 1894 to the Present.* Kampala: Fountain Publishers Ltd.

Kategaya, E. T. (2006). *Impassioned for Freedom,* Kampala: Wava Books Ltd.

Ker Kwaro Acholi (2009). *Strategic Plan 2009-2014.*

Kingma, K. (ed.) (2000). *Demobilization in Sub-Saharan Africa: The Development and Security Impacts,* London: Macmillan Press Ltd.

Kisamba-Mugerwa, W. (2001). 'Institutional Dimensions of Land Tenure Reform',in, Hansen, H.B. & Twaddle, M. (eds.) *Changing Uganda,* Kampala: Fountain Publishers.

Kjaer, A. M. & Olum, Y. (2008).'From Confronation to Acquiescence? The Role of Civil Society and the Media in the 2006 Elections in Uganda,' in, *Electoral Democracy in Uganda: Understanding the Institutional Processes and Outcomes of the 2006 Multiparty Elections,* Kampala: Fountain Publishers.

Kostelny, K. (2006). 'A Culture-Based, Integrated Approach: Helping War-Affected Children', in, Boothby, N. & Strang, A. & Wessells, M. (eds.) *A World Turned Upside Down: Social Ecological Approaches to Children in War Zones.* Bloomfield: Kumarian Press, Inc.

Kumar, R. (2005). *Research Methodology: A Step-By-Step Guide for Beginners,* (Second Edition)London: Sage Publishers.

Ladegaard, L. & Otto, H. (1999).*Fighting for a Childhood: About Child Soldiers in Uganda and their Struggle for a Life Without War,* Copenhagen: Save the Children Denmark.

Latigo, J.O. (2008). Northern Uganda: Tradition-based Practices in the Acholi Region, in, *Traditional Justice and Reconciliation after Violent Conflict: Learning from African Experiences,* Stockholm: International Institute for Electoral Assistance (IDEA).

Lederach, J.P. (1995). *Preparing for Peace: Conflict Transformation Across Cultures.* New York: Syracuse University Press.

Lederach, J.P. (1997). *Sustainable Reconciliation in Divided Societies,* Washington, D.C.: United States Institute for Peace Press.

Lucima, O. (2002). *Protracted Conflict, Elusive Peace, Initiatives to End Violence in Northern Uganda.* London: Conciliation Resources.

303

Machel, G. (2001). *The Impact of War on Children: A Review of Progress Since the 1996 United Nations Report on the Impact of Armed Conflict on Children,* London: Hurst & Company.

MacKay, S. & Mazurana, D. (1999).*Where are the Girls? Girls in Fighting Forces in Northern Uganda, Sierra Leone and Mozambique: Their Lives During and After War,* Montreal: Rights & Democracy, International Centre for Human Rights and Democratic Development.

Makara, S. (2007). 'Uganda's 2006 Multiparty Elections: Consolidating Democracy and Building Peace?' In, Tumushabe, G. (ed.) *East African Journal of Peace and Human Rights,* Kampala: Makerere University, Faculty of Law, Human Rights and Peace Centre.

Makara, S., Rakner, L. & Rwengabo, S. (2008). 'Administering the 2006 Multiparty Elections: The Role of the Electoral Commission, in, Kiiza, J., Makara, S. and Rakner, L. (eds.)*Electoral Democracy in Uganda: Understanding the Institutional Processes and Outcomes of the 2006 Multiparty Elections,* Kampala: Fountain Publishers.

Mamdani, M. (1976).*Politics and Class Formation in Uganda.* Kampala: Fountain Publishers Ltd.

Masina, N. (2000). 'Xhosa Practices of Ubuntu for South Africa', in, Zartman, W.I. *Traditional Cures for Modern Conflicts: African Conflict 'Medicine.* London: Lynne Rienner.

Mason, J. (2002). *Qualitative Researching,* (2nd Edition) London: Sage Publications.

Mazrui, A.A. (2008). 'Conflict in Africa: An Overview', in, Nhema, A. & Zeleza, P.T. (eds.) *The Roots of African Conflicts: The Causes and Costs, Zimbabwe, Lethetho, Kenya, Sudan, Uganda, The Horn of Africa. Pretoria:* UNISA Press.

Mazrui, A. Ali (2001) 'Constitutional Change and Cultural Engineering in Africa's Search for New Directions'in, Oloka-Onyango (ed.) *Constitutionalism in Africa: Creating Opportunities Facing Challenges,* Kampala: Fountain Publishers Ltd.

McCallin, M. (1998).*Community Involvement in the Social Reintegration of Child Soldiers,* in, Bracken, P. & Petty, C. (Eds.) Rethinking the Trauma of War, New York: Free Association Books.

McKay, S. & Mazurana, D. (1999).*Where are the Girls? Girls Fighting in Northern Uganda, Sierra Leone and Mozambique: Their Lives During and After War.* Montreal: A Publication of the International Centre for Human Rights and Democratic Development.

McKay, S. (2006). 'Girls Stolen: The Plight of Girl Soldiers During and After Armed Conflict', in, Boothby; Strang, A. & Wessells, M.G. (eds.) A *World Turned Upside Down: Social Ecological Approaches to Children in War Zones,* Bloomfield: Kumarian Press, Inc.

Mudoola, D. (2001). 'Institution-building: the Case of the NRM and the Military 1986-9', in, Hansen, H.B. & Twaddle, M. (eds.) *Changing Uganda,* Kampala: Fountain Publishers.

Muggah, R (2004). *Analysis: The Anatomy of Disarmament, Demobilization and Reintegration in the Republic of Congo. Conflict, Security and Development,* Volume 4, Issue 1 April. York: Routledge, pp. 21-37.

Muggah, R. (2004). *The Anatomy of Disarmament, Demobilization and Reintegration in the Republic of Congo,* International Policy Institute. York: Carfax Publishing.

Mugyenyi, J.B. (2001). *IMF* 'Conditionality and Structural Adjustment Under the National Resistance Movement', in,Hansen, H.B. & Twaddle, M. (eds.) *Changing Uganda,* Kampala: Fountain Publishers.

Muravchik, J. (1996). 'Promoting Peace Through Democracy', in, Crocker, A.C.; Hampson, O.F. & Aall, P. (eds.) *Managing Global Chaos: Sources of and Responses to International Conflict,* Washington, DC: United States Institute for Peace Press.

Murithi, T. (2008).'African Indigenous and Endogenous Approaches to Peace and Conflict Resolution', in, Francis, D.J. (ed.) *Peace and Conflict in Africa,* New York: Zed Books.

Murithi, T. (2009).*The Ethics of Peacebuilding,* Edinburgh: Edinburgh University Press Ltd.

Museveni, Y. K. (1997). *Sowing the Mastered Seed: The Struggle for Freedom and Democracy in Uganda,* Oxford: Macmillan Publishers Ltd.

Mutibwa, P. (2008). *The Buganda Factor in Uganda Politics,* Kampala: Fountain Publishers.

Mwesige, P. & Muyomba, L. (2007).*Deepening Democracy in Uganda: Legislative and Administrative Reforms Ahead of 20II Elections,* Kampala: ACODE Policy Briefing Paper, No. 19, 2007.

Nhema, A. & Zeleza, P.T. (eds.) (2008).*The Roots of African Conflicts: The Causes and Costs, Zimbabwe, Lethetho, Kenya, Sudan, Uganda, The Horn of Africa,* Pretoria: UNISA Press.

Nsibambi, A. R. (2001). 'Resistance Councils and Committees: A Case Study from Makerere', in, Hansen, H.B. & Twaddle, M. (eds.) *Changing Uganda,* Kampala: Fountain Publishers.

Obote-Odora, A. (1999) *Legal Problems with Protection of Children in Armed Conflict,* International Law Articles, Volume 6, Number 2 June.

Okello, L. (2002). (ed.) *Protracted Conflict, Elusive Peace: Initiatives to End Violence in Northern Uganda,* London: Conciliation Resources & Kacoke Madit.

O'Leary, Z. (2007). *The Essential Guide to Doing Research,* Lodon: Sage Publications.

Oloka-Onyango, J. (ed.) (2001) *Constitutionalism in Africa: Creating Opportunities, Facing Challenges,* Kampala: Fountain Publishers Ltd.

Osaghae, E.E. (2000). 'Applying Traditional Methods to Modern Conflict: Possibilities and Limits', in, Zartman, W. (ed.) *Traditional Cures for Modern Conflicts: African Conflict 'Medicine'* London: Lynne Rienner.

Owen, J.M. (1997) *Liberal Peace, Liberal War: American Politics and International Security.* London: Cornell University Press

Ozerdem, A. (2002). *Disarmament, Demobilization and Reintegration of Former Combatants in Afghanistan: Lessons Learned from a Cross-Cultural Perspective,* Third World Quarterly, Vol 23, No 5, pp 961-975. York: Carfax Publishing.

Pankhurst, D. (2008). 'The Gendered Impact of Peace', in, Pugh, M.; Copper, N.; Turner, M. (eds.) Whose Peace? *Critical Perspectives on the Political Economy of Peacebuilding,* London: Palgrave Macmillan.

Paris, L. (2004). *At War's End: Building Peace After Civil Conflict,* Boulder: Cambridge University Press.

Peters, K. & Richards, P. (1998). 'Fighting with Open Eyes: Youth Combatants Talking About War in Sierra Leone', in, Bracken, P. J. & Petty, C. (eds.) *Rethinking the Trauma of War,* London: Free Association Books.

Petty, C. & Jareg, E. (1998). 'Conflict, Poverty and Family Separation: the Problem of Institutional Care', in, Bracken, J.P. & Petty, C. *Rethinking the Trauma of War,* New York: Free Association Books Ltd.

Porto, J. G., Alden, C. & Parsons, I. (2007). *From Soldiers to Citizens: Demilitarization of Conflict and Society,* Hampshire: Ashgate Publishing House Ltd.

Prendergast, J. & Plumb, E, (2002). 'Building Local Capacity: From Implementation to Peacebuilding', in, Stedman, J. S., Rothchild, D. & Cousens, M. *Ending Civil Wars: The Implementation of Peace Agreements,* London: Lynne Rienner.

Prunier, G. (2009).*From Genocide to Continental War: The 'Congolese' Conflict and the Crisis of Contemporary Africa,* London: Hurst Publishers Ltd.

Pugh, M. (ed.) (2000).*Regeneration of War-Torn Societies,* London: Macmillan Press Ltd.

Pugh, M.; Cooper, N. & Tunner, M. (2008). (eds.) *Whose Peace? Critical Perspectives on the Political Economy of Peacebuilding,* London: Palgrave Macmillan.

Rukooko, A. B. (2005). 'Protracted Civil War, Civil Militias and Political Transition in Uganda Since 1986', in, Francis, D. J. (ed.) *Civil Militia: Africa's Intractable Security Menace?* Burlington: Ashgate Publishing Limited.

Ramsbotham, O. Woodhouse, T. & Miall, H. (2005) (2nd Edition) *Contemporary Conflict Resolution,* Cambridge: Polity Press.

Refugee Law Project & Human Rights Peace Center (2008).*Conflict, Justice and Reconciliation in Teso: Obstacles and Opportunities.* Refugee Law Project & Human Rights Peace Center, Faculty of Law, Makerere University: Kampala.

Reychler, L. & Paffenholz, T. (2001).*Peace-Building: A Field Guide,* London: Lynne Rienner.

Reyntjens, F. & Vandeginste, S. (2001). *Traditional Approaches to Negotiations and Mediation: Examples from Africa.* In, Reychler, L. & Paffenholz, T. Peace-Building: A Field Guide, Boulder: Lynne Rienner.

Richards, P (2005). (ed.) *No Peace, No War: An Anthropology of Contemporary of Armed Conflicts,* Oxford: Ohio University Press.

Robson, C. (2002). *Real World Research*, (Second Edition) Oxford: Blackwell Publishing.

Rosen, D.M. (2005). *Armies of the Young: Child Soldiers in War and Terrorism*, London: Rutgers University Press.

Ross, M.L. (2000). 'Oil, Drugs, and Diamonds: The Varying Roles of Nature Resources in Civil War', in Ballentine, K. & Sherman, J. *The Political Economy of Armed Conflict - Beyond Greed and Grievance*, London: Lynne Rienner.

Sarantakos, S. (2005). *Social Research*, (3rd Edition) Hampshire: Palgrave Macmillan.

Save the Children (1999). *Fighting for a Childhood: About Child Soldiers in Uganda and their Struggle for a Life Without War.* Copenhagen. Save the Children Denmark.

Seale, C. (2004). (ed.) *Social Research Methods*, New York: Routledge.

Sembuya, C.C. (2009).*The Other Side: Idi Amin.* Kampala: Sest Holdings Ltd.

Sendabo, T. (2004).*Child Soldiers: Rehabilitation and Social Reintegration in Liberia*, Uppsala: Life and Peace Institute.

Sesay, A. (ed.) (2003). *Civil Wars, Child Soldiers and Post Conflict Peace Building in West Africa*, Ibadan: College Press and Publishers Ltd.

Shorr, L. (2007). The Post-Conflict Treatment of Child Soldiers: A Case Study of Liberian Child Soldiers, in, Tumushabe. G. (ed.) *East African Journal of Peace & Human Rights.*Vol. 13, No.1.

Silverman, D. (2005). *Doing Qualitative Research*, (2nd Edition) London: Sage Publications.

Singer, P.W. (2006). *Children At War*, Berkeley: University of California Press.

Soto, R.C. (2009). *Tall Grass: Stories of Suffering and Peace in Northern Uganda*, Kampala: Fountain Publishers.

Spear J. (2002). 'Disarmament and Demobilisation', in, Stedman, J., Rothchild D. & Cousens, M.E. (eds). *Ending Civil Wars: The Implementation of Peace Agreements*, London: Lynne Rienner.

Strauss, A. & Corbin, J. (1990).*Basics of Qualitative Research: Grounded Theory Procedures and Techniques*, London: Sage Publications.

Strauss, A. (1987). *Qualitative Analysis for Social Scientists*, Cambridge: Cambridge University Press.

Summerfield, D. (1998). 'The Social Experience of War and Some Issues for the Humanitarian Field', in, Bracken, J.P. & Petty, C. (eds.) *Rethinking the Trauma of War.* London: Free Association Books Ltd.

The Constitution of the Republic of Uganda, 1995.

The Republic of Uganda, Ministry of Gender, Labour and Social Development (2009) *Child Protection Recovery Strategy for Northern Uganda 2009-2011*, Kampala: Ministry of Gender, Labour and Social Development.

The Republic of Uganda, Office of the Prime Minister (2007).*Peace, Recovery and Development Plan for Northern Uganda (PRDP) (2007-2010)*, Kampala: Republic of Uganda, September.

The Uganda Peoples' Defence Forces Act, 2005.

Tumushabe, W. G. And Bainomugisha, A. (2004).*Constitutional Reform and Environmental Legislative Representation in Uganda,* Kampala: ACODE Policy Research Series, No 10.

Uganda Debt Network (2004).*Will NUSAF Deliver Northern Uganda out of Poverty?* Policy Review Newsletter Vol: 4, Issue 3.

Vigh, H. (2006). *Navigating Terrains of War: Youth and Soldiering in Guinea-Bissau,* Oxford: Berghahn Books.

Wessells, M. (2006). 'A Living Wage: The Importance of Livelihood in Reintegrating Former Child Soldiers', in, Boothby, N. & Strang, A. & Wessells, M. *A World Turned Upside Down: Social Ecological Approaches to Children in War Zones,* Bloomfield. Kumarian Press, Inc.,

Wessells, M. (2006).*Child Soldiers: From Violence to Protection,* London: Harvard University Press.

Wessells, M. (2006). 'The Importance of Livelihood in Reintegrating Former Child Soldiers', in, Boothby, N., Strang, A. & Wessells, M. (Eds.) *A World Turned Upside Down: Social Ecological Approaches of Children in War Zones,* Bloomfield: Kumarian Press, Inc.

Woodward, P. (2001). 'Uganda and Southern Sudan 1986-9: New Regimes and Peripheral Politics', in, Hansen, B.H. & Twaddle, M. (eds.) *Changing Uganda,* Kampala: Fountain Publishers.

World Vision International (2005).*Pawns of Politics, Children, Conflict and Peace in Northern Uganda,* World Vision International.

World Vision Uganda (2001). *Peace and Reconciliation for the Children of War: Healing the Wounds in Northern Uganda,* Kampala.

Zartman, W. (2000). (ed.) *Traditional Cures for Modern Conflicts: African Conflict 'Medicine,'* London: Lynne Rienner.

Electronic Sources, Newspapers, Magazines and Reports

Agreement on Accountability and Reconciliation between Government of Uganda and Lord's Resistance Army/Movement, 29th June, 2007. Available at: http://www.beyondjuba.org/peace_agreements/Agreement_on_Accountability_And_Reconcilition.pdf. Accessed on 24/5/2010.

Afako, B. (2002). 'Reconciliation and Justice: 'Mato Oput' and the Amnesty Act'. *Conciliation Resources.* Available at: http://www.c-r.org/our-work/accord/Northern-uganda/reconciliation-justice.php. Accessed on 12/4/2010.

Allen, T. & Schomerus, M. (2006). *A Hard Homecoming: Lessons Learned from the Reception Centre Process in Northern Uganda,* An Independent Study produced for USAID & UNICEF.

Amnesty International (1999).*In the Firing Line: War and Children's Rights,* London: Amnesty International, United Kingdom.

Annan, J.; Blattman, C. & Horton, R. (2006).*The State of Youth and Youth Protection in Northern Uganda: Findings from the Affected Youth.* Kampala: A Report for UNICEF, Uganda.

Amnesty International (2012).Landmark ICC verdict over use of child soldiers. Also available on Internet at: https://www.amnesty.org/en/latest/news/2012/03/landmark-icc-verdict-over-use-child-soldiers/ Accessed on 13/10/2018.

An Agenda for Peace, Preventive Diplomacy, Peacemaking and Peacekeeping (17 June 1992). Available at: http://www.unrol.org/files/A_47_277.PDF. Accessed on 2 May 2010.

A Summary of Geneva Conventions and Additional Protocols. Available at: http://supportgenevaconventions.info/library/geneva_conventions_summ ary.pdf: Accessed on 29/4/2010.

Ayugi, C. (2007). *Pardoned Former LRA members, who allegedly hid their weapons from authorities, are being blamed for a series of gun crimes across Northern Uganda.* Institute of War and Peace Reporting, Norwegian Council for Africa, Oslo, Norway, 06 December. Available at: http://www.afrika.no/Detailed/15590.html. Accessed on 27/5/2010.

Baines, E.; Stover, E. & Wierda, M. (2006).*War Affected Children and Youth in Northern Uganda: Towards a Brighter Future: An Assessment Report,* May.

BBC News, (2004) *Ex-child Soldier's Path to Hope,* Available at: http://news.bbc.co.uk/1/hi/uk/3733349.stm Accessed 15/9/2009.

BBC interview with Uganda's President Museveni on, *The involvement of children in armed conflicts in Uganda.* Available at: www.youtube.com/watch?.v=up1tvcxw_gk. Accessed on 28/6/2010.

Blattman, C.; Fiala, N. & Martinez, S. (2009). *Impact Evaluation of the Northern Uganda Social Action Fund Youth Opportunities Project, Uganda.* Available at: http://www.iza.org/conference_files/ELMPDC2009/martinez_s4899.pdf. Accessed on 8/5/2010.

Brock-Utne, B. (2001).*Indigenous Conflict Resolution in Africa.* Available at: http://www.africavenir.com/publications/occasional-papers/BrockUtneTradConflictResolution.pdf. Accessed 8/5/2010.

Civil Society Organizations for Peace in Northern Uganda (CSOPUN) (2008).*Learning from Past Experience, Designing a Better Future: Towards a Successful Disarmament, Demobilization, Reintegration & Resettlement in Northern Uganda,* Kampala: CSOPUN.

Coalition to Stop the Use of Child Soldiers (2004) *Child Soldiers Global Report.* Available at: http://www.child-soldiers.org/library/global-reports. Accessed on 14/4/2010.

Coalition to Stop the Use of Child Soldiers (2008).*Child Soldiers Global Report.* Available at: http://www.childsoldiersglobalreport.org/. Accessed on 15/5/2010.

Conciliation Resources (2006).*Dealing with the Past: Experiences of Transitional Justice, Truth and Reconciliation Processes After Periods of Violent Conflict in Africa,* London: Conciliation Resources. Available at: http://www.c-r.org/our-work/uganda/documents/Dealing_with_the_Past.pdf. Accessed on 21/9/2010.

Convention relating to the Status of Refugees, Available at:http://www2.ohchr.org/english/law/pdf/refugees.pdf. Accessed on 24/9/2010.

Daily Monitor September 15, 2009 *I am not Responsible for Buganda Crisis-Museveni.*

Daily Monitor September 4, 2009 *Kanyeihamba Criticises Museveni Over Elections.* Available at: http://www.monitor.co.ug/artman/publish/news. Accessed on 16/6/2010.

Daily Monitor September 8, 2009 *Stop Defending Corrupt Bush War Comrades.* Available at: http://www.monitor.co.ug/artman/publish/news/stop_defending. Accessed on 16/6/2010.

Daily Monitor (2010). LRA Victims should be Compensated- Ocampo, Tuesday June 1. Available at: http://www.monitor.co.ug/News/National/-688334/929644/-/x0ab2i/-/index.html. Accessed on 2/6/2010.

Daniel, Y. (2003). *The International Criminal Court's Trust Fund for Victims: Analysis and Options for the Development of Further Criteria for the Operation of Further Criteria for the Operation of the Trust Fund for Victims.* Available at: http://www.redress.org/downloads/publications/TFVReport.pdf. Accessed on 16/6/2010.

Denov, M. (2007).*Is the Culture Always Right? The Dangers of Reproducing Gender Stereotypes and Inequalities in Psychosocial Interventions for War Affected Children,* London: Coalition to Stop the Use of Child Soldiers. Available at: www.child-soldiers.org. Accessed on 23/6/2010.

Dolan, C. (2002). *Which Children Count? The Politics of Children's Rights in Northern Uganda.* Available at: http:www.c-r.org/our-work/accord/Northern-uganda/which-children-count.php. Accessed on 17/6/2010.

Dzinesa, G. (2008). *The Role of Ex-Combatants and Veterans in Violence in Transitional Societies.* Centre for the Study of Violence and Reconciliation: Johannesburg. Available at: http://www.nipsnepal.org/pictures/integration/QCT_excombatants1108%5B 1%5D%5B1%5D.pdf. Accessed on 18/5/2010.

Guyot, J. (2007).*Suffer the Children: The Psychosocial Rehabilitation of Child Soldiers As A Function of Peacebuilding.* London. Coalition to Stop Child Soldiers. Available at: http://www.child-soldiers.org/psycho-social/Linked_Guyot_2007.pdf.Accessed on 4/11/09.

Gulu District NGO Forum & Liu Institute for Global Issues (2007). *The Cooling of Hearts: Community Truth Telling in Acholi-Land,* July.

310

GUSCO (2003).*What Else Have I Known in My Life Apart from War and Gun?* The Child Trumpet, Vol 3 April-June.

GUSCO (2006).*What is My Fate?*The Child Trumpet. A Quarterly Publication of GUSCO.

ICRC (2004).*What is International Humanitarian Law?* Available at: http://www.ehl.icrc.org/images/resources/pdf/what_is_ihl.pdf.Accessed on 6/7/2010.

HaLevi, E (2006). *Hamas Launches Website Encouraging Kids to Become Martyrs.* Available at: http://www.israelnationalnews.com/News/News.aspx/99839. Accessed on 2/11/09.

Hamilton, C. & Tabatha, Abu El-Haj. *Armed Conflict: the Protection of Children Under International Law.*Available at: http://www.essex.ac.uk/armedcon/story_id/000577.html. Accessed on 25/09/2009.

Harvey, R. (2003). *Children and Armed Conflict: A Guide to International Humanitarian and Human Rights Law.* A publication for The Children and Armed Conflict Unit, Children's Legal Centre, Human Rights Centre of the University of Essex and The International Bureau for Children's Rights. Available at: http://www.essex.ac.uk/armedcon/story_id/000044.pdf. Accessed on 6/7/2010.

International Crisis Group (2002). *Capturing the Moment: Sudan's Peace Process in the Balance.* Africa Report No 42, 3 April. Available at: http://www.crisisgroup.org/en/regions/africa/horn-of-africa/sudan/042-capturing-the-moment-sudans-peace-process-in-the-balance.aspx. Accessed on 20/5/2010.

International Crisis Group (2004). *Northern Uganda: Understanding and Solving the Conflict.* Africa Report No 77, 14 April. Available at: http://www.crisisgroup.org/en/regions/africa/horn-of-africa/uganda/077-Northern-uganda-understanding-and-solving-the-conflict.aspx. Accessed on 20/5/2010.

International Crisis Group (2001). *Rwanda/Uganda: A Dangerous War of Nerves.* ICG Africa Briefing, 21 December. Available at: http://www.crisisgroup.org/en/regions/africa/central-africa/rwanda/B007-rwanda-uganda-a-dangerous-war-of-nerves.aspx. Accessed on 22/5/2010.

International Crisis Group (2008). *Northern Uganda: The Road to Peace, With Or Without Kony,* Africa Report No 146 (10 December). Available at: http://www.crisisgroup.org/home/index.cfm?action=login&ref_id=5804A ccessed on 24/5/2010.

International Crisis Report (2007). *Northern Uganda: Seizing the Opportunity for Peace.* Africa Report N0 124-26 April. Available at: http://www.crisisgroup.org/en/regions/africa/horn-of-africa/uganda/124-Northern-uganda-seizing-the-opportunity-for-peace.aspx. Accessed on 26/5/2010.

International Service Volunteers' Association (AVSI) & UNICEF (1997).*Resilience in Conflict: A Community-based Approach to Psychosocial Support in Northern Uganda.* AVSI & UNICEF.

IRIN (1999).*Special Report on the ADF Rebellion.* Available on the Website: htt://www.africa.upenn.edu/Hornet/irin-120899c.html. Accessed on 26/5/2010.

Jareg, E. (2005). *Crossing Bridges and Negotiating Rivers: Rehabilitation and Reintegration of Children Associated With Armed Conflicts.* London: Coalition to Stop the Use of Child Soldiers. Available at: www.child-soldiers.org/resources/psychosocial. Accessed on 26/5/2010.

Kaihura, K. (2000). *Uganda: The Integration of Child Soldiers into the School System,* Association for the Development of Education in Africa (ADEA) International Institute for Educational Planning. Available at: http://www.adeanet.org. Accessed on 8/10/2009.

Ladu, I. M. (2010).*LRA Victims should be Compensated,* Ocampo, Daily Monitor, Tuesday June 1. Available at: http://www.monitor.co.ug/News/National/-688334/929644/-/x0ab2i/-/index.html. Accessed on 2/6/2010

Liu Institute for Global Issues, Gulu District NGO Forum & Ker Kwaro Acholi (2005).*Roco Wat 1 Acoli, Restoring Relationships in Acholi-land: Traditional Approaches to Justice and Reintegration,* Kampala: Published by Liu Institute for Global Issues, Gulu District NGO Forum & Ker Kwaro Acholi.

Makerere University, Faculty of Law, Refugee Law Project & Human Rights and Peace Centre (2008).*Is The PRDP Politics As Usual? Update on The Implementation of Uganda's Peace, Recovery and Development Plan.* Briefing Note N0 2 December. Available at: http://www.internal-displacement.org/8025708F004CE90B/(httpDocuments)/2FD0B4097013990EC12575220042C436/$file/PRDP_Briefing_Note.pdfAccessed on 13/5/2010.

Makerere University, Faculty of Law, Refugee Law Project (2004).*Behind Violence: Causes, Consequences and the Search for Solutions to the War in Northern Uganda.*Working Paper No 11, February. Available at: http://www.refugeelawproject.org/working_papers/RLP.WP11.pdf .Accessed on 17/5/2010.

Makerere University, Faculty of Law, Refugee Law Project (2005).*Whose Justice? Perceptions of Uganda's Amnesty Act 2000: The Potential for Conflict Resolution and Long-Term Reconciliation.*Working Paper No.15. Available at: http://www.refugeelawproject.org/working_papers/RLP.WP15.pdf. Accessed on 17/5/2010.

Makerere University, Faculty of Law, Human Rights & Peace Centre & Liu Institute for Global Issues (2003).*The Hidden War: The Forgotten People: War in Acholiland and its Ramifications for Peace and Security in Uganda.* Kampala,

312

March. Available at: http://huripec.mak.ac.ug/Hidden_War.pdf. Accessed on 21/9/2010.

Mallinder, L. (2009). *Uganda and Crossroads: Narrowing the Amnesty?* Working Paper No 1 From Beyond Legalism: Amnesties, Transition and Conflict Transformation,Institute of Criminology and Justice, Queens University Belfast. Available at: http://www.qub.ac.uk/schools/SchoolofLaw/Research/InstituteofCrimin ologyandCriminalJustice/Research/BeyondLegalism/filestore/Filetoupload ,152141,en.pdf. Accessed on 4/7/2010.

Mao, N (2009*). Has the Government Moved a Vote of No Confidence in Itself?* The New Vision Newspaper 9 February. Available at: http://www.friendsforpeaceinafrica.org/norbert-mao/345-has-the-govt-moved-a-vote-of-n. Accessed on 14/5/2010.

Maputo Declaration on the Use of Children as Soldiers of 22 April 1999. Available at: http://chora.virtualave.net/Maputo-declaration.htm. Accessed on 15/5/2010.

Michael, G. Wessells (2008). *'Do No Harm: Challenges in Organizing Psychosocial Support to Displaced People in Emergence Settings.'* Refuge 25 pp.6-14. Available at: http://www.yorku.ca/refuge. Accessed on 6/6/2010.

Ministry of Finance, Planning and Economic Development (2003).*Post-conflict Reconstruction: The Case of Northern Uganda.* Discussion Paper 7 (Draft). Available at: http://www.finance.go.ug/docs/Post-conflict%20Reconstruction.pdf. Accessed on 13/5/2010

Ministry of Finance, Planning and Economic Development (2004).*Post-conflict Reconstruction: The Case of Northern Uganda.* Discussion Paper 8, March. Available at: www.finance.go.ug. Accessed on 17/5/2010.

Moncrieffe, Joy (2004). *Uganda's Political Economy: A Synthesis of Major Thought.* Report Prepared for DFID Uganda (Final Draft). Available at: http://www.gsdrc.org/docs/open/DOC44.pdf 18/9/09. Accessed on 20/4/2010.

Morales, F.J.A. (2005).*ThePsycho-Social Care of Demobilized Child Soldiers in Columbia: Conceptual and Methodological Aspects.* Available at: www.child-soldiers.org/resources/psychosocial. Accessed on 20/5/2010.

Namuyonjo, J. (2004). *Conflicts, Poverty and Human Development in Northern Uganda.* Paper presented at the WIDER Conference on Making Peace Work in Helsink, June. Available at: http://62.237.131.23/conference/conference-2004-1/conference%202004-1-papers/Nanyonjo-3105, Accessed on 15/5/2010.

News & Noteworthy (2006).*Uganda's Amnesty Commision in Final Phase of Issuing Resettlement Packages to Ex-Combatants,* N&N no. 12 May 18. Available at: http://escolapau.uab.cat/img/programas/desarme/mapa/uganda08i.pdf. Accessed on 10/5/2010.

Northern Uganda Rehabilitation Programme (NUREP) Guidelines for Grant Applications. Available at:http://ec.europa.eu/europeaid/tender/data/d28/AOF79428.pdf. Accessed on 11/5/2010.

Obote-Odora, A. (1999). *Legal Problems with the Protection of Children in Armed Conflict*, Murdoch University Electronic Journal of Law, Volume 6, Number 2 (June). Available at: http://www.murdoch.edu.au/elaw/issues/v6n2/obote-odora62_text.html. Accessed on 16/5/2010.

Odama, B.J. (2008).*Reconciliation Process (Mato Oput) Among the Acholi Tribe in Northern Uganda.* A Paper presented at a Ceremony for 21st Niwano Peace Prize Award in Japan. Available at: http://www.npf.or.jp/peace_prize_f/21/speech_e.pdf. Accessed on 15/5/2010.

Oketch, (2009).*Uganda Oil Discovery Stokes Ethnic Tensions.* Available at: http://www.groundreport.com/world/uganda-Oil-Discovery-Stocks-Ethnic-Tensions/2907422. Accessed on 1/7/2010.

Olupot, M. (2010).*Aliker Raps Otunnu Over LRA War Case*, The New Vision, 16 June, 2010. Available at: http://www.newvision.co.ug/D/8/12/722921. Accessed on 17/06/2010.

Olupot, M. (2010).*ICC Failed the Kony Talks, Says Oulanyah*, The New Vision, 27May, 2010. Available at: http://www.newvision.co.ug/D/8/13/721001. Accessed on 24/9/2010.

Otim, P.W. (2009). *An interactive Media: Reflections on Mega FM and its Peacebuilding Role in Uganda:* Available at: http://www.beyondinteractability.org/case_studies/mega_fm.jsp?nid=6814 . Accessed on 28/5/2010.

Oryem, O. H. (2009). *Peace Talks andProspects for Peace in Northern Uganda*, A Keynote Address at the Prayer Breakfast Organized by Advocates Coalition for Development and Environment (ACODE), Inter-Religious Council of Uganda at Serena Hotel, Kampala: Uganda.

Project Hope: Northern Uganda Youth Development. Available at: http://www.thecommonwealth.org/Internal/152816/152834/177193/proj ect_hope__Northern_uganda_youth_development_ce/. Accessed on 10/5/2010.

Projects Gulu District NGO Forum. Available at: http://www.humanrightsuganda.org/ngo-forum/projects-gulu-district-ngo-forum. Accessed on 11/5/2010.

Report of the Expert of the Secretary-General Ms. Machel, G. (1996) *The Impact of Armed Conflict on Children.* Available at: gopher://gopher.un.org/00/ga/docs/51/plenary /A51-306.EN. Accessed on 18/5/2010.

*Report of the Secretary-General on Children and Armed Conflict in Uganda, 15 September 2009.*Available at:
http://daccessdd.un.org/doc/UNDOC/GEN/NO7/298/63/PDF/N072
9863.pdf?OpenElement. Accessed on 19/5/2010.

Research Centre for Constructive Conflict Management (2006).*Traditional Approaches to Conflict Transformation- Potentials and Limits*, Available at:
http://www.berghof-
handbook.net/documents/publications/boege_handbook.pdf. Accessed on 6/7/2010.

Robinson, M (2000). *Community Driven Development in Conflict and Post-Conflict Conditions: The Northern Uganda Social Action Fund (NUSAF) Project.* Available at:
http://www.google.co.uk/#hl=en&source=hp&q=World+Bank%2C+Apr
il+2000%2C+Northern+Uganda+Reconstruction+Project%3A+Performa
nce+Audit+Report%2C+Operations+Evaluation+Department.+Report+
No.20664&btnG=Google+Search&aq=f&aqi=&aql=&oq=&gs_rfai=&fp
=74aa98f7d3a65fd7 Accessed on 8/5/2010.

Stuart, V.H. (2009). *The ICC Trust Fund for Victims: Beyond the Realm of the ICC.*
Available at:
http://static.rnw.nl/migratie/www.rnw.nl/internationaljustice/specials/co
mmentary/090204-ICC-TFV-redirected. Accessed on 2/6/2010.

Summary of Geneva Conventions and Additional Protocols. Available at:
http://supportgenevaconventions.info/library/geneva_conventions_summ
ary.pdf: Accessed on 29/4/2010.

Sunday Monitor August 30, 2009 *'Strong Leaders will Stop Acholi Land Grabbers'.*

Tebajjukira, M. (2008). *Shs 2.5 Billion (US$ 1,129,964) NUSAF Funds Missing.*
New Vision 10 July. Available at:
http://allafrica.com/stories/200807110006.html. Accessed on 14/5/2010.

Tebajjukira, (2009).*Land Conflicts High in Buganda.* Available at:
http://www.allafrica.com/stories/2009021200786html. Accessed on 1/7/2010.

The Amnesty Commission Report (2007-2008). *Reconciliation in Action*

The Children Act 1997.

The Independent Newspaper (2010).*Mao's Election and Secession of the Nile State,*
September 11. Avaialble at:
http://www.independent.co.ug/index.php/column/guest-column/68-
guest-column/2590-maos-election-and-secession-of-the-nile-state. Accessed
on 11/9/2010.

The Independent Newspaper (2010).*ICC Bill: Why did Mps trap Museveni and Save Kony?* 31March. Available at:
http://independent.co.ug/index.php/column/insight/67-insight/2702-icc-
bill-why-did-mps-trap-museveni-and-save-kony. Accessed on 18/6/2010.

The Independent Newspaper (2010).*International Criminal Court: Africa beware of 'new' legal colonialism*, 14 June. Available at: http://independent.co.ug/index.php/column/opinion/86-opinion/3032-international-criminal-court-africa-beware-of-new-legal-colonialism-. Accessed on 18/6/2010.

The Independent Newspaper (2010*). ICC Bill: Why did MPs trap Museveni and Save Kony?* Available at: http://independent.co.ug/index.php/column/insight/67-insight/2702-icc-bill-why-did-mps-trap-museveni-and-save-kony. Accessed on 2/6/2010.

The UN (Machel) *Report on the Impact of Armed Conflict on Children (1996).* Available at: http://www.unicef.org/graca/. Accessed on 23/9/2010.

The New Vision, *ICC Failed the Kony Taks, Says Oulanya.* Available at: http://www.newvision.co.ug/D/8/13/721001. Accessed on 28/5/2010.

The Rome Statute of the International Criminal Court. Available at: http://en.wikipedia.org/wiki/Rome_Statute_of_the_International_Criminal_Court. Accessed on 20/9/09

Bugembe, A. (2009). *Uganda: Election Laws Won't Change – Museveni,*The New Vision 21, June. Available at: http://allafrica.com/stories/200906220090.html Accessed on 23/9/2010.

The Republic of Uganda (2002). *The Peace Agreement Between The Government of the Republic of Uganda and The Uganda National Rescue Front II, December.* Available at: http://www.beyondjuba.org/peace_agreements.php Accessed on 2/6/2010.

The Republic of Uganda (2006).*United Nations Development Programme, Programme Action Plan 2006-2010 for Uganda.* Available at: http://www.undp.or.ug/whatwedo/14. Accessed on 2/6/2010.

The Republic of Uganda (2007).*Karamoja Integrated Disarmament and Development Programme 2007/2008-2009/2010.* Available at: http://www.ugandaclusters.ug/dwnlds/0204Karamoja/KIDDP.pdf. Accessed on 10/5/2010.

The Republic of Uganda Office of the Prime Minister (2008).*Northern Uganda Rehabilitation Programme.*Annual Report.

The UN Declaration on the Protection of Women and Children in Emergency and Armed Conflict was proclaimed by the United Nations General Assembly under the United Nations Resolution 3318 (XX1X) on the 14 December 1974. Available at: http://www.cidh.org/Ninez/pdf%20files/Declaration%20on%20Protection. Accessed on 10/6/2010.

Uganda – US-UN-LRA Disarmament Bill. Available at: http://www.invisiblechildren.com/news-press/news/detail.php?pID=235739135. Accessed on 18/2010.

Uganda (Amnesty Act, 2000-08). Available at: http://escolapau.uab.cat/img/programas/desarme/mapa/uganda08i.pdf Accessed on 10/5/2010.

Uganda Human Rights Commission (2005) *Annual Report.*

Uganda Human Rights Commission (2006*) Annual Report.*

Uganda Human Rights Commission (2007*) Annual Report.*

Uganda Human Rights Commission (2008) *Annual Report.*

UNICEF (2006). The *State of Youth and Youth Protection in Northern Uganda: Findings from the Survey for War Affected Youth.* Kampala: A Report of UNICEF Uganda.

UNICEF (2006).*Machel Study 10 - Year Strategic Reveiw: Children and Conflict in a Changing World,* UNICEF. Available at: http://www.un.org/children/conflict/machel/english/preface.html. Accessed on 23/9/2010.

UNICEF (1997).*Cape Town Principles and Best Practices on the Prevention of Recruitment of Children into Armed Forces and on Demobilization and Social Reintegration of Child Soldiers in Africa,* April 27-30. Available at: http://www.unicef.org/emerg/files/Cape_Town_Principles(1).pdf. Accessed on 10/9/2010.

United Nations, Office of the Special Representative of the Secretary-General for Children and Armed Conflict (2018) Available on Internet at: https://childrenandarmedconflict.un.org/sudan/. Accessed on 11/10/2018.

United Nations Department of Peacekeeping Operations: Disarmament, Demobilization and Reintegration of Ex- Combatants in A Peacekeeping Environment: Principles and Guidelines. Available at: http://www.un.org/depts/dpko/lessons/DD&R.pdf Accessed on 5/10/09.

United Nations Development Programme (2006).*Programme Action Plan 2006- 2010 For Uganda.* Available at: http://www.undp.or.ug/aboutus/8. Accessed on 11/5/2010.

United Nations, Report of the Secretary-General on Children and Armed Conflict in Uganda. Available at: http://www.un.org/children/conflict/english/index.html. Accessed on 23/9/2010.

United Nations, Report of the Secretary-General on Children and Armed Conflict in Burundi. Available at: http://daccess-dds-ny.un.org/doc/UNDOC/GEN/N09/494/21/PDF/N0949421.pdf?OpenElement. Accessed on 23/9/2010.

UN Security Council Resolution 1261. Available at: http://www.un.org.News/Press/docs/1999/199990825.sc6716.html Accessed on 29/6/2010.

UN Security Council Resolution 1314. Available at: http://www.crin.org/law/instrument.asp?Inst1D=1056 Accessed on 29/6/2010.

USAID, (2005).*Democracy and Governance Assessment: Republic of Uganda,* USAID.

Verhey, B. (2001). *Child Soldiers: Preventing, Demobilization and Reintegrating, Africa Region.* Working Paper Series, Available at: http://www.worldbank.org/afr/wps/index.htm. Accessed on 7/5/2010.

Vines, A. (1998).*Disarmament in Mozambique,* Journal of Southern African Studies, Volume 24, Number 1, March, pp. 191-205. Available at: http://www.informaworld.com/smpp/title-content=t71346095. Accessed 6/5/2010.

Wessells, M. G. (2006). *Do No Harm: Challenges in Organizing Psychosocial Support to Displaced People in Emergency Setting.* Coalition to Stop Use of Child Soldiers: Available at: http://www.child-soldiers.org/psycho-social/Wessells-_Do_No_Harm-2008.pdf. Accessed on 23/6/2010.

Wikipedia, *Gacaca Court.* Available at: http://en.wikipedia.org/wiki/Gacaca_court. Accessed on 2/11/09.

Wikipedia.International Criminal Court. Available at: http://www.en.wikipedia.org/wiki/International_Criminal_Court. Accessed on 2/6/2010.

World Bank Report (2008). *Analysis of Post Conflict Policy and Land Administration: A Survey of IDP Return and Resettlement Issues and Lessons in Acholi and Lango Regions.* Available at: http://www.oxfam.org.uk/resources/leaving/land right/downloads/Northern_uganda_land_study_acholi_lango.pdf. Accessed on 1/7/2010.

World Vision in Uganda, Available at: http://www.worldvision.org.uk/server.php?show=nav.1652 Accessed on 11/5/2010.

Unpublished Sources

Bigirwa, E. & Komakech, L. *Profiles of NGOs and CBOs Involved in the Implementation of the Peace, Recovery and Development Plan (PRDP) for Northern Uganda.* ACODE Policy Research Series (Forthcoming).

Index

Israel, 31, 41, 51, 133

J

Juba Peace Process, 155

K

Kadogos, 27, 47, 59, 172, 173, 174, 175
Kahira, Andrew, 174
Karamoja Integrated Disarmament and
 Development Programme, 207,
 208, 316
Karimajong, 27
Kashmir, 31
Kenya, 27, 39, 145, 177, 301, 304, 305
Ker Kwaro Acholi, 133, 237, 267, 268,
 282, 312
Khmer Rouge, 31
Kings African Rifles, 148
Kitgum Concerned Women's
 Association, viii, 219, 264
Kony, Joseph, 12, 75, 175, 176, 177,
 178, 186, 189, 262, 270, 272, 281,
 311, 314, 315, 316

L

Lakwena, Alice, 12, 177, 256, 299
Lango sub-region, 16, 262
Latin America, 28, 128
League of Nations Declaration on the
 Rights of the Child, 63
Liberal peace approach to
 peacebuilding, 14, 127, 291
Liberia, 32, 34, 35, 41, 55, 57, 75, 83,
 91, 100, 104, 187, 195, 247, 307
Liu Institute for Global Issues, 109,
 110, 111, 118, 180, 195, 230, 251,
 256, 280, 296, 310, 312
Lome Peace Accord, 83
Longitudinal study, 114
Lord's Resistance Army, viii, 11, 12,
 54, 75, 139, 154, 155, 159, 174, 175,
 178, 186, 208, 262, 302, 308
Lule, Yusuf, 145, 146
Luwero, 147, 173, 174, 221

M

Madrassah schools, 45
Makerere University, 153, 155, 160,
 198, 208, 277, 302, 304, 306, 312
Maputo Declaration on the Use of
 Children as Soldiers, 81, 82, 313
Masai, 39
Mazrui, Ali, 144, 147, 162, 165, 166,
 304
Middle Ages, 24
Middle East, 28, 31
Moshi Conference, 145
Movement for the Liberation of
 Angola, 97
Mozambique, viii, ix, 32, 55, 60, 73, 91,
 94, 96, 97, 106, 107, 108, 113, 114,
 172, 195, 274, 297, 304, 318
Mozley, Michele, iv
Mugyenyi, Onesmus, iv, 150, 151, 305
Muhwezi, Winstons Wilson, iv
Museveni, Yoweri, 12, 15, 27, 46, 49,
 50, 59, 76, 141, 142, 144, 145, 146,
 147, 148, 149, 150, 151, 152, 154,
 155, 156, 157, 158, 159, 160, 161,
 162, 163, 164, 165, 166, 168, 170,
 171, 172, 173, 174, 175, 177, 183,
 186, 194, 197, 198, 199, 205, 221,
 262, 281, 305, 309, 310, 315, 316
Myanmar, 30

N

National Resistance Army, viii, 12, 15,
 27, 46, 49, 50, 147, 149, 164, 171,
 172, 173, 177, 221
National Union for the Total
 Liberation of Angola, 97
Nigeria, 167, 253
Non-Governmental Organizations,
 viii, 173, 189, 192, 220, 230
Northern Uganda Reconstruction
 Programme, viii, 196, 201
North-South problems, 147

O

Obote, Milton, 26, 50, 70, 84, 86, 90,
 141, 143, 144, 145, 146, 147, 149,

www.ingramcontent.com/pod-product-compliance
Lightning Source LLC
Chambersburg PA
CBHW070558270326
41926CB00013B/2351